Brother Keshavananda;
I hope you find some insp[...]
from my life stories, MA[...] [...]at
continue to guide you[...] [...] — God Bless
you —
W.H. McDonald
"Bill"
July 2004

A Spiritual Warrior's Journey

The Inspiring Life Story of a Mystical Warrior

By

W.H. McDonald Jr.

© 2003 by W.H. McDonald Jr. All rights reserved.

No part of this book may be reproduced, stored in a retrieval system, or transmitted by any means, electronic, mechanical, photocopying, recording, or otherwise, without written permission from the author.

ISBN: 1-4140-1449-X (e-book)
ISBN: 1-4140-1450-3 (Paperback)

Library of Congress Control Number: 2003097126

This book is printed on acid free paper.

Printed in the United of States America
Bloomington, IN

Foreword and Editing by Jan Hornung

1stBooks - rev. 10/18/03

Acknowledgments

I want to thank all those who helped me have the courage to share my story. It wasn't a comfortable thing for me to do.

I will be forever grateful to Jan Hornung for her belief in what I had to say. It was through her patient editing that she taught me so much about the art of storytelling. Her humor and skilled eye for grammar were greatly appreciated. She has been a friend on my spiritual path.

I would be remiss if I didn't thank Cheryl and Patrick Fries for the wonderful journey they provided this little ole veteran. I think of them both as fellow travelers and the dearest of friends.

My life would not have had the same fullness and joy it has now if it were not for my son and daughter. Josh and Daya, I love you both. I hope this book gives you a clearer understanding of your father. Pass it down to your children so that they will have this history of their grandpa.

My wife, Carol, who has endured all the worst of my ego, my wild sense of humor, and my sensitive mood swings; I would not be who I am today without having had you in my life. I love you beyond measure.

My Guru, Paramahansa Yogananda, you have taught me the value of love! I am forever your devotee.

Dedicated To:

Carol, my first and only love, who has always been there for me in sickness and in health, for better or for worse; all the guys at The Hidden Valley Ashram, and fellow Vietnam veterans and devotees, Brahmachari Carl and Brahmachari Lee; all former members, living and dead, of The 128th Assault Helicopter Company—I will always be a "Tomahawk Warrior"; my friend and high school classmate, Karen Wilson, who has been supportive of me and my dreams all these years; my children and their families: Daya and Mark, Josh and Syd, and all my grandchildren, now and in the future; my best friends from Sunnyvale High School: Mahaila, Bob Brooks, Bob Amick, Bill Martin, Jim Carter, Bruce Hughes, Sidra, Becky, Rita Jo, Brenda, Dennis, Ed, Dondee, Pat Lawyer, Anne Franklin, Marianne, Jim Laub, Sharon, Nancy "Romy" Hallmark, Linda Provance, and all of the Class of 1964; all my friends from church, especially my spiritual brothers: Mike, Robert, Fred, Lynn, Haig, Rick, Guillermo, Allen, Tony, TJ, Howard, and Lee; Paramahansa Yogananda, "the pole star of my life"; all of the crew of old Huey 091, The Shadow; Patrick and Cheryl Fries; The Peace Patrol: Richard Webster, Robert Reese and Dave Gallo; all of the Robin Hoods; Doug and Leilah Ward; Aurence and Biegun, and White Dog; Earl Waters, Ernie Dogwolf and all the veterans I met at Angel Fire, New Mexico; Vietnam veterans Johnny Hobbs, Keith "Hacksaw" Bodine, Brian Wizard, John B. Givhan, and Rodney Riley; my old Tomahawk pilots who brought me back alive from Nam, the world's greatest Huey pilots and my "guardian angels": Bob Codney, Ed Ewing, and Ben Powell; Reginald—his body may be imprisoned in Soledad, but his mind and spirit are free; my Postal Service friends: Marty Topper, Jack Green, Dave Diab, Mike Hoover, Sean, Sam, Rick, Roger and Frank Maruyama; my father, whom I have never known but have missed forever; and especially my relatives: Gary, Linda, Marsha, Melody, Dawn, Billy, Todd, Kim, Mike, Darlene, and Gina; and to all those who have ever tolerated me, encouraged me, laughed at my jokes, or listened to my stories over the years, you are all a part of me and these memories.

Without any one of you, this life adventure would not have been the same.

I dedicate this book to all of you.

Table of Contents

ix

I Wanted the World

I wanted to travel
When I was just a child.
I wanted to reach out
Across seas, skies, green valleys,
Climb tall mountains,
Walk crowded city streets
Filled with beautiful young maidens
Who lived only on poetry and oranges.

I wanted to touch
Souls of people
Who were not like me.
I wanted to see and be in places
That were foreign to my young being.
I wanted to live in places
That I only saw and felt in dreamland.
I wanted to taste foods and life
As it was experienced someplace else.
I wanted to hold snowflakes
From Himalayan mountaintops
On my tongue
And dance naked across virgin beaches
On some uncharted island.

I wanted the world
When I was just a child.
I wanted to find
Some enlightened poet
Who could show me
How to find the rainbow's end.
I wanted to understand why, and how,
And find that truth
That lay hidden
Under layers of forgotten karma
And other lost dreams.

I wanted so much
When I was just a child.
I wanted the world back then,
But now,
All I want is you
And me!

October 1966, Berkeley, California

"Kick the Skids and Light the Fire!"
Jan Hornung, former Army helicopter pilot.

Foreword by Jan Hornung

We each have a special gift offered to us from a greater being. I choose to believe that being is God. As we grow physically, mentally, and spiritually, we are blessed to discover our gift or gifts. The happiest folks, I believe, are those who have found their gift and share it with others.

Someone's gift might be nothing more than a bright smile. Yet this one person's smile may enhance or change the lives of hundreds. Others may have the gift of imagination. These are the people who have brought medicines, technology, and beauty to our lives. There are no small gifts. There are only small people such as those who use their gift for evil, or those so self-absorbed they have not found their gift.

As we travel through our lives, we make choices to discover, to use, and to share our gifts. Many people blindly stumble along, not even knowing they have these choices. Others actively seek out their gifts. And when they discover them, they give thanks to that greater being and pray for guidance in using and sharing them. Bill McDonald is such a man. Since he was a boy, he has known that God had gifts for him. Bill has spent the past 50-plus years seeking his gifts, asking for divine guidance in using them, and most important, sharing them with others.

This collection of stories from Bill's life will take you on his search for love as a child, his search for himself in early adulthood, through the Vietnam war, and into marriage, parenthood, and now as a grandfather. Search for your own spiritual awareness, your own gifts, as Bill takes you through the pains, the loves, the wisdoms, the inspirations, and the epiphanies of his divinely-guided life.

I first met Bill through e-mail while I was compiling stories for my book *Angels in Vietnam*. As we chatted, I could see that Bill was a special person. Special in the sense that he was caring about and sensitive to others. As I read some of his stories on his website, I became intrigued with his love for mankind and God. In addition to being writers, we had something else in common; Bill had been a Huey crew chief, and I a Huey pilot.

I was excited and honored when Bill asked me to edit this book. While reading Bill's stories, I cried, laughed, prayed, and reflected. Some stories scared me, while others made me ecstatic. Even the sad stories caused me to reflect on the good that comes from all experiences, if we only take the time to look for it.

Bill McDonald's love for life shines through in each of his stories. From haunted houses to magical rainbows, heavenly angels to unearthly beings, horrific war to blessed weddings, out-of-body soaring to helicopter flight, Bill takes us there with each of his told-from-the-heart tales.

Now sit back, relax, and prepare to run the gauntlet of your emotions as you enjoy the journey of one man's incredible life—one man who has touched so many other lives, as he will yours.

Jan Hornung
Author/editor, Huey pilot, Army wife
Angels in Vietnam: Women Who Served
This Is The Truth As Far As I Know, I Could Be Wrong
If A Frog Had Wings…Helicopter Tales
KISS the Sky…Helicopter Tales
Spinning Tails
www.geocities.com/vietnamfront

Introduction To My Journey

This book is not about war, even though it does contain many stories related to that experience; this book is about the spiritual journey that my life took before, during, and after my tour of duty in Vietnam. I must warn you that this book is not like any other book you have ever read in your life—it will challenge your very ability to remain open-minded and will perhaps even assault your own basic concepts of what you thought reality is. This book will leave you with more questions than answers, but in any case, it will change forever the way you view your own life.

I have written the chapters in this book so that you, the reader, can begin anywhere you like, for each story is a complete and separate experience by and of itself. Some will make you cry, get angry, or become frightened; a few will provoke a smile or perhaps a laugh; while others might leave you with a sense of wonderment or inspiration. There are some stories, however, that just do not fall into any neat categories for our understanding—and frankly, you may find them totally unbelievable because they deal with events that none of us can truly understand or conceive as even possible. If you were telling me some of these same experiences, I would not believe you if I had not been there myself. Then, there are some emotional stories that I've told only to give you a better understanding of how my spirit was altered in some way by what happened. This journey has many different shades of life experiences, and each chapter takes you on a new and unexpected turn. You will never read another book quite like this one—this is a unique, one-of-a-kind life story that will compel you to think about your life in a much different way. This book could lead you down new roads you have not spiritually or emotionally taken before, so be careful and realize that what you are about to read may very well alter your own views of life as you know it.

There are many stories that I have deliberately left out of this book. It was not my intention to create a fully detailed account of my life, but rather to share the emotional and spiritual footprints of my journey.

Some events in my life have left me unable to explain what really happened. I do not fully comprehend the meaning of everything I have experienced, so I do not try to explain why or how these sometimes mystical and sacred moments take place. I just know that they have happened as I have written them down. Some readers will think that these were just accidents of fate or that I have been an extremely lucky or blessed person. You might even want to believe that whatever happened to me could somehow be explained away with some good logical reasoning. Who knows? I certainly cannot offer any answers, and you are welcome to draw your own conclusions.

I am not trying to convert anyone to my own way of thinking. I just want to share some of the events from my own life experiences that I thought might perhaps inspire you to seek out the basic mysteries of your own life such as: "What is the real meaning of life?" and "Why am I here?"

You have your own set of perceptions and beliefs, which will taint how you read and emotionally digest each of my stories. I ask only that you put yourself in my shoes while you are holding this book. Read my words and thoughts and try to feel the experience on another level. Disengage that part of your logical mind that doesn't believe in the mystical possibilities of life, and join me on this journey as you read stories where miracles and angels, and love and war coexist in my world.

To more fully appreciate and understand who I was when I arrived for my tour of duty in South Vietnam in October 1966, I feel you need to know a little about my life prior to becoming a participant in that war. I just didn't all of sudden become who I was; there were emotional and spiritual roots that helped create the very me that arrived in Nam. I was a product of my country, my generation, my dysfunctional family, and some very mystical and supernatural experiences in my life. However, there was no way I could have been prepared for what I found there or for the emotionally and spiritually troubling reception that I received when I came back home again.

I began my life as a part of the Baby Boomer Generation, born on March 16, 1946, in San Francisco, California. I was the third born of my mother's six babies. Although we grew up together, I do not share the same father with any of my siblings. My brother, Gary, was born in 1939 during my mom's first marriage. My sisters, Melody, born in 1943, and Marsha, born in 1948, had the same father. Melody was born while my mother was divorced from her first husband. Melody's father eventually returned from the war and became my stepdad. My father married my mother and had been supporting the whole family, but when my stepdad came back into the picture, she chose to divorce my dad.

I know almost nothing about my real dad's life other than he was once a promising All-American baseball player in high school and had even signed a professional contract before his generation's "war to end all wars." He was wounded in World War II and never played professionally. I also know that he was born and raised in San Francisco. Since he never chose to visit or make any contact with me after their divorce, I never got to know my dad at all. I also never heard from his parents or siblings, even though they all lived in San Francisco. Even after 57 years, there is still a very large hole in my heart. I admit to feeling a little rejected, unwanted, and unloved.

My mother immediately married my stepdad as soon as the divorce papers were dry. My stepdad was an alcoholic who could at times become very violent. He created and ruled a household built on fear and intimidation, subjecting our family to tremendous emotional abuse. Growing up, I always thought that he personally hated me; then, it dawned on me when I was an adult that he really hated everyone, including himself. It was nothing personal at all.

My mother was considered a gifted psychic by some people. She could be a fairly accurate fortuneteller at times. She did have a special gift for being able to read people and know things about them. She had a small following of people that she used to read the cards for. Her own mother was also gifted with abilities to know and see events that had not yet happened. Going back several generations on my mother's side in Italy, there are many family members with various psychic abilities.

We basically grew up in the San Francisco Bay Area, although we lived in Coos Bay, Oregon, for a two-year period before eventually settling down in the little rural town of Sunnyvale, California. Back before the computer chip boom, Sunnyvale was just an orchard and farm community with plenty of open space between the closest towns.

Lots of things happened to me growing up that molded my outlook on life, as it is with all of us. As you read each of these stories, you will notice that I did not necessarily bridge them together with any connective paths of personal data or history. These stories are meant to be individual snapshots of some of my life experiences. I wrote each of these individual memories that I thought were significant in some way to my whole life journey and would be of interest to you. There are not many names, dates, or lots of reference data mentioned. I want to share the emotional and spiritual moments of my life and not necessarily present a complete autobiography. I feel this will enhance your reading experience by getting straight to the action.

I make no claims other than what is stated in each story. They say there are no accidents in life, therefore, the fact that you now have this book in your hands means that there is something of value within these pages that your spirit needs to know in order to help you along your own spiritual journey. I hope you find whatever it is that your higher self came looking for. God bless you.

Bill McDonald

Fort Campbell, Kentucky, 1966.

Part 1

Before Nam

My Childhood, 1946–1965

The Journey Begins!

"Current scientific thought supports the limited nature of our present vision. Quantum mechanics is discovering that there is a "spiritual" realm within the cosmos. We say "spiritual" because that is the realm of the invisible and non-experiential. Scientists are discovering a world of extra dimensions where the laws of space and time no longer apply, a supernatural world, a world in which anything is possible. The biblical words are being proven, "Nothing is impossible" (Luke 1:37).

Dr. Robert A. Schuller, from his book *Possible Living.*

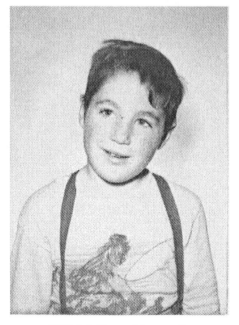

Bill McDonald, age 8.

Bill with siblings in 1948.
Melody with the doll, Gary holding Marsha.

Author's note: It is not easy to find the right place or moment to begin this journey with you, so I am sharing one of the first, if not the strangest, encounters of my young life. I am not sure how best to describe all the events that took place at our Lake Street house. When I read this story myself, it all seems so unbelievable. If I had not lived through these actual events, I would never believe it happened. I would certainly be very skeptical and doubtful should you be telling me this same story. However, I wrote it down as best I could remember it, along with some added recollections from my older brother, Gary, who almost died himself in this house. I have no idea what really happened. This all took place at such a very young age, and now here I am trying with my adult mind to figure and sort it all out. I am not sure that it is even possible to bring a basic understanding to what events had actually transpired back then, so all I can do is share how I remember it. Choose to believe what you will. Your own theory of what happened is as good as any. You do not have to believe anything, but realize that I, as a frightened, young child, certainly did!

Our Haunted House on Lake Street

(Around 1948–1950)

During the late forties, we lived on Lake Street in San Francisco. We had a large three-story house, if you counted the garage on the bottom floor. My father had purchased the house in a partnership with my grandmother. She lived in the upstairs flat, while all of us occupied the downstairs unit. My stepdad inherited and took over the house when my mother divorced my father and married him. It was in this house that our family experienced many unexplainable and frightening happenings. It was also in this same house that my two baby brothers died. Actually, one died in the house; the other was taken to the hospital where he died later. My oldest brother, Gary, told me many years later how he had almost died in this house from being unable to breathe. He said it felt as if someone were physically trying to choke him to death, but no one else was in the room with him at the time.

Most people who know our family do not know anything about my two baby brothers, or that they ever existed. Bruce and Roger Engelking each lived for less than a year. I remember the day that they took out the body of one of my brothers. The house was eerily quiet and sad. There was no evidence of crying; no tears from my mother, at least none that any of us saw. I am sure that it must have affected her. I believe that she became very depressed because she tried to repress it all and not show any emotions. She handled the burden of her two dead children all by herself; she never confided in anyone or had any kind of counseling. People just didn't do that back then. My stepdad made her feel guilty, as if it were somehow her fault; back then there was very little understanding about crib deaths (Sudden Infant Death Syndrome, SIDS). He had wanted to have sons and all he got from their relationship was two daughters, my sisters, Melody and Marsha. His only two sons had both died as infants. He felt that there must have been something that my mother was doing wrong that had in some way contributed to those deaths. He had expressed this belief to her in one of his drunken rages as he destroyed yet another layer of her self-worth and esteem.

She did mange to take out her anger on the weakest target she had, my poor brother, Gary. Moments after they had taken the body out of the house, she was still standing alone in the room where her baby son had just died. The crib was empty, and the crocheted blankets were still laying there. This was her second baby to die in less then two years. Who knows what thoughts were going on in her head at the time; she was just staring at the crib saying nothing. When my 11-year-old brother approached her to give her some emotional comfort, she turned around and looked my brother right in the face.

"It should have been you that died!" she screamed at him.

My brother still feels the hurt from that misplaced moment of rage and anger even all these years, and he is now in his 60s as I write this. He was only a child wanting to help his mother. I do not think my mother ever realized how much hurt and emotional damage she did that one day to her living, loving, and oldest son, Gary! When he told me this story a few years ago, I wanted to cry for him.

5

This house was also a place where many strange and supernatural events took place. It was downright scary at times. No one seemed to know what was going on, or why; worse yet, no one could stop what was happening there. It seemed as if this house were either haunted or being visited by some unknown beings, each and every night. It was a place of great mystery, but much greater fear. It all seemed to begin shortly after my stepdad moved into the house.

The only history we knew about the house was that someone had once died there sometime before we had moved in. The room where the death occurred was always very physically cold; it was the "almost see your breath" kind of cold. If we spent any time in that particular room, we became emotionally depressed. It was the very same room that one brother had died in, the other got ill in and then later died, and where Gary was almost suffocated by some unknown source of trouble. This was also the room where my normally meek and passive mother went a little berserk and into a fit of anger against my brother. The room always had a feeling about it that could only be called gloom and doom. It was not a cheerful place to be in and every one of us avoided going in there.

It wasn't too long after my stepdad moved into this house that all the troubles began. Every night there were odd sounds and noises, as if someone or something were walking or moving down the hallway and going into some of the rooms. It was the sound of footsteps and doors opening and closing. These ever-present visitors, or ghosts of some kind, were in our house every night. We could hear whatever it was very clearly, night after night. We would hear someone walking past our bedroom door, stand there, then move on down the hallway.

It almost drove my stepdad insane. My mom remained very composed throughout all of this. I do not understand or know why that was so, but she kept telling all of us that it was just our nightly visitors again and not to worry about it.

Of course, none of this was a normal situation. Almost any normally functioning family would have questioned these events with much more curiosity and authority. Perhaps, being motivated by some well-deserved fears, anyone else might have had the good sense to move out of the house! Not our family—for whatever the reasons, we stayed there. One of the strange parts about all of this was that we accepted it as a part of our normal routine.

My grandmother never had any problems upstairs. It only involved the first and second floors of the house that the rest of us occupied.

When my stepdad moved into our house, he brought with him a large handgun. He was a World War II veteran who had seen a lot of combat. Today, he would be diagnosed as having a bad case of Post Traumatic Stress Disorder, PTSD. He pulled out his gun every night and took it to bed with him. Actually, under the circumstances, I am not too sure that this wasn't a sane and rational reaction for him. When he heard the sounds, he would jump up out of the bed with his fully loaded pistol and dash out into the hallway to catch whomever it was. He did this night after night; he was always ready for combat. It was very odd that he wandered all around the house and never saw anything. All of us children stayed in our rooms. It would have been dangerous for any of us to venture outside our bedroom doors at night, not because of the nightly intruders, but because we could have possibly become an inadvertent target of this very frightened and lethally-armed man. This activity of his finally stopped after several months, without his finding any evidence of intruders. Why he never found anyone and why he gave up, I do not know.

We never saw anything ourselves, or better stated, we never remembered seeing anything. I do know that there was someone or something, coming and going each night. I am not sure if they actually came into any of our rooms. I was very young at the time and remember only pieces of events. I cannot figure out if this "someone" ever visited me or any of us. There was a collective non-memory of nothing other than knowing that we were visited each night. It strikes me as odd that we allowed this to continue as we passively went off to sleep until the morning. I can remember being very tired each morning when I got up, so sleep wasn't as good as it could have been.

I often wonder if more was happening to us than we can remember. The most amazing part of all this was how my parents could have slept through the nights with someone or something wandering around the house while their own children lay helplessly alone in their beds. If it were my children, I could not have slept.

We may have been visited again over the years, even after leaving that house. I remember dreams of places and beings, but nothing more than dreams. Anything that might have happened is a lost or, perhaps,

7

a repressed memory. There is no doubt in my mind that there was some type of unearthly activity going on there. No one really explored with me what it might have been.

I do remember my stepdad telling me that he once saw someone, or what appeared to be the backside and legs of someone, going through a window. It was odd that our parents did not more actively question all this at the time. My brother and I have discussed this a few times with each other over the years. We both remember it as I have stated, but the questions about the why of it still remain unanswered and a complete mystery. My brother and sisters just accept it as a fact. I seem to be the only one wanting to dig below the surface of it. At the time, I knew it was happening, but I also knew that there was nothing we could do to stop the visits. Something happened to me, but I am not sure what. I have no memories of anything beyond what I have stated. It is just an uneasy feeling about it all.

There are many large holes in my memory of these events. I was around four years old, so it was hard for me to realize what I was seeing and hearing. Maybe my brother, Gary, knows more but is unable to remember? Maybe this whole experience was just some nightmare that we all somehow lived through and shared? What was the truth? Why didn't my parents take some kind of action?

I have no answers to any of these questions. Do you?

#

In the backyard of our Lake Street home in 1947.
Gary, Melody, and Bill.

Bill's mother sitting next to his dad who is in uniform, 1944.

Author's note: I decided to follow up the story of one strange encounter with another because they both have a similar quality and seem to be connected. We moved from San Francisco to Coos Bay, Oregon, around 1951. But some things never change, as you will see when you read this hair-raising encounter. I shared this life experience with both of my sisters Melody, who was eight years old, and my little sister, Marsha, who was only three years old at the time this all took place. No one talked about this night until almost 50 years later. It seems odd to me that no one has ever discussed or wanted to talk about it, and they still don't. I share this experience with you as it happened one very scary night to the three of us very frightened children.

Strange Beings

(Around 1951, Coos Bay, Oregon)

We sold our house in San Francisco and headed north to Oregon. My stepdad took all the money they made from the sale of the house and used that to make the move. We stayed at a cheap motel for a while, but we began to run out of money very fast while my stepdad was out looking for work and a place to put us. He was a logger but was out of work most of the time.

It was around this time that my parents drove by an old abandoned government-housing complex in Coos Bay. It was sitting in a large field of uncut grass and dirt. There were about 18 units of three-bedroom apartments that were once used to house military dependents. There were three of these units in each section or triplex. They were all completely boarded up with large "Warning! No trespassing—Government Property Keep Out" signs posted on the doors and windows. We were not welcome to come in for sure.

My mother got the very bold idea that we could move into these buildings and claim squatters' rights. She called the local newspaper and media to tell them that we were breaking into one of the units that afternoon with the entire family. She went on to say, which they printed in the local newspaper, that her husband had earned the right as a veteran. She said that we would have to be removed by force if they wanted us out of there. The local newspaper ran this story on its front page with a photo of the entire family inside one of the units unpacking our belongings. After radio newscaster Walter Winchell took up the story and broadcast it on his national radio show, there was a crowd of people wanting to move into the rest of the apartments. The entire complex was taken over in less than one day after the story aired. By the time the city council figured out what had happened, my mother was a citywide and national hero, and nobody wanted to give the order to the police department to remove this poor veteran's family. So, we won the battle and found a place to live. We spent several days cleaning it up and fixing some small things that were wrong with it. We got the lights and the water turned on, and we had ourselves a real home. We didn't have much money, but we didn't pay rent to anyone.

Things did not remain quiet for very long, however, as life began to get ghostly weird in that house. We found ourselves back in almost the same kind of frightening situation that we had just moved away from in our last house. But this time it was not nightly, and it was a whole different experience for us.

What happened on this particular night, around 1951, made me very afraid for a long time. You might think at first that this was all just someone's bad dream or the creation of a young child's wild imagination, but my two sisters were witnesses to what happened on at least this one occasion. I ask no one to believe any of this. Again, it is one of those crazy stories that I wouldn't believe myself if anyone else were telling me that this was his own true-life experience. So, I present to you another hard-to-define and much harder-to-believe moment from my young life.

I recall going to bed late one night. I lay there trying to sleep while my brother was already asleep in the other bed. Looking around the bedroom into the darkness, I felt very uneasy, as if someone were watching me. I noticed that the room temperature had changed; it seemed much cooler. I pulled up the blankets to get warm, and I noticed that in the darkness there was some movement—I saw something move across the room.

I became very frightened and yelled out for my parents. I kept calling out to my mom, waking up everyone except my brother in the process. My stepdad came in, and, of course, he was angry that I had awakened him. Whatever had been there was gone when he came in and turned on the lights. He told me not to call him again as he turned off the lights and left me in the darkness.

I listened to my stepdad's retreating footsteps until they finally fell silent. I heard him close his bedroom door. Several more anxious moments passed before my eyes adjusted to the darkness. I could clearly see that they were still there waiting for me. I was terrified!

Whatever they were, they came back as soon as he left the room. I could see several of them in what appeared to be matching uniforms or jumpsuits. They were small childlike figures, not much bigger than I was at that age. I did not, however, get the impression that they were actually children. They stood several feet away from me and stared with huge owl-like eyes. I saw their lips moving and thought they were talking, but I didn't hear or understand anything.

I was terrified of what I was seeing, and worse yet, no one was coming to rescue me even after I began screaming loudly again. Gary, for whatever reason, remained in an almost death-like sleep. With all my piercing screams I should have awakened everyone in the house, even our neighbors, but I didn't. I was yelling at the top of my lungs, screaming in great fear, yet no one heard me except my two sisters in the other room. But they were too afraid to move or to come help me. I have never understood how my brother could have slept right through all my screaming or why the beings left him alone in his bed. Why didn't he wake up? Why couldn't my parents hear me?

These beings looked kind of human, but not exactly, since I could see light through them. I knew that I was seeing "beings" (for lack of a better term) and that they wanted to do something to me. I felt that they wanted to take me away from my home for reasons I did not understand. I could not hide from them, nor could I make them go away.

These beings were in my closet and around my bed. I saw them while I was wide-awake; this was no dream. I tried to hide from them under my covers, but it was as if there were an x-ray machine at work because I could actually see light and their images right through the blankets.

They, about five of them, had some type of tool in their hands that reminded me, at that age, of a fishing pole. They were trying to touch me with it. Two of these creatures were sitting on top of a shelf in my closet; they were using the pole to shoot what appeared to be bubbles down onto me.

Each bubble had a hook or sharp object in it. I felt they were doing something to me, and I did not understand it at all. I was overcome with the horror of it and was no longer able to scream. I was frozen to my bed by sheer terror, unable and unwilling to move. Then, in a moment of extreme bravery coupled with manic fear, I was finally able to jump off my bed, bolt out of my bedroom and into my sisters' room. My two sisters were awake and wide-eyed with fear. They saw a slight glowing of light behind me, and then they saw these same creatures coming into their room. We were trembling in terror.

Our last memory in the bedroom is of the beings standing directly in the doorway, blocking our potential escape. Our next memory is in the early morning. The three of us were standing behind the sofa in the front room, where we waited for them to come after us.

Our collective memory goes from seeing them enter the bedroom to seeing them come out of the bedroom while we were in the front room. The elapsed time doesn't make any sense because everything started around nine at night, yet several hours passed without our remembering anything that happened. There is a major gap of time from when we saw them enter the bedroom until we remember hiding behind the sofa, which was at sunrise. Just as the dawn's early light came shining through the windows, we saw them walking toward us. They smiled sympathetically like a mother smiling at her crying child, and they held up their hands as if they were saying goodbye to us. As they stood next to the sofa and stared at us, they transfixed me with their oval-shaped eyes. As frightened as I was, I found it difficult not to stare back into those lidless eyes. I had the feeling that they did not want to harm us, but I still felt angry at them for scaring me.

They were not that much bigger than we were, and we could see through them when they moved across the floor toward us. Then, as the light from the windows hit them, they all disappeared, slowly fading away until we could no longer see them at all. My sisters and I stood there ever so silent for a long time, afraid to move back to the bedrooms. We all saw what happened that night, but we did not speak about it again for many decades. We never shared it with our parents or with anyone else at the time.

It was around this time that I began to get frequent, terrible nosebleeds for no apparent reason. I often woke up in the morning with blood on my pillow from my nose. I used to think that the change in weather, or something easily explained, brought it on. But no one ever figured out why my nose bled as often as it did. I do not remember hitting it or doing any damage to it. I also found that certain of my paranormal psychic skill levels increased greatly around this same time period.

I began to sense that "others" were visiting me at night. I often woke up and felt the presence of "others" near me, but I would fall back to sleep. I never remembered anything except the feeling that someone had been there and that I had not been in my bed all night long. I got the sense that I had journeyed some place during the night. I had a lot of strange dreams about places and journeys, but I had trouble relating any of them to the real world that I woke up to in the morning. I just accepted this as normal at the time and did not really question any of it until almost 40 years later.

#

Author's note: On the surface, this experience seems to have nothing really supernatural about it as it gives a look at one of the emotional and physical traumas of my childhood. I experienced several health issues as a child, yet my mother always seemed slow and even reluctant to take me to a doctor for any treatments. This is one incident when I was badly burned, and yet I was never treated by any physician. It created within me certain emotional messages about my self-worth and doubts about how much my mother really loved me—if at all. The good news about this story is that I did experience love from a woman who acted as my own personal "guardian angel" and saved my life.

I Walked on Fire

When I was around five years old, we still lived in Coos Bay, Oregon. There were no Kindergarten classes at the local schools nor was I enrolled in any preschool, so I spent all my time just hanging around our housing project. I must have believed at that age that I could walk through fire. That is exactly what I did one day, and I almost got myself killed.

One afternoon I was fooling around outside, playing next to a large pile of burning trash. It was a common practice for some of the residents at this project to burn their household garbage on the open ground between the rows of housing. There were never any adults around to guard it or to ensure that it didn't get out of control. Most of the preschool children in the project enjoyed playing around the fire, throwing sticks and leaves into it as small children normally do. It was like our own campfire. We gathered around it and pretended that we were camping or that we were cowboys and Indians.

For whatever reason, I chose this one particular day to wander very close to the trash fire; then, I actually decided to walk through the flames. I wasn't trying to walk on hot coals, I am talking about piles of burning garbage.

While I was walking through the pile of trash, red fingers of fire leaped up. Suddenly, one of my pants' legs caught on fire. Within a few quick seconds my clothing was fully engulfed. Flames shot out from my clothing as I ran around the housing project screaming and

15

crying. Of course, the faster I ran the more the flames grew. Luckily for me, my yelling reached the ears of an older neighborhood woman. She ran out of her apartment so fast that she couldn't have had time to think about her actions. She raced to where I was running around screaming and looking like a red fireball. She outright tackled me hard enough to knock me down on the ground as if she were a football player. She threw dirt on my blazing body and rolled me around on the ground. She picked me up and looked straight at me. She was visibly shaking and seemed more afraid of what had happened than I was. I remember she had tears flowing down her checks as she stood there wondering what to do next. I felt so much love coming from the woman's eyes as she looked at me. I believe that she may also have gotten some small burns on her hands in the process of saving me. She had used her own bare hands to pat down the flames. But it was her motherly look of worry that I have never forgotten. I would have been totally disfigured for life or perhaps even dead if she had not taken such swift action when she did. I do not remember ever seeing her before or after this incident. She was just there when I needed her and then was no longer around. Who she was I am not sure of, but I do know that she loved me.

My leg was badly burned, and other parts of my body also were reddened by the fire. I was in great pain. The woman had stripped me of most of my clothing by the time she got me back to my apartment. She tried to carry me as gently as possible, but I felt as if I were still on fire. I was crying and screaming in agony.

My mom did not panic when she saw me. In fact, she was rather emotionless as she took me from the arms of the woman. My mother finished taking off the remaining threads of clothing and cleaned me up. She did the best she could without taking me to see any doctors. I was still in great pain, and I had blisters all over my legs. My right leg in particular looked like cooked meat. I eventually recovered from the burns without any medical attention or pain medication. I still have a large circular scar on the inside of my right leg from the burn that day. We were very poor back then, so I assumed that my mother couldn't afford to pay for a doctor visit. Later, as an adult looking back at my childhood, the message seemed to be that I wasn't important enough to her.

I was extremely fortunate that someone was watching over me that day. Whoever that woman was, I will always remember her as my first guardian angel!

#

Author's note: This was a period in my life when I came very close to death for the second time. It also was a time for many emotional and spiritual changes.

I Became a Ward of the County Hospital

My schooling never really got off on the right foot. I began first grade a couple of weeks after the school year had started. I was not only the new kid with no friends, I also was behind in the schoolwork from the first day. To make matters even worse, I never attended any preschool or Kindergarten classes, so this was my very first day ever in any school. I did not know my numbers or letters, and I couldn't read a word. I was overwhelmed that first day and didn't want to look stupid, so I became the class clown and joked around to cover what I didn't know.

We had moved back to San Francisco from Oregon and were living in my grandmother's house. She had a three-bedroom place, so that meant she had one room, my parents another room, my two sisters took the third bedroom, and my brother, Gary, and I had to sleep in the front room. I had a rollaway bed. It was not an ideal situation. I knew my grandmother was not very pleased about our being there in her living space; we had even brought our dog into her house. But it was our home until we would move again.

I finished the first grade; then, I went off to another new school with all new kids for the second grade. I went for only a few weeks there before we moved to Sunnyvale and into our new house. I began class not knowing anyone, and I was jumping right into the class after several weeks of the school year had already passed. Once again, I had no clue as to what was going on in the classroom. To make matters even worse, my mother had decided to have me use my stepfather's last name, Engelking, for this new school. When the teacher asked me to write my name on my papers, I didn't know how to correctly spell my new last name. My teacher and the students thought I was really stupid. I began my new class feeling totally overwhelmed and with zero confidence.

They used to have a snack time with graham crackers and milk each afternoon. All the students brought in their milk money each

18

Monday. The teacher then bought the milk and crackers. The students sat there each afternoon at snack time drinking their milk and eating their crackers—that is, everyone but me. I did not have the milk money each week to give for the food and drinks, so I did not get any. I sat there watching everyone else. The teacher asked me why I wasn't buying any milk. I said something about not being hungry. They were not very sensitive to poor kids back then; there were no free snacks or free lunch programs. I felt like an outcast.

After surviving second grade, which best describes that whole ordeal, I began third grade right on time—a first for me. I actually knew some of the students from the year before and felt much better about the school year ahead. There was a problem, however, with my health. I developed a high fever, and my face swelled up like a balloon. I was peeing blood for weeks, and I lost a tremendous amount of weight. My skin was pale, and I looked like a POW. I went to class with this high fever, totally out of it. I was in pain, and I was dizzy almost all of the time.

It wasn't until my teacher finally took notice and sent me to the school nurse that anyone in my family paid any attention to my health condition. The fact was that I was slowly dying, and no one even noticed that I was in pain. The teacher sent me home and told my mother not to send me back until I was well. She recommended to my mother that she take me to see a doctor. It was not until my aunt came for a visit about a week later that anyone did anything about my health. She took just one look at me and demanded that my mother call a doctor at once! Up until that moment, I had been just lying in bed every day, getting weaker and thinner. I was also getting a little closer to death.

Finally, someone did call the doctor. He came out to the house and took one look at me and ordered my parents to take me to the San Jose County Hospital. They took me that same night to the hospital admitting room. When the doctors saw me, they immediately began a series of tests and x-rays. They told my mom and stepdad that there was a good possibility that I could die, since I was already so far gone.

My frail, little nine-year-old body, fastened down with leather straps onto a hospital gurney, was wheeled down a hall away from my family. I did not have any time to say goodbye to them because it was

19

all happening so fast that first night. I can still remember looking up at the ceiling from the gurney, the bright lights hurting my eyes, as a nurse pushed me through the halls. Feeling like a prisoner immobilized on the stretcher, I was confused, sick, and scared.

The nurse took me into a separate facility outside the main hospital building to the isolation ward. I wondered why I had to be kept alone. Was this a treatment or punishment? No one had time to explain much to me.

In the room the nurse finally wheeled me into, I saw a metal table with a lot of long needles on it. They were the longest ones I had ever seen. The nurse informed me that they were going to stick them in my back and into my lungs to draw out fluid. It hurt like hell, but they kept sticking me over and over again. It went on for the longest time, with me sitting backwards on this cold metal chair in my underwear while they went about their job of suctioning fluids from around my lungs. When they finally finished, they left me sitting there alone for a few moments until a nurse came back to put me in bed. No one hugged me or even said that she was sorry. In fact, the nurse didn't say a word to me as I cried myself to sleep. That turned out to be just the first night of a very long and lonely year as a ward of the San Jose County Hospital.

#

Author's note: This was the longest year of my life—ever. I was restricted to total bed rest and not allowed to walk around or even to leave my bed. I spent most of the time alone without any other children. I had nothing for entertainment except my imagination. I had family visitors only once a week for about 10 minutes on Sunday afternoons. I learned so much about myself during this time that it was really the greatest education I could have gotten. It was a painful and lonely one, but one I would never trade for anything. The pain and discomfort became the spiritual vehicle for the many gifts that came into my life from this experience. This was the most defining moment of my young life before Vietnam.

My Mind Was My Only Playground

While spending that year in the hospital, I had only my imagination as a playground. No one provided me with any forms of entertainment such as reading material, toys, television, coloring books, or radio. I was very much alone and isolated almost all of the time. There rarely were any other children patients to talk to. Almost all my conversations for that entire year were with adults, and that was limited to the medical staff. That meant that I had to endure some very long days with nothing more to do than daydream and think. Time went very slowly. Every minute and each hour seemed to be the same, day after day, for almost a full year.

I was hurting inside for some attention and friendship, but I found none. I was on my own in that hospital and realized that the staff really didn't give a damn about me as a person. I was just a part of their job, someone that they were paid to medically care for.

I went for treatments everyday. Someone wheeled me in one of those old wooden wheelchairs over to the main building for x-rays and blood tests everyday. The people taking me around in the wheelchair rarely ever talked to me to see how I was feeling emotionally or what I was thinking about. Almost all the conversations were based on what medical information they needed to know from me and what they wanted me to do.

There were those continual shots into my lungs to extract fluid. This happened about six or seven more times over the first several

21

weeks. One day, as the nurse rolled me into the main building, she opened up a door and wheeled me onto a wooden platform stage. When I looked around, I saw rows of doctors seated in a small theater-like room. No one had prepared me for what this was all about. I had no idea what was in store for me.

The nurse undressed me and sat me down in front of all those strangers so they could see the procedure I was undergoing. It was humiliation time for me. Perhaps they thought I had no feelings. No one ever asked my permission to do anything. Had someone asked, I would have told him that I did not want to be displayed like some animal in an experiment in front of a crowd.

I took my mind away from all that was happening to me so I would not have to endure all these people watching me suffer. I refused to cry out when it hurt because I did not want them to enjoy my pain. It became a battle for my own dignity. I endured, but I did not win any prizes. I was always being reminded that the adults ran that place, and what a nine-year-old child wanted or felt was not important to any of them. When they did things to me, they talked about me as if I were not even a person or not even there. I was angry inside about what they were doing, but I didn't express it because I knew that yelling or complaining would be a futile emotional exercise. I practiced what I had learned very well from all my dealings with my stepdad—I suppressed my anger.

The procedure took much longer than usual since they stopped to lecture about the process as they went along. They even had some members of the audience come up and try sticking me with needles. They practiced by stabbing me through my back and into my lungs with long needles. Not all of them hit the right place or did it correctly, and the doctor in charge instructed them to do it again.

It hurt me both physically and emotionally sitting there enduring this procedure in front of everyone. I was being spiritually raped of my manhood right there on that stage by those uncaring doctors. No one even thanked me or apologized when they were finally finished. They just left me sitting on the platform stage in my underwear while they finished talking about the procedures. Finally, someone rolled me offstage and back to my ward where I lay alone in my bed and softly cried, unheard by any of the staff. Nobody stayed around to talk to me, and no one checked in on me or asked me how I felt. No one held my hand or hugged me. I was alone and abandoned.

#

Author's note: This is a hard concept to believe let alone accept, but almost everything major that has happened in my life up till now and even beyond this moment that I am writing this, I dreamed about while lying in my hospital bed many years ago. I have recalled some of those dreams just a short time before they became reality years later; others, I remembered for years before the "real" event happened. While sleeping in that hospital bed, it was as if someone showed me the future of my life—a dream at the time—if, in fact, any of them were just dreams. I even dreamed how my life will end some day, but that memory, mercifully, is blocked from my conscious mind. I do know I will remember it again, however, just before it happens.

Dreams of Future Events

I entered the hospital when I was only nine years old and stayed six months past my 10th birthday. I was there for all of the holidays. Thanksgiving was meaningless since nothing special happened, and I had few visitors. During Christmastime, someone dressed up as Santa, and he came into my room to say, "Hi." But this Santa brought me no toys, only some candy that the nurses promptly took way from me after he left. My own family didn't do anything special for me for any of the holidays; they didn't even bring me any gifts. Besides Santa, the staff did absolutely nothing special for any of the kids on the holidays. The only Christmas decorations were down the hallway at the nurse's station. In my room, there was nothing, not one single piece of tinsel, to designate that it was a holiday. I did my best to think of the real reason for the celebration—Christ and his birth. For me, a small child, however, being alone at Christmas was a lonely and depressing experience that year. I could hear Christmas music playing down the hall at the nurse's station, along with an occasional laugh from one of the staff, but this only added to my sadness.

The staff woke me every day at five or six in the morning when the shift changed. The long, dull hours stretched endlessly before me. I had no clock, so I never knew what time it was. I didn't know the date or even the day of the week. I spent my time going within my mind to keep myself entertained. I had many vivid dreams about people, events, and places that many years later I recognized in real

24

life. Many of these dreams became reality some five, 10, 20, and even 40-plus years later. To this day, things are still unfolding from these long-ago dreams that I had as a child.

Even at the young age of nine, I felt things inside me about love and God. I knew that there must be a purpose to all that had happened to me. I refused to think of myself as a victim. I knew that this experience would make me a different, better person. How I looked at life, after this time in the hospital, was altered forever.

I could not physically leave the hospital, but I had the freedom to think and dream. Free inside my mind, I searched for the deeper parts of myself. I prayed and talked to God. As my confidant, I thought he was perhaps the only real friend that I would ever be able to count on and trust. In many ways, I was blessed that all this had happened to me because it gave me a new perspective on my life.

I developed a hunger to change myself into a better person. I might have been physically in the hospital, but I was never mentally or spiritually a captive of that place. I took my mind on magical trips into new worlds and on great adventures. I created stories and did anything I wanted to in my mind. I found that the harsh world that held my body as a prisoner did not exist for me in my inner world. I learned a lot by keeping silent and lying still on my bed. I quieted my thoughts and emotions. I felt at peace.

Author's footnote: I had several things wrong with me due to a bad case of the mumps that I had developed and no one treated. Both of my lungs became infected and I developed bacterial pneumonia, which caused fluids to surround my lungs, a condition called pleurisy. In this weakened condition, I developed Bright's Disease or glomerulonephritis, a kidney disease. I was peeing blood, my blood pressure soared, and I had tremendous chest and back pains. I was dizzy all the time, and I couldn't stand up straight.

#

Author's note: If you like stories about love and dogs and angels, then this one is for you.

Angels and Dogs

The year was 1956, and I was 10 years old. I had just returned home from my long stay at the San Jose County Hospital where I was a captive for almost a full year of my young life. I had been through some long treatments and a year of complete bed rest. I was just glad to be alive and home again.

I was looking for ways to make myself better, not just physically but spiritually as well. Even though I was very young, I felt a strong urge and need to draw closer in my personal relationship with God. One of the first things I remember doing was taking a vow never to eat meat again. My thinking was that if the Catholics did not eat meat on Fridays, then I could go without it altogether. After all, I had so much to be grateful for. My mother was supportive of my decision, but she did suggest that I eat some fish and fowl since otherwise there would not be much for me to consume.

Shortly after making this personal decision, I shared a strange yet beautiful experience with my mother. The moment still stands out brightly in my heart and mind today. We were resting on the sofa in the living room when I began to hear what sounded like the singing of a church choir. I had never in all my life heard singing as wonderful as this. The multitude of muted feminine voices seemed to be coming from all around us, even from inside of me. The sound and feel of the sensuous music was soft—very holy, very sacred. I had never heard any church music sound so inspiring or so beautiful.

At first, I had thought that someone may have left on a radio or a record player. I could tell from the look my mother gave me that she was hearing the singing also! We both got up and searched the entire house, but we could not locate the source of this beautiful singing. No matter where I went, the music followed me. Outside, it seemed to be coming from the sky itself. A pleasurable, blissful chill came over my entire body, and a joyful shiver raced up my spine. It was like being loved and being in love.

No matter where we went, the music remained the same volume as if it were a part of us. The voices were everywhere, singing, praising, loving. My mother and I finally stood side by side, listening. Peace washed over both of us. I embraced the feeling of love that blossomed within myself. I felt as if I were being hugged by a divine being. Neither I nor my mother could offer any explanation for the singing, so we just absorbed all that awesome peace. Finally, after a blissfully long time, the voices gently faded.

My mother and I both felt lightheaded and joyous for several days following that event. Later, when my mother suggested to me that we had perhaps been blessed to hear the angels themselves singing, I fully accepted that as a fact. And it felt right.

Just a short while after this shared experience, a passing car hit one of our dogs. He could barely move when I found him lying there in the street. I tearfully carried him inside the house to the sofa where I knelt down on my knees and prayed. I prayed with all my heart and soul for God to heal my dog. With all my faith, I tensed up my entire body; then, I gently laid my hands on the dog and wished with all my strength for God to transfer that energy to him. It felt like electricity jumping from my fingertips into the dog's body. To my astonishment, my dog suddenly jumped off the sofa. He paraded around the house as if nothing had ever happened. He was healed! I believed that God healed my dog because I had trusted and believed in Him. My faith in God had healed my dog.

More strange and wonderful experiences began to unfold after that healing. I found that I was aware of events in the future, not just my own future but in the futures of other people I didn't even know.

At the time, I did not realize what was unfolding or why these things were happening to me. Back then, I was but a small, trusting child who somehow was graced to have experienced the magic and holiness of God's angels. I heard them sing, and they touched my heart and soul forever!

#

W.H. McDonald Jr.

Author's note: Sometimes small kindnesses are never forgotten.

A Neighbor's Love

When I was 11 years old, I used to go to a friend's house every day after school. It was about six blocks from where I lived. I do not think my mother knew where it was because she never asked for an address, a family name, or a phone number. I stayed there for as long as I could each day. My friend and I watched TV and played with his toys until it was time for his dinner. I sat in front of their TV set while they ate, and I did not take their hints to leave because I did not want to go home.

One day as I was finally leaving their house, I paused in front of their closed garage door and heard his mother lecturing my young friend about my being there all the time. She said that she didn't want me to come over so often. She also made some unkind remarks about my family and me, and she asked her son if I had a home to go home to. Her remarks hurt me deeply because I thought I was a welcomed guest. Heck, I didn't cause any trouble, and all I wanted to do was stay there and enjoy their family.

I ran home, feeling rejected and hurt by the mother's words. I vowed never to visit them again, which I never did. Looking back, I know that I overstayed my welcome. I was just a lonely little kid looking for love, some friendship, and a safe refuge from my own dysfunctional family life. Besides, they had a TV set and we didn't.

Later, a new family moved into our neighborhood four houses down from us. They were the nicest people I had ever met up to that time. The young mother may have sensed that I needed some attention because she gave it to me. She let me talk to her, and she actually listened to me as well. I told her what I thought about life and other important stuff. She also let me play with her children's toys. One day when she saw that I was attached to an old cowboy outfit and a couple of beat-up toy guns, she asked me if I would mind taking them home with me since her children didn't need them anymore. I was overjoyed.

Sometimes, she baked cookies for me and gave me milk. When she did this, it was the most enjoyable experience of the day for me. I

28

really loved this woman and her whole family. Her children were much older than I was, but she let me come over to play and just hang around even when her own children were not there.

She lived a wholesome lifestyle and projected an image of stability that my family certainly did not. She was the best thing for me at that age because she made me feel good about being me. I did not worry about saying or doing something wrong around her; I had the feeling that she would always like me no matter what I did. I visited her often, and she always treated me as if I were a part of her family. I certainly felt welcomed and loved there.

They lived on our block for only a short time. When she told me that they were moving, I took the news very hard. I stopped going over to their house. The funny thing is that I have absolutely no memory of the day she and her family moved. My memory draws a total blank on any of the details of their leaving. After she was gone, it was as if she had never been there. My mind just wrote off the whole history of that relationship and those memories. I guess I did not want to feel abandoned once again, so I did not mourn her moving away. She was one of the most positive people in my young life, yet I find it so very odd that I wrote off the whole experience of that relationship after she moved away. I had no feelings about it until now as I think about her and remember her influence on me. It was almost the same kind of reaction and response I had in Vietnam to death, battles, and relationships. I guess I learned early in life how to shut off my emotions in an attempt to protect myself.

#

Bill McDonald, 9, and Gary Rech, 17;
Marsha, 7, and Melody, 13, Engelking.

We Were Just Wildflowers

We were
Nothing more
Or less
Than random seeds
Scattered
Into a willing womb.

A product of passion
Not love.

My brothers
And sisters
And I,
Nothing
More
Or less
Than
Wildflowers
Along the road
Of life.

#

Author's note: As a young child, the art of listening to an insane, drunk man holding a gun to my head was a hard-learned lesson in how to deal with anything life threw at me.

Lessons in Listening from a Drunk

When my stepdad got drunk, he sometimes exploded with great anger and rage, aimed at the entire world around him. He did not always erupt into violence, but the fearful anticipation and anxiety that he created in me was 100 percent of the time. We didn't want to find ourselves anywhere near him after he had been drinking, which was almost all of the time he was awake and wasn't at work. A mean-spirited drunk, he was verbally abusive to anyone and everyone around him, but most especially to family members. It was hell to be around the house when he was home. I tried to stay away as much as possible when I was young.

He used to carry a bowie knife, hidden under the back of his shirt. The knife was at least a foot long. He had a leather sheath case for it that he tucked into his belt. He had no problem moving around with it. When it got in the way, he pulled it out and put it on the bar counter next to his drink. He also carried a loaded .357 Magnum pistol in a concealed holster under his jacket. It was a huge gun that he wore all the time, except at work when it was in his car. The very image of Dirty Harry's evil alter ego, he was always prepared for war with anyone.

One time, after he had disappeared for several weeks from our home, he returned to explain that he had been under investigation for shooting someone in the head with a shotgun. He told the cops that it was an accident, that it happened when he was cleaning the gun. He had witnesses testify that was what happened. The truth, he said, was that he had been paid by the witnesses to do it, a murder for hire. This was just one more killing he got away with, if you believed him. I certainly did. I knew that he could do something like that very easily to anyone.

He was involved in a knife fight in a bar in Palo Alto when I was about 12 years old. He had cut and sliced up some poor guy who ended up in the hospital. He claimed self-defense, and once again, he beat another rap.

He got mad one night at home. He took out a leather bullwhip and began to use it on our family dog, a large German shepherd who did not like my stepdad. He began to tear the animal's flesh apart with the leather whip. There was blood everywhere on that poor animal. The dog barked in great fear and pain, but he kept hitting the dog again and again. I couldn't take it any longer. I went into my parent's bedroom where he was whipping and beating this poor animal, and I told him to stop. He turned and looked at me with rage in his eyes. He told me to stay away or he would take the whip to me next. I ran in front of the dog to prevent further beating. He raised his arm and I waited for the blows, but he hesitated and dropped his arm. He then cursed me and walked away. The dog was bleeding badly. I wanted to cry for my dog, and I should have, but I couldn't. I was angry at my stepdad for what he was doing to our poor dog; but I dared not show that emotion outwardly, knowing that it might well lead to more violent consequences. I stood quietly, thinking how insane my stepdad was.

My stepdad came back into the room and told me that if I told my mom what had happened, he would personally kill me. I wasn't so sure he wouldn't have done it, so I did not want to take the chance. I figured my mom could see what had taken place by all the blood on the bedroom floor and on the walls, and by the huge, raw bloody marks on the dog. The dog continued to bark and cry softly as any hurt animal does.

On another occasion, he pulled his pistol out and put it right to my forehead. He then pulled back the hammer with his thumb. It was fully loaded and cocked, ready to fire. I could see the actual bullets in each cylinder, just inches from my face. I remember looking at each of them and wondering what it would feel like if he really did pull the trigger and those bullets penetrated my forehead.

He talked to me for what seemed like an hour, but in reality it must have been only a couple of minutes. It could have been a lifetime. I attentively listened without making any comments. I stood there not moving, breathing slowly and shallowly. I wasn't afraid as I should have been; I was tranquil and at peace. He reached up with his left hand and gently put down the gun's hammer to its resting position

33

on the cylinder. He pulled the gun away from my forehead and put it on top of a shelf in the hall closet as if nothing had ever happened between us. I stood there very still, not wanting to make any sudden or wrong moves. I was concerned about what this crazy man might do next, but he just walked away. I felt no emotion at all. I went to my bedroom and listened to records as if it were just a normal day. No fear, no tears, and no anger!

One night, I was awakened from a sound sleep by the "thunk!" of a large knife hitting the wall just above my head. He was drunk and was coming in to talk to me about his life and his sad childhood. He repeated this knife throwing on several other occasions; luckily, he always hit the wall. I learned to be a great listener at a very young age in order to survive. I listened to all his stories about beating, robbing, and even killing people. I never really knew what to believe, but I did not doubt the possibility that he would and could have killed as many people as he claimed. I never wanted to test him on this issue.

I respected that territorial line that separated his evil personal world from that of other normal human beings. Crossing it would have been dangerous at best, so I chose not to openly judge him or confront him with the obvious nature of his insanity. I left him alone both physically and emotionally, and I avoided any confrontations.

His own friends were actually afraid of him, too. No one gave him any lip. No one crossed him, and everyone just left him alone. He could be very evil and nasty when he was drunk. Most people just wanted to keep to themselves, staying quiet and cool-headed around him, so as not to set him off on some raging binge of violence and anger. I just listened and tried to become as invisible as I could.

#

Author's note: Never make promises to a child unless you plan on keeping them. They will remember it forever if you don't keep them. I know.

Promises Not Kept

My stepdad always promised to do things with me when he was drunk or feeling guilty about something, but he never came through with any of them. He meant well and talked a good talk at times. I always wanted to believe him, but I finally learned that it was just that—talk.

My Uncle Johnny (I only knew one uncle) once gave me his own personal shortwave radio. It was a transoceanic radio that could pick up stations from around the world. I was thrilled to get it even though it didn't work. It needed some minor work, a tube or something. My stepdad promised to get it fixed for me and packed it into his car one day shortly after my uncle gave it to me. Months went by, and every time I asked about it he told me to be patient. He said he had some guy working on it, but the part was not there yet. A full year or more expired when I finally asked him for the last time about the radio—my radio! He told me to stop bugging him about it. He went on to state that it wasn't that great a radio, so he gave it to a friend at a bar as a favor.

I guess he felt a little guilty about the radio episode, so he promised to take me fishing for the first time in my life. On the Saturday we were to go fishing, I got up before sunrise, ready and eager. I was at the kitchen table waiting for him to get up, have his breakfast, and take off with me in tow.

He came in and saw me sitting there all dressed for the fishing trip with my pole and equipment against the wall. My brother, Gary, had given me a beat-up, old fishing pole and a metal box that had a handful of small fishing hooks and lures in it that he said he didn't want anymore. He had never gone fishing that I knew of.

My stepdad told me that he had to go do a small job first thing that morning. He told me to hang around the house and wait because he would be right back for me. I waited all morning and all afternoon for him to return.

35

He finally came home after six o'clock that night. He said he had forgotten about me, but we would still go fishing. We got into the car and drove to Stanford University, where he worked at the time. He said he had to stop at a bar first to see a guy who could tell him where there was a good fishing spot. He returned to the car about an hour later and said the guy did not know of any good places to fish, but he said he knew of one. He drove to a fenced off area behind the university with large "No Trespassing" and "No Fishing" signs posted. He said there was a small lake just a short walk from the fence. We went over the barbed wire fence and walked to a lake. I didn't feel good about trespassing and was worried that someone might bust us and take my fishing pole. We both stood and looked at the water for a few minutes. He then declared that there were no fish in the lake, so we should go home. I never even got my fishing line wet.

We never fished, and I never asked to go anywhere with him again. I did not show any anger at the time and told him it was okay. I knew I had been screwed once again, but I decided to let it pass. My mother never said anything nor did anyone else. The fishing pole sat unused in my bedroom closet until years later when I finally gave it away. I have never had the desire to go fishing again, and I have not been fishing to this day.

#

Carol and Bill at the Christmas Prom, 1963.

Author's Note: This was one of many predictions that I made when I was young. It was another defining moment in my life and for all of my generation.

JFK Dreams

When I was a senior in high school, I kept having recurring dreams about President Kennedy getting shot. Not only shot, but killed. I saw images of people crying and watching television. I sensed from my dreams that the President was going to be killed very soon. I was bothered by the dreams, but I only shared my dreams with a few close friends at school.

On November 22, 1963, I felt very uneasy; I knew something was going to happen that day. I wasn't totally sure if it was related to all of my dreams I had been having for several weeks, but my uneasiness did make me vigilant that something was going to happen that morning.

While sitting in my government class, we heard the announcement over the school intercom about the shooting. The words came out slowly and brought a hushed silence to the class. Some kids softly cried while listening to the announcement of the president's death. It was such terrible news for us to hear.

Later that morning we heard a live radio broadcast from the United Nations. The radio announcer said the delegates were standing up for a minute of silent prayer in honor of the fallen President. So, I stood up by my school desk and was soon joined by others in the class, including the teacher.

The principal came over the intercom and told everyone that school was over for the day. We hung around the halls, talking quietly and trying to figure out what had happened and what was going to happen next.

I met up with Carol, and we walked to my house to watch the TV and see what was happening on the news. All the stations had coverage on the shooting and the follow-up stories. I was glued to the television set for the next three days. It was as if I were watching footage from my dreams—it was so unreal. The black and white images on the television screen were reflecting what I had already seen in my dreams many days before.

I felt I had lost a friend, and I was angry at the world for taking away my hero. It was hard to go back to school and still be excited about football and basketball games and school dances. None of it seemed that important to me anymore. Life did go on at school, but it took a little while and it was not the same. I got back into the grind of finishing out the school year, but my heart and soul were never in it again.

#

Author's note: I left for the Hawaiian Islands within 24 hours of my last day in high school. What a naive young man I was! I went on to meet an old Hawaiian kahuna,"Papa" David K. Bray, who had written, at that time, about 30 books on the Hawaiian history and culture. (Only one of his books is still in print, "The Kahuna Religion of Hawaii," coauthored by Douglas Low.) He also had been in an old Hollywood movie with Louis Jourdan and Jeff Chander in 1951, called "Bird of Paradise," which can still be purchased on DVD and video. He tried to instill in me the fundamentals of Hawaiian mysticism; although I was able to absorb and learn much, I made a very conscious choice not to go down this path with my life. Papa Bray showed me that he also had a dark side to his spiritual quest. He was not above using his psychic and mystical powers in negative and harmful ways. Unfortunately, a short time after I left the islands, my mother formed a spiritual alliance with him and his cohorts, unbeknownst to me until her death some 20 years later. She knew that I would have never approved; that is why she never told me.

Hawaiian Adventure

My plan was to purchase a one-way ticket to the Hawaiian Islands, go there, and just let my life unfold each day. I was very naive about a lot of things. This ideal of finding my fortune and fame in Hawaii was one of those innocent adventures in which I followed my heart and dreams.

I was able to buy a one-way ticket on an airline called, USOA, United States Overseas Airlines. The airplane had four propeller-driven engines, much like the airplanes in old black and white movies. In other words, this was an old airplane, even by 1964 standards.

My family did not give me any extra money. They had made a point of telling me that I was on my own when I left home. The flight departed from Oakland Airport the day after my high school graduation. A group of my friends went to the airport, along with my mom and stepdad. I was leaving with no return date. At that time, I was not sure if I were ever going to come back home again. I had $40 cash, one suitcase of clothing, and a lot of big dreams. As backup insurance in case I had problems, my sister Marsha gave me the address of her boyfriend's grandfather. Even though he would not know me, she wanted me to have an emergency contact there.

My mom made a point to tell me that if I got into trouble, I was not to call her because they had no money and could not help me out; I was on my own. Then, she went over to the flight insurance machine and purchased one hundred thousand dollar's worth of life insurance on me. I saw her doing this, and it made me sad. There she was betting on my life with money she could have given to me. I was worth more dead than alive to her.

When I got on the plane, I almost cried. I felt so alone heading off to somewhere I had never been. I did not know what I would find there. I was both excited and saddened by my mom's words and actions.

The flight took more than eight hours. When we landed, they rolled out a ramp so that we could deplane. Some FAA officials came out and put locks on the airplane's wheels. That was their last official flight. The airline went out of business; they were shut down.

I caught a bus for Waikiki Beach on the island of Oahu. There, I hooked up with a guy who was about my age that I had met on the airplane. I paid him $10 so that I could sleep on the floor of his hotel room for a couple of nights. It was just a block from the beach, so I put on my shorts and went for a walk that first night along the ocean's edge. It was already late at night, but the water was the warmest I had ever experienced. I waded and walked about four miles, drinking in all the sights and sounds of the beach and the people who were wandering around.

My money couldn't be wasted on things like food, so I began to fast. I knew that with only $30 left, I had better come up with a plan of action very quickly. I decided it would be wise to look up Marsha's boyfriend's grandfather. I hoped that he might assist me in some way with my job search or might know someplace I could flop on a sofa for a few days.

I had his address, so I walked out of the hotel and onto the street to seek directions. The first person that I asked told me to look up at the street sign. The grandfather lived on the same street as the hotel, less than 100 feet from where I was staying. My luck seemed to be once again working for me, as always!

41

I knocked on his apartment door and was met by an old Hawaiian kahuna. David Kaonohiokala Bray was the real thing. I had never met a real-live kahuna priest before, but he certainly looked every bit like I thought one should.

Papa Bray, as the locals called him, was a local god to the people on the islands. He had written many books on the history and religion of the Hawaiian Islands and its people. He was dark skinned and fat in a Buddha-like way with his stomach hanging over his belt. He and I both stood about 5' 7" tall, and his sea salt-like hair was all wild and white.

When he opened the door, he looked through me as if he were searching my very soul for who I was. It was a penetrating gaze that focused on my eyes. I was a little uncomfortable with him looking at me that deeply. I felt spiritually naked. He followed my brief introduction, in which I told him my name and my circumstances, with a long moment of silence.

He finally invited me into his apartment. Inside was like a strange New Age native church. On one wall, there was a large painting of the Hawaiian goddess Pele coming out of a volcano. There were strange artifacts, seashells, and Hawaiian paraphernalia all around the room. We sat down and talked as if we knew each other already. He offered to let me stay at his apartment for a few days and assist me in finding employment.

Those first few days we talked for countless hours. I listened to him talk about his thoughts on life and God. I told him about some of my feelings and dreams. He was the first person who really seemed to understand me. I felt I had found a long lost piece of the puzzle to my inner self. This man seemed to know things about me that no one else ever had. He stated his desire to have me follow in his path. He went on to tell me that he had been waiting for me to come to him for many years. For some reason, he made a point to tell me that he felt I was gifted with much more spiritual energy than he had. I was unsure of why he was telling me all this, but my youthful ego was flattered. I really did not know or even care if he were right, it just sounded good to have someone believe in my abilities.

All kinds of people came to his apartment for prayers and blessings at all hours of the day and night. The movie *In Harm's Way* with John Wayne, Kirk Douglas, and other famous actors was being filmed in Honolulu. (This movie came out in 1965, but they were filming it in Hawaii in 1964.) At night, some of the cast and crew came by to see and spend time with Papa.

I saw him using his occult powers in ways that brought about healings and good results, but he also had a dark side. He did have supernatural powers, which he activated by chanting or by prayers. I could see that his power was slowly becoming corrupted by his ego and sensual living. It is hard to explain all that happened over several months time in my association with him. There was a lot of good in the man's soul. He asked me to begin an apprenticeship with him so that he could pass on his powers and knowledge. He showed me many strange and wonderful things such as how to cure people of certain aliments through the use of herbs, chants, and potions made from frog hearts and ground-up corral. He could also cast spells for success and even love. I did learn much, however, I did not want that kind of power and told him so. I was looking for my own personal enlightenment, and I did not want to become a leader of any cult. His dark side convinced me that what he was doing could become dangerous for me and others. I did not want to promote that kind of spiritual path.

He did get me a couple of jobs on Oahu. The first one was on the other side of the island in Kailua. I lived in a small cabin on the beach and worked at a restaurant nearby. While working in the kitchen one day, I spilled a large pot of boiling rice on myself. A large amount of the hot rice splashed on my stomach and chest. My immediate reaction was to drop the whole pot, which landed right on my legs and tennis shoes. It stuck to my clothing and shoes, badly scalding my skin. Big blisters formed all over my legs and feet. I was unable to wear anything except a swimsuit for several weeks afterward. I was unable to wear any shoes for about four months. I could not afford to go to a doctor, so I suffered with large fluid-filled blisters all over my legs for several weeks.

The next job, as a custodian for a school, came after a long period of unemployment. I was paid $1.25 per hour and worked full-time. I was able to save enough to buy an airline ticket for San Francisco.

When my time came to leave, Papa told me several things about what would happen to me in the future. (These all proved correct.) He then told me that we were long lost friends from a past life on these very islands where we were both big kahunas. I listened to him and at some level believed what he had to say, but I could not afford, either financially or spiritually, to stay there any longer. It was time to close this chapter on my life and move on.

When I left the islands, I got a big sendoff from Papa and some Hawaiian girls. I had several garlands of flowers, leis, draped around my neck as I boarded the plane. I wore my suit, with the leis swagged across my chest, but I was not wearing shoes or socks. It was rather interesting in that years later, my look reminded others of the way The Beatles dressed on the *Abbey Road* album with their bare feet and suits.

In San Francisco, I was the last to get off the airplane. When I did emerge, I saw a large crowd. My friends were sensitive to how I felt when I left for Hawaii, so they took it upon themselves to be there to welcome me home. They cheered when I got off the airplane, and other people came over, thinking that I must be a famous person. Soon, there was a small mob of people, many of them total strangers, trying to get a look at me. I loved it all. I felt I had been very successful on my first journey away from home. However, I really didn't want to go home again. I vowed that this was going to be just a rest stop before I left again on another adventure.

Author's footnote: "Papa" David K. Bray spent his lifetime exploring what was beyond the horizon of our material world. In 1968, his spirit sailed out from these shores for the last time to embrace that other reality that so few of us in our busy daily lives ever attempt to explore or even understand.

#

Author's note: This, I suppose, could have been classified as a miracle in that I should have been killed in this incident, but I wasn't even injured. I really do not understand why I wasn't. Someone seemed to be looking after me.

Asleep at the Wheel

In the spring of 1965, I was just a young man of 19. I had dreamed of traveling and seeing the world, but I had come from a poor family. I did not have much money, but I was not going to let that stop me from broadening my personal horizons. I set off on what must have looked to others as a foolishly-conceived adventure, hitchhiking across the country from San Francisco to New York City. I was going to catch a flight out of New York for Europe, which meant that I had a deadline in order to get on my airplane.

I had been hitchhiking almost nonstop for three days. I only slept for a few hours when I was in someone's car, and I was very tired. I could hardly keep my eyes open. The only thing that kept me from falling asleep was that I was standing on the roadside. There was a cold Indiana wind that was beating up my body and chilling me inside and out. I was totally exhausted, but I could not afford to spend a night at a hotel. I needed to keep moving closer to New York. If I got a ride, I could sleep while the guy drove; anyway that was my plan.

It must have been around midnight, and I had been standing for a couple of hours watching car after car pass by me in the darkness. My mind was thinking about how my own family didn't seem to care where I was or what might happen to me. I began to feel alone and a little depressed. I wanted to travel not so much just to see things, but I also realized that I was trying to escape from my family. It was a very low point in my life. I was cold, tired, and lonely. I felt that no one loved me. It was the lack of sleep getting to my normally upbeat and happy self.

Finally, a car pulled over and some guy in a business suit honked the horn and waved for me to get in. I ran the distance between us in the darkness and jumped in his warm car. I was looking forward to falling asleep and just going for a ride to get out of the cold wind.

45

However, when I got in, he asked me to drive. He said he was very tired, and he needed me to drive so he could sleep.

I was not in any mental shape to drive, but it was either drive or keep hitchhiking in the cold, so I figured I could do it. I put my backpack in the back seat and got in the driver's seat. I pulled back onto the highway and got the speed of the vehicle up to about 70 mph. The businessman was already falling asleep as I was moving along the interstate.

I was having a difficult time staying awake. I kept drifting back and forth between sleep and being awake. After a while, I was not sure if I was still awake or dreaming. Then, I stopped drifting and fell completely asleep. I was driving perhaps as fast as 90 or 100 mph when the car left the paved highway and began to spin around and around, creating a huge cloud of dust. I had somehow managed to spin the car around more than a half dozen times before it came to a complete stop—all on its own.

I had done nothing but hang onto the steering wheel. I had not even applied the brakes. I was now fully awake as I surveyed my surroundings. The businessman was wide-eyed awake, too. We both stared out the windows. No one said a word. I could tell he was upset, and my heart was still pumping wildly.

We could see that somehow the car had managed to spin around and through a dense forest. There were trees all around the car, most were only a few feet apart. It was impossible for the car to have avoided hitting trees; they were everywhere and there were no straight lines to drive into or out of where we found ourselves in this forest.

It seemed that the car had actually spun around and changed directions several times, and in doing so, it avoided hitting anything. We both got out of the car to take a closer look around. We could see the tracks and skid marks that wrapped themselves around several trees. It was an amazing sight, and neither of us could figure out why we were not dead or seriously injured from a crash into any one of those trees. There was just no way anyone could have driven into this forest at any speed, even wide awake and in the daylight, and not have hit something!

The man was now fully alert. He also was not too happy with my driving skills, and he moved himself back into the driver's seat. Getting out from where we were took us several minutes of backing up and pulling forward just to avoid hitting anything. When we finally pulled out of the woods and onto the side of the highway, the guy just looked at me, shook his head and said, "You're one very lucky kid. We should have both been killed back there; somebody upstairs must really love you!"

His words hit me. Yes, Somebody does, and I drifted off into a relaxing, peaceful sleep in the back seat of his car.

\#

Author's note: I very much wanted to see Europe when I was a young man. Although I had big desires, I had little money. Nevertheless, this was the beginning of my journey around Europe. I went on great faith that things would all work out for me, and of course, they always did.

Europe on a Dollar a Day

When I got off the plane, I had no idea where in the world Luxembourg was in relation to the rest of Europe, let alone the world. I was, however, ready for anything and everything. I felt as if I were going home—not like the one I had left, but like the one of my dreams where people who love me, welcome me and make me comfortable. I left the airport and walked out to the road and looked at the several possible directions I could take, and since I had not been to any place in either direction, I went with my feelings and walked down the road to the east.

I ended up at the edge of Luxembourg City where I met a young traveler from England. He told me about youth hostels and how I could stay cheaply in them. I followed him to the hostel where he spoke for me, telling the clerk that I had lost my membership card. I felt very fortunate to have run into this guy because I ended up using my "replacement" card all over Europe. But, in life, there are never any accidental meetings.

I was wide-eyed with excitement at seeing so many new things and meeting people from far off places. The first night at the hostel I was staying with a group of German, Italian, and English students. We spent several hours singing both American and German folk songs. The group was very open and friendly to me as they gave me their best advice on how to make my money last, on where to go, what to see, and even what to do and not to do. I took mental notes and was thankful that I was lucky to have found a hostel and so much information the first night I was in Europe.

It did strike me as odd that my family wasn't worried about my whereabouts some 6,000 miles away. I had no address or any way for them to contact me. They did not even know if I had made it safely to New York. Yet there I was, a 19-year-old adventurer, alone with about $130 cash in my pocket and still as optimistic as any sane person dares to be. I knew that Someone was looking after me. I really believed that everything would turn out okay for me if I just kept the faith and stayed within the boundaries of my own moral code. That first night I went to sleep feeling really free for the first time in my life. I did not have to be any place at any time and I was debt free. I had no one depending on me for support. I also was as free as the wind to fly off in any direction I chose. It would be the only time in my life that I was truly free of obligations. I felt good about it and knew that this was the right time and place for me to make this journey. It felt right both spiritually and intuitively.

The next day I was off exploring the city and watching the people. Someone was always able to speak enough English, so I had little trouble communicating my needs. Fed and rested, I began my day's adventures at an old castle high up on a cliff. There were guided tours for about 25 cents, so I went along. When they came to several passageways under the castle, I took my own path (both metaphorically as well as physically) to explore a different route from the tour group. I saw all kinds of additional passageways that kept twisting and backtracking under the castle. There was a familiar feeling about the place, so I was never worried, even after several hours of wandering produced more tunnels and dungeon-like rooms. I finally found the main passage again and joined in behind the last group leaving the castle before the guards locked up for the night.

I loved this city; it really looked like the Europe that I'd seen in the movies and on old postcards. I wandered around the city for several more days; then, I decided to go to Paris to see the flowers that bloomed in April. The old song "April in Paris" kept playing in my head, so I wanted to be able to say that I was in Paris during April.

I walked out of the city and country of Luxembourg and headed south. I had no maps and very little sense of where I was, but in my heart I knew I would end up where I wanted to be.

It was around one in the morning, and it was very dark and isolated on the backcountry road I had taken heading south. There were no lights anywhere, and I had a feeling, which was more a fear, that someone or something was watching me. It was so dark that I could not even see my feet as I walked along the middle of the road. My surroundings began to stimulate my imagination. I thought there

49

were aliens from a UFO watching me and preparing to take me away with them. My conscious mind knew it couldn't be a real possibility, but I had an inner fear that made my heart pound at the thought of it. I stood still in the middle of the road and felt the weight of eyes on me. I wanted to get out of there as fast as I could. The only sound I heard was from an owl. Normally, the sounds of an owl brought me a good deal of comfort. In my heightened state of paranoia, however, I thought about how much an owl's eyes resembled what I imaged an alien's eyes looked like. I figured this was not where I wanted to spend the night alone. The more I walked down the road, the more I felt someone's eyes watching me. I could not shake the feeling, which made it impossible for me to stop and camp in my sleeping bag in the open fields.

Finally, getting tired and sleepy, I mentally dozed off and lost track of time. The next thing I remember was a truck driver stopping for me. He did not speak any English, so I tried to explain where I wanted to go. He let me crawl into the back of his truck and sleep while he drove south to within six or seven miles of Paris.

It was raining hard and the dark skies shot out massive displays of lightning. The truck driver let me out on the road about five in the morning, in the cold rain. I began to walk up a hill, and when I reached the top I saw lightning strike the Eiffel Tower in the distance. It was beautiful. The whole skyline was aglow with the lightning strikes. It was like a movie, and I was getting to see and be a part of it during the filming. I felt alive and in love with this city of lights that lay ahead of me. I knew that good things awaited me there.

I walked around the city all day long until almost midnight. I was soaked from the rain, but I did not care about getting cold or wet. I was in Paris, and I had never felt so alive with energy. It felt very holy and sacred, and I was very much at peace within.

I bought a large loaf of French bread that must have been over three feet long and put it in my pack. I also bought a small bottle of wine so I would have a container to put water in after I emptied it. I was not fond of wine, but it was the only thing I could find to drink that I trusted. I ate and drank as I walked all over the city and watched the people. I felt very comfortable there, and I had no trouble finding my way around.

I never did get very tired. I found that each street and turn I took brought me new and exciting discoveries. Paris was everything I had expected and so much more. I was in love with this city and felt it loved me back.

I finally decided that I needed a room so I could get some sleep. I found a rundown hotel next to the Seine River, and I got a room for five francs or about $1.25. I had the top-floor room, up 13 flights of stairs. It had no restroom or shower; those were down four flights from the room. The room was around seven or eight feet long and six feet wide, about the size of a small walk-in closet. The ceiling came down to five feet at the window and was just above the door. It was clean and had a bed. There was a window that I hoped would have a lovely view of the city come first light. Although I could look out of the window only while lying on the bed because of the height of the window and the wall, I was pleased. I dropped of to sleep without any effort at all.

I woke up early the next morning, and I looked out of my window expecting to see the city. Instead, I had a view of the roof and art studio next door. I was even joyous over this; for this too was Paris and it was perfect. I thanked God for my being there. I meditated, wrote poetry in my journal, and I got dressed to go out to see the city. I left my belongings in the room so as not to be encumbered with my backpack and sleeping bag as I had been the day before. I could really travel around the city now.

The first thing I wanted to do was to find old churches and museums. I had no trouble finding any of them. I sat for some time in each church, feeling and absorbing all the energy of devotion and prayers by so many people over hundreds of years. There is something very special about old churches, for they bring much inner peace to the heart and soul. I said my prayers of thanks to God and my guru for taking such good care of me. I wanted to stay in each church I visited, but I also hungered to see many other sights. I felt I knew each church as an old friend that I had come back to visit. I had never felt so at peace in my whole life up till then.

Next, I went to the famous French museum of art, the Louvre. The place was huge. It was so large that I had to come back over the next three days to see it, and I still saw less than three-quarters of it.

I wanted to see the famous painting of the "Mona Lisa," but I found out that for the first time in its history it was not there. It was on loan to New York City for the 1964–1965 World's Fair. I never got to see "her" and thought it was odd that the painting was in New York City when I was there.

I remember tourist buses coming to the museum and all those people rushing to see the entire place in less then an hour. There was a joke I heard at a youth hostel about a young track star from Japan who did a sub-four-minute tour of the Louvre. I thought at the time it summed up how many people visit museums and churches. They do not sit and spend time absorbing the energy of such magnificent places, and therefore, they miss out on the true experience.

I next went to see that grand church that sits so saintly along the Seine River, Notre Dame. I was totally awed by its beauty and sacredness. It was truly a sanctuary for God. I went inside and looked for a stairway that would take me up to the roof. I found one that was hidden from the public, and I went up as far as it took me. There was a window from which I was able to climb out onto the roof. I then climbed even higher onto the utmost top part of the structure. The view was all that I had dreamed it would be. I sat down on the roof, so as not to be seen from the ground, and meditated for some time. I felt the holy vibrations of that great church coming up and all around me. I spent a great part of the day up there. I can still see the view in my mind today.

One cultural problem I had to learn about was how the French people used the restroom. I needed to go, and a helpful man told me that the funny looking structure on the corner of the street was a men's water closet (restroom). It consisted of a metal wall that was only about six feet tall, but it had no wall structure from the ground up to about two feet. I had to walk inside this rounded metal fence and pee on a wall with water flowing down it.

I was not sure how private it was going to be with hundreds of people walking past, but I decided "when in Rome, do as the Romans do." Well, this was not Italy, but I figured the same applied to this situation. I finally relaxed and was standing at the wall when the traffic light turned red and a double-decker bus, loaded with young college-age American students, pulled up next to the wall. The next thing I realized was that cameras were sticking out of the bus windows as the students shot photographs of me standing at the "peeing" wall. I did not know if I should smile or hide. I did not move, and I waited until the light changed green before pulling myself away from the wall to zip up and leave. I guess I must be famous in someone's photo album back in Kansas or Iowa.

I stayed in Paris for several weeks. I never got enough of watching the nightlife or the street artists' creating their chalk masterpieces on the sidewalks during the day. I spent many enjoyable hours in the outdoor cafés where I sipped French coffee, wrote poetry, and talked with strangers who sat next to me. I thought of myself as a beatnik, and I told myself that I was absorbing the whole emotional experience around me for future poetry and writings. Which, as it turns out, I really was.

#

W.H. McDonald Jr.

Author's note: I wrote binders full of poems when I was traveling around Europe. I sat and watched people coming and going from my vantage point at some sidewalk café while drinking coffee. The following is one that reflected my young thoughts about the busloads of noisy, photo-taking tourists that filled some of the churches. I enjoyed the off-main street churches that attracted local devotees, what I thought to be true worshipers. I wrote this poem in Paris, April 1965.

Satisfied Is Not a Place

Churches and temples
Seem so empty and void of angels
When they are only filled
With tourists.

Visiting,
And being a part of
Something
Are not the same.
I can find no satisfaction
In just looking at a river.
I need to fully immerse
In its cool current
To really know
And understand it.
I must become
A part of it.

#

Paris, 1965

Author's note: I wrote this while stuck for hours on an isolated road outside of Luxembourg, waiting for someone to stop and give me a ride to Paris or anywhere that was out of the rain.

Hitchhiking Across Luxembourg

May, 1965

People traveling past me
Looking through me
As their journey melts
Into the horizon's
Frozen stare.

The real gurus
Wait somewhere else tonight.
They do not have to contend
With sense pleasure thoughts, or worries,
Nor any cancer-coffin fears,
While standing cold and wet
And spiritually naked
On some rain-soaked, lonely highway of doubts.

The real gurus tonight
Are inwardly seeking some divine mistress
Beyond this conscious world.

While I continue to spend my moments
Alone on this garbage highway
Hitchhiking
Across this material world,
While praying that some
Beethoven-Shakespeare-Christ
Will find me
And give me a ride
And perhaps some wisdom.

#

W.H. McDonald Jr.

Author's note: I found Italy, Rome in particular, to be so soul satisfying that I really did not wish to leave. I had little money to see the big tourist sites, so I mingled with the local people. My 19-year-old eyes found this a very exciting place to visit. My adventure in the Vatican could never take place today with all of the new security concerns, but I am glad I had my chance to explore all that I did. At a youth hostel, I had teamed up with an English medical student who was on break from college. He had brought over an old London taxicab that we drove around the city.

Roman Holiday

In Rome, my new English friend and I took in all the sights and even explored the catacombs along the old Apian Way, where early Christians had hidden from persecution. The tunnels and caves were quiet reminders to me of how the love of God could not be killed off by any man. Thousands of those early believers were killed in the Roman Coliseum for fun and sport. I wandered through those tunnels and felt I was walking on holy ground. There were several early popes and saints entombed in some of the ones I explored.

The city of Rome was full of things to see and do, and we saw everything over several days. We even stopped at the Spanish Steps and ran up and down all 137 of them. The church, Trinità dei Monti, at the top of the steps, was built about the time America was discovered.

I wanted to explore Vatican City and perhaps catch a glimpse of the Pope if he were home. I was young and not too smart in the ways of the world. So, my friend and I went off to explore the Sistine Chapel where Michelangelo painted the ceiling.

I wandered around, and my friend followed me as I went to the room where the College of Cardinals elects the new popes. We saw the potbelly stove that they burned the ballots in. We next wandered down the halls and explored the other rooms and buildings.

I actually wandered unnoticed into the area where the Pope resided. There is just no way that this should have happened. There were security guards, but no one took notice of two bold, young men strolling around the Pope's residential compound.

We spent several hours having fun and feeling at home until a Swiss Guard finally asked us what we were doing there. We explained we were lost. By this time we were ready to leave anyway, so we allowed him to escort us out of that area. Looking back, I do not understand how anyone could have just walked around the Vatican as we did. We had actually gone inside a home and looked inside a huge walk-in closet that had what looked like the Pope's ceremonial robes. It was almost as if no one could see us as we wandered wherever we wanted to go without any concern. It was a wonderful experience; however, I know that it is something that no one would be able to do today, given the security concerns of these modern times.

Later, we decided to pick up some women at the Rome airport with our old London taxicab. This turned out to be a big mistake and not a very smart decision for us. It seems that taxi drivers the world over have á competitive edge that makes them unwilling to let young punk kids take business away from them.

We were parked at the airport when a group of Australian flight stewardesses called out to us for a ride. They thought it would be fun to ride in a London cab, so they all jumped in and we took them to their hotel. When we got there, we could see trouble was brewing for us. There were about three or more taxies following us. Worse yet, with every street that we passed we picked up more taxies, joining the parade of cabs behind us.

We began to drive faster, but they were on our bumper and pushing us. We turned the corners as fast as we could and headed out of the city. However, they continued to follow us no matter how fast we went. The road got narrow and there were high cliffs going down to the ocean to our right. We knew we had to try to talk some sense into the taxi drivers before they forced us off the cliff. We pulled over. They stopped next to us, in front of us, beside us, and all around us, blocking the entire road with at least a dozen cabs.

They got out and quickly surrounded us, looking angry and mean. Some of them had knifes in their hands and a couple had metal tools and car jacks. I knew it would take some fast talking and some good old McDonald luck to get out of this mess.

We tried to explain in English that we were not charging money and that we were just passing through Rome. They told us to never come back, or they would kill us. They sounded serious about it. Yet, my young English friend, after waiting just a couple of hours after the taxis cleared the highway, turned his London cab around and drove right back into the city. I was a little concerned to say the least, but I trusted my luck and went along for the ride. We tried to be as invisible as possible with our old London cab, even though it had a large and easy-to-see "TAXI" sign bolted right on top of the roof. We went to a party that evening where we met some young women. We took them on as fare-paying passengers, which paid for our gas and food. We left early the next morning, heading north on the Italian coastal roads to Pisa and as far away from Rome as we could.

#

Author's note: In my beloved city of Paris, where I ran out of money, a rich and powerful family fed and took care of me. The wife was the highest ranking female judge in France and a personal friend of the president of France. They really took great care of me and then sent me on my way to the coast so I could catch my ship to New York. This story takes up right after I left Paris and began hitchhiking again.

Waiting for My Ship

I had spent the day hitchhiking and being rather lucky. Everyone who gave me a ride, also fed me and gave me something to drink. I finally ended up in a small village along the banks of the Seine River. I was getting hungry again and needed a place to spend the night. I had no money except for a few loose coins in my pocket and the ticket for my trip back to America, so buying food or paying for a room were not options.

I figured God had provided for me very well that day with a free breakfast, a free lunch, and plenty of drinks and snacks. Now, I felt He should take care of my dinner needs as well. And while He was at it, I thought He should get me a place to sleep for the night, too. I had the greatest faith that my needs would be met.

I sat down on the street curb in the small village. I looked at my watch and decided I was going to give God just three minutes to take care of my needs. I knew He would provide for me, so I began my wait. Within two and half minutes a beautiful young lady, about 28 or 30 years old (I later learned that she was a local schoolteacher), came over and asked me why I was sitting on the curb. I told her I was waiting for dinner and a place to stay.

She no doubt thought I was crazy and needed her help. She told me to follow her into a building where a community meeting was going on with the people in the village. She sat me down in the back of the room and went to talk to the people running the meeting.

They all stopped talking and turned their heads to look me over. They motioned to an older woman who came over, took me by the hand, and led me outside. The schoolteacher explained to me that the older woman was a sea captain's wife who was going to take me home with her. She did not speak any English, but some of her nine children did. She was a kindly woman who treated me like one of her own sons.

I was welcomed not only in her home, but the whole village took an interest in my situation and me. Each day, as I wandered around the streets of this small village, someone gave me a copy of an American newspaper. Also, people gave me food and pastries all day long.

The schoolteacher who had helped me requested that I spend some time helping her classes with their English lessons. I went to her school a few times where I had conversations with the young students in English. I was only slightly older, 19, than the 16- to18-year-old students. It was a lot of fun for everyone, including myself. I told them about surfing, American football, and dating in the good old U.S.A. In return, they told me about dating, sports, and their favorite music in France.

I tried to be helpful around the sea captain's house since I was a guest. I did yard work and helped to paint the house. I did not realize that some of her flowers were not weeds, and I pulled them. She tried not to show that she was upset about it, but I felt bad. She gave me a big motherly hug and tried to make me feel okay about it.

Several villagers gave me tours of the surrounding countryside. Someone also took me to see the famous beaches of the D-day invasions. It was while I was there, overlooking one of the beaches, that I had a strange sort of flashing dream. It was like a memory that popped into my mind.

What I felt from this "memory dream" that flashed inside me was the struggle and fears of a young American soldier who was wounded and drowning in the surf of that beach. I felt an instant sorrow and then relief. I somehow felt all that young man had thought and feared as he rolled, dying, in the surf that day. I felt the loss he felt at having never seen France and having died without ever getting to fight in the war.

I realized at some level within, that I was that same man coming back to where it had ended 21 years before. I felt strange about it and wasn't sure if it were real or just my imagination. It was such a strong dream and feeling, I believed it had to be me I was seeing and feeling that day.

When I left the town, the people arranged for me to stay with an old college professor and his wife. They told me that they had waited 21 years to repay an American for freeing their city and kicking out the Germans. He told me personal accounts of the invasion as he saw it from his residence. He saw the dead GIs floating in the waves and his heart went out to them. He made a point to show me everything that he could. He treated me as his token American so that he might pay gratitude to this karmic debt.

I still felt the regret of that American GI whom I "remembered within" at the beach. He was still very much within my heart. He had wanted to see Europe and to fight the war, but never got off the beach alive. I somehow knew and felt that through me his desire had now been fulfilled, even if it took a second lifetime to do so.

#

W.H. McDonald Jr.

Author's note: I was inspired to write these lines of poetry while standing in the graveyard above the beaches at Normandy. It was an emotional place for me.

Sunrise Over Normandy—21 Years Too Late

The cool June air rushing over and through my clothing
Chills me on this June day.
One can almost still sense the blood
As it must have flowed
Across these killing fields of sand.

This is where
The death machines of war
Ate up all those young souls.
I can hear the birds nearby,
Crying out in their collective remembered fears,
Of grown-man-children losing their lives
On those very beaches below.

I am cold and nothing seems able to warm me
Not even my woolen jacket can bring me any relief
From the coldness of war's huge footprints on this land.

There is a part of me here and a part of you.
A part of every man who has stood
In harm's way trying to free others
While risking his own life.

I feel cold wetness rolling down my cheeks.
I look around to see if anyone is near
Who might be watching me
Drowning in memories
And history of what happened here.
But it matters not,
I cannot hide
From myself

Or God.

#

Written on the beaches of Normandy, June 5, 1965

W.H. McDonald Jr.

Part 2

My Tour of Duty

My Army Years, 1965–1968

March 1967, South Vietnam
"War is thus divine in itself, since it is a law of the world.
War is divine through its consequences of a supernatural
nature… War is divine in the mysterious glory that
surrounds it and in the no less inexplicable attraction that
draws us to it…"
Joseph De Maistre (1753–1821), French diplomat, philosopher.

Author's note: This really was the beginning of the end of my childhood—nothing would ever be the same again for me.

The Draft—The End of My Childhood

When I got back home from my trip to Europe, there was not enough room for me in my family's apartment. They had moved to a small apartment after they sold their home. Now I needed to figure out what exactly I was going to do with my life. I wanted to get away and leave the area again, so I began to explore the possibilities. Over the next several weeks I took the physical examinations for the Army, Navy, Marines, and Air Force at the Oakland Induction Center. I was trying my best to get into any service, and I was not having any success with the results. I kept getting rejected, classified 4-F. They based it all on my childhood medical history and my chest x-rays. They believed that I was trying to defraud the system by enlisting, and then going after a pension from the military for medical reasons that they felt I was hiding from them. It was really bizarre thinking based, I think, on the fact that everyone else was trying not to join.

I realized that I had to do something with my life, so I went to San Francisco and signed up for the Military Sea Transportation Service, better known as MSTS. It was the old Merchant Marine Service. The jobs paid good money, and they went to the Far East. Ports of call included Saigon and the war zone areas. I went down and got my overseas and Asian shots and had all the paperwork done. They were ready to ship me off to Vietnam when they mentioned that I needed to be cleared by my draft board.

I felt this would be a mere formality since the services considered me physically unfit to join. At the draft board, they told me that I needed to take a complete predraft physical to establish my draft status and rating. I figured this would be no problem, since I had just spent the last couple of weeks failing the same physicals in Oakland. Now, I was going back to see the same doctors.

I reported for my free bus ride to Oakland at 4:30 a.m. at the San Jose Draft Board offices. They took all of us young men on a fleet of five chartered buses to the Oakland Induction Center. It was very quiet on the bus trip. The day at the center was a very long and boring process—even more so for me since I had gone this medical examination route several times already. We stood in long lines all day in just our underwear. We were poked and prodded as we handed over our paperwork from one doctor to another. They asked me the same old questions about my health and medical history. I gave them the same answers to their medical questions that I had given them when I had failed these same physical exams a few weeks before. These were the same doctors, but this time, the results were different. They felt that I was trying to get out of the draft, so they discounted all my medical history and said I was classified as 1-A, and fully fit for military service. What a kick in the butt that was. I stood there totally surprised and a little angry at the same time. What a farce all this was. I could see that I was at the whim of these men and women in white. How could I be unfit five days before, and then the same doctors with the same information determine me to be fit for duty when nothing had changed except their decision.

I found out that my draft board had listed me as a volunteer for the draft. This wasn't just a casual classification draft physical but an induction physical. That meant that I could be inducted at the end of the physical I had just taken.

I was thinking over the situation, not sure what to do, when an Army recruiter who happened to be in the same building approached me. He told me that I would be smart to join for an extra year, so I could get some good career schooling. His idea of good training was helicopter maintenance. He told me that this would be good civilian job training for later when I got out of the Army.

I signed up for the extra year in the good old U.S. Army. I was given the oath, fed a meal at a cheap restaurant, and then loaded onto another bus that was heading for basic training at Fort Ord, California. I didn't even have a toothbrush or a change of underwear with me. Welcome to the Army!

Author's footnote: My basic training was at Fort Ord, California, from November 8, 1965, to January 1966. Then, I went to Fort Rucker, Alabama, for three months of aviation schooling to learn how to work on Hueys and other aircraft. I was assigned to Fort Campbell, Kentucky, after that, where I volunteered for Vietnam. I got orders to leave in October 1966. I returned from Vietnam a year later, and finished my Army career at Fort Benning, Georgia. I departed the Army November 7, 1968.

#

Author's note: Once I realized that I would eventually be going to Nam, I wanted to go and get it over with. I had actually believed in all the reasons we were fighting for over there. I had taken Far Eastern history classes and read numerous books on French Indochina history including all of Dr. Tom Dooley's books. I had some knowledge of what had happened there over the years, but it still didn't prepare me for what I found. This story is about getting ready to go over. I was on leave and said all my goodbyes to my friends and family. I felt as if I were going over to fight the great holy crusade against communism. Yes, I was a true believer.

Orders for Nam—Home on 30-Day Leave

I finally had my orders, as did another guy in my company at Fort Campbell, Kentucky. We decided to head home to California together since we were both from there. We took the trip in his old car, and we split the gas cost. On the cross-country drive, we talked about how proud we were that we had volunteered to serve our country and rid the world of the evils of communism. We looked forward to doing our part in what we both thought was going to be a quick little war in Asia. We even put a sign on the car that read, "Vietnam Bound."

Our families both lived in the San Francisco Bay Area, so we traveled all the way to Hayward where he lived. I managed to get a ride home to Sunnyvale, which was just a few miles down the road.

My family had moved out of our old house and into an apartment building. I did not know anyone there. The apartment really did not have enough room for me to stay in it comfortably, but for three weeks it would have to do.

I found out that one of my high school classmates, Mike Harrison, was not only home on leave before going to Vietnam (on the same day I was to report), but he was also getting married to another classmate, Donna Dixon. They invited me to their wedding before we both had to leave for the war.

The wedding was a rather sad affair for me since it was just days before we were shipping out for a year, assuming that we didn't get ourselves killed or maimed in the process!

I tried to find some small pleasures in visiting friends and relatives before I went away, but I did not. I experienced and suffered through a series of judgmental and negative comments from almost everyone, even my relatives, who questioned the war and why I was going there. It was not a friendly exchange of hugs or well wishes, but more like small lectures from people. Everyone felt that they had the right to give me a hard-ass lecture about the morals and ethics of this war. After a few days of this crap, I decided to relax by going to San Francisco to spend some time doing what I enjoyed best—walking around Broadway mingling with the crowds. At night, I often sat in a coffee shop writing my poetry on napkins or any scrap of paper that I could find.

One foggy night, Karen, an old high school friend, accompanied me on one of my sojourns into China Town and then up to Telegraph Hill where there was a great view of the bay and all the lights of the city. We talked about Mike and Donna's marriage and how they would be separated from each other. We also talked about the dangers of the war and the possibility of something actually happening to one of us while we were there. It was a rather sad night. It ended when we drove to a fortuneteller's place where I had the seer read my palm. She told me that I would come back from Nam, get married to a woman with dark hair, and have two children, a boy first and then a girl. At the time, we thought it was funny and figured she was thinking that Karen was my girlfriend, which she was not. (I did come home. I did have two children, one boy and one girl. I also married my high school sweetheart, Carol, who has black hair.)

While I was home, I visited my ex girlfriend, Carol. (We married in 1970 and are still married today.) She was going to Cal (University of California) and lived on the campus at Berkeley. It was not much of a conversation. I felt the worse for having gone to see her. She was in college and had a whole new life. She let me know that I was not a part of any of her future plans. I was still trying to get things patched up so we could get back together, but she felt it was over for good and there was no way we would ever get back together again. There seemed to be nothing left between the two of us according to her. She told me that she wasn't going to write to me. If I wanted to write to her mother, however, she would keep track of what was happening with me from her. I was emotionally torn up inside about the outcome

71

of our meeting as I said goodbye. She left me feeling rather hopeless and depressed. It almost killed me to think that she wasn't even going to write me a letter.

Mike and I had to report to the Oakland Army Base at 0600 hours on a balmy October day in 1966. We had orders for the same place, so we decided to go together. I rode in the car with Mike and Donna, and my good friend Karen came along to give both of us her best wishes and prayers. Since she was Donna's best friend, I assumed she would also be there for Donna's moral support when we said goodbye and left.

We pulled up in front of the gates while it was still dark outside. Donna took me aside and made me vow to look after Mike and bring him back home safe and alive. I promised her I would take care of him as best I could. But I knew it was up to God, not me.

Mike and Donna embraced for a long time. I felt bad for them, but I was also a little envious that they had each other for loving support. Karen did give me a friendly hug, and then we had to leave. Mike and I walked slowly from the darkness toward the lights of the entry gate, dragging our duffel bags. We looked back at Donna and Karen standing next to the car and waving a final goodbye to us. Donna was softly crying; her face was all wet and shined in what little light there was.

I noticed a slight wet sparkle coming from Mike's eyes, so I did not look him in the face as we both reported in and waited for our flight to Nam. Neither of us was very talkative as we walked in silence inside the base. We hoped that next year we would both be standing here together again.

#

PFC Bill McDonald camping out during
Operation Cedar Falls, 1967.

W.H. McDonald Jr.

Author's note: Written on top of Telegraph Hill in San Francisco while on 30-day leave, October 1966. I penciled this poem on the back of a bar napkin that Karen and I had picked up at Mike's Pool Hall, which was in North Beach.

On Leave Before Going to War

San Francisco, 1966

Standing alone with so many others
On Telegraph Hill
I searched the incoming fog
For answers.
I could find none.
The lights of the city below
Burned through the darkness.
I could hear the mute sounds
Of people around me.
Some may have been lovers,
Perhaps, having to say goodbye.
Others may have been voices
Of angels chanting prayers for peace
In the foggy mist.

I saw myself
Like that lonely fog
That hugs the city for its very life,
Hoping that some
Future wind doesn't blow it away
Before it can fully taste life.

This is my city,
My home,
My place of birth.
This is where I began my journey.
This is where I will begin a new one.

I have felt this city breathe
And I've heard her cries
As she bid farewell to countless
Departing warships,
Each filled with young virgin warriors
Venturing off to some distant war-stained shore
To meet themselves and their fate
On some battleground graveyard.

I love this damned city
Filled with so many lost souls,
Suicides, broken dreams,
And lonely poets
Who hate to say goodbye.

\#

W.H. McDonald Jr.

Author's note: This was absolutely the worst commercial flight of my life—it was a physically and emotionally draining experience. Of course, getting to our final destination was certainly not like going to Disneyland or Hawaii. So, we were not too concerned about getting there on time for the war.

Flight of the Damned

Flight to Vietnam—October 1966

Mike and I boarded a commercial airline out of Travis Air Force Base (AFB) in northern California, which was just a short bus ride from the Oakland Army Base where we had in-processed. I remember looking out of the bus windows at people whizzing by us on the freeway—people who were totally unaware or did not give a damn about this busload of young virgin warriors.

At the airfield, we walked up the ramp and flight stewardesses in miniskirts greeted us. This was before the liberated times that changed everything from their job title (now, a politically correct "flight attendant") to men doing this job. I think all of us young soldiers preferred the miniskirt look, which for some men was their last look at an American woman.

Mike and I sat next to each other and exchanged some small talk for the first hour or two of the trip; then, we each fell into a reflective silence. What we would find when we got to Vietnam was all a big mystery as well as a great adventure into the unknown. So, our feelings of excitement were mixed with our concerns about our own personal safety. We had no clue as to what awaited either of us there.

The plane developed engine trouble within a few hours, and it was directed to land at Honolulu International Airport. It was a very pleasant surprise. As we got off, however, I noticed that there were MPs (military police) watching the exits where we were waiting. Perhaps they thought we might attempt an escape and run away. I was a little annoyed with being treated like a prisoner, but I couldn't do anything about it. The layover lasted about four hours. We just hung around the airport lounge and talked.

The plane was eventually fixed, and we were on our way again. However, the same engine problems that they had fixed in Hawaii acted up again. This time we landed at night on the island of Guam. It was really muggy and hot when we departed the plane. We were taken to an old airplane hangar where they left us to stand around and wait. No chairs, no air conditioning, and no food—only an old water cooler that didn't cool and made the water taste funny. Worse yet, we were still wearing the same clothing that we had on at the start of the trip. We were beginning to smell ripe. We spent five or six hours sitting on the hangar floor before we climbed onboard again. No one had fed or given us any drinks in Guam or Hawaii. The food onboard was old and stale from sitting too long because of the repairs.

Then it happened again—the engine had more problems, and we landed at Clark AFB in the Philippine Islands. Once again, someone took us to a hangar, where it was even hotter and more humid than it had been in Guam. The same fate awaited us there—no special services for us of any kind and no food or drinks. After about six hours, they rounded up our group and put us back on our plane. I noticed that the crew was no longer polite with us. In fact, they were all tired and smelly themselves. I thought they just wanted to finish this damned trip and get some sleep. Our flight had flown more hours than scheduled, and there was no more food, unless you happened to believe that peanuts are a dinner. They were even out of soft drinks.

We flew several more hours on what had turned out to be the continuing voyage of the damned. I was miserable, and the clothing I was wearing was wrinkled and had large wet stains under the armpits. I looked bad and felt even worse. The flying time should have been about 25 hours back then, but with all our detours and stops for repairs we had been traveling the better part of two full days. Yet, I held out great hope that Saigon was near. I had visions of debarking from this prison flight and setting our feet, once again, on terra firma.

My great hopes of getting off that plane were shattered after we began the short approach to the Saigon airport. The aircraft abruptly pulled its nose up and turned away from the airfield. I looked out of the window and could see how close we had come to touching down. The wheels were down and locked for landing, yet we were heading off in a new direction—and it wasn't Vietnam. The pilots didn't get paid for subjecting themselves to any combat dangers. When snipers fired off a few rounds at our aircraft on the approach, the pilots pulled out of the pattern and headed for Thailand, of all places.

A few hours later we were sitting in the airplane on the tarmac at Bangkok Airport. They needed to save fuel, so they shut down the engines. We just sat there for over two hours in the tropical sun as the temperatures inside the aircraft kept climbing higher and higher. I felt like a small child locked in a car with the windows up in a shopping mall parking lot on a hot summer day. It was so unbearable that all of us began to loudly complain that we wanted off. I think the crew thought that we were about to get violent. They opened the door and had a ramp put next to the plane so we could go into the air conditioned terminal.

We were all starved, since they had run out of food and drinks before we even left Clark AFB. However, neither the crew nor the U.S. Army was providing anything for our comfort or hunger. Several of the guys went to the restaurants inside the main terminal and waited in line until they got tables. As luck would have it, there was an announcement made in English on the public address system informing all the men on my flight to report back to the aircraft for immediate takeoff. I was fortunate that I had very little money, so I had not ordered anything to eat. But the poor guys who did order, got stuck paying for the meals that they were never served. There were airport police there to ensure that they all paid. Some of the guys were really pissed at this point. I thought we would have an airport riot. But cooler heads prevailed, and we got back on the plane. We lifted off once again, heading back for Vietnam. Except this time, we were heading east instead of west.

When we finally landed, it was three days after we had left California. We had been wearing the same underwear and clothing the entire time. It was around noon when we stepped off the plane, and it was much hotter and muggier than we had expected. The heat as well as the smells made it difficult for us to breathe. It hit me really hard and almost knocked me over when I took that first whiff of hot, smelly Nam air. There has never again been another moment like that in my life.

Because of our late arrival, there was no one there to greet us or to pick us up. I mean, no one at all. We all just wandered off the aircraft and stood around waiting for someone to tell us what to do or where to go. The asphalt was soft from the heat and so hot that it burned the bottom of my feet inside my shoes! We stood around in the direct sunlight waiting and waiting. The flight crew left us, and the ground crew dumped our duffel bags into a couple of huge piles on the hot asphalt tarmac. All the bags looked the same, but we had all day to sort though them and find our own.

Finally, we decided to walk over to the side of the airport next to the building; we put our duffel bags under our heads and fell asleep. It wasn't until the next morning that a bus came for us. Unlike the bus that took us to Travis, this one had wire mesh and bars across the windows to keep hand grenades and bombs from being tossed inside. Thus began our first day of our tour of duty in Nam.

#

W.H. McDonald Jr.

Author's note: I wrote this on the way to Vietnam from California, to report for my tour of duty in October 1966.

On the Flight to South Vietnam

A young poet
Goes to war
Laughing at the uniform
He now wears,
And
Cries
Because
He must.

Not totally aware
Of why,
He goes
Because
It is his duty
And
Tries to understand

And
Cries
Because
He cannot!

#

October 1966

Author's note: This is not the way they would have greeted John Wayne! This was my rude introduction to my combat unit and Thanksgiving Day in the Nam. This was not the way I had expected it to be.

I Am the FNG (The New Guy)

My introduction to the 128th Assault Helicopter Company, the Tomahawks, was a rather rude one at best. I had been shipped around Vietnam to several different locations, including a week at Nha Trang along the South China Sea, before getting my final orders to report to the 128th AHC. I had no clean clothing to wear, no money, and I needed a haircut. Frankly, I looked terrible and didn't smell too good either.

When I reported to the company I was not met with any fanfare. I was just told to go find a bunk in the maintenance hooch and do the best I could at settling in. I was to report right away for duty in maintenance, where I ended up working all night long fixing Hueys. There were few introductions and little formalities, besides telling me where the toolboxes were. Everyone was too darn busy. To be honest, I really didn't know what in the heck I was doing yet. I didn't remember much of anything from my weeks of training at Fort Rucker, Alabama. I was actually more concerned about not knowing my job than I was about the war at this point in my tour.

The next morning came, but we worked past the sunrise. When I finally got off work, I managed to stagger back to the mess hall for breakfast. When I got there, I found out that my company had let all the nationals who worked for us off for the Thanksgiving Day holiday. I was new in country, but I knew it wasn't their holiday, it was ours. I was a little angry about their getting the day off for "my holiday." I was going through the breakfast line when someone signaled me to go see the mess sergeant. He had selected me to fill in on KP to help wash pots and pans and clean up the kitchen area.

I couldn't believe it; here I was exhausted from my extra long trip getting to Vietnam and being bounced around in country for almost three weeks. Then, I had worked my entire first night while desperately in need of a shower and some sleep. Now, this high school dropout, lifer-sergeant was making me wash pots and pans—on my Thanksgiving Day!

I was willing to do my tour of duty and had even volunteered for Vietnam, but I saw right away that this war was all screwed up. I mean this was my holiday—not a holiday for a bunch of Vietnamese peasants who lived out in the countryside and had never even heard of Thanksgiving Day. So, why did we give them the freaking day off and I had to work?

I was lucky that I was really much too tired to mouth off, and being the new guy, it didn't seem right to do so. I was very willing to fight and even die for my country. Washing dishes in Vietnam, however, on Thanksgiving Day was not what I had envisioned John Wayne ever being asked to do for his country. It was just about the worst Thanksgiving Day I had ever had. I was spending the day away from home and family with no friends to share the meal. I had been up all night working on helicopters and getting dirty. I smelled so bad that I hated being next to me. I was desperately in need of the blessings of a good, long, warm shower. By the time I had finished cleaning up the kitchen and was ready to take a shower, I was told that all the shower water was gone for the day. I dragged my hot, stinky body back to my hooch.

It was late afternoon by the time I got "home," and I found that everyone else was now up and moving about. They had been able to get some sleep and shower after breakfast. Several of the guys were listening to their individual brand of music, which they were playing loudly from several different record players and radios. I glanced around at the guys and tried to introduce myself to some of them. Then, I lay down on my bunk bed with my dirty uniform still on, which was soaking wet with sweat and dirty from the grease and oil. The temperature and the humidity were unbearably high, but I didn't care anymore, I just needed some sleep. All I remember is being awakened some four hours later for another night of maintenance work.

I moaned something about needing to rest, and some joker yelled out to me, "Hey FNG, welcome to The Nam!"

#

Bill McDonald test-firing new M-16 rifle.

Author's note: This was not the way I envisioned that our soldiers should be acting. This was not the way to win hearts and minds!

Outraged at My Fellow Soldiers

I was in the company just a few weeks, and already I was feeling the need to get out of the maintenance platoon. I, like so many others, was just waiting for my shot at eventually getting an assignment as a crew chief to my own aircraft. I wanted to get out of the base camp and see the country and meet the people. This desire prompted me to volunteer for some local community work details.

I went one day to the local community hospital to paint it and to do some repairs. It felt good working with the locals. The clinic was run by a group of Vietnamese Catholic nuns, and I spent an entire day enjoying my labor there. I felt this was part of the winning hearts and minds that General Westmoreland had told us was a part of our mission. He told us that we were there not only to win on the battlefields, but also to engage in the process of winning the hearts and minds of the South Vietnamese people. That belief was something that would later become shattered by the reality and futility of that conflict.

At the end of the day our company truck came by to pick me up and take me back to the base camp. I was riding in the back with four short timers, guys who had less than 90 days to go in country. They all had M-14s at this time. (M-16s were not issued until I was there a couple more months.) They were having lots of fun scaring the hell out of the local peasants by pointing their rifles at them as we drove down the road. The people would get huge eyes and freeze, afraid to move forward or backward or make any sudden moves. These bozos thought that was a really funny game to play with these people. Then, they began firing off rounds at farm livestock, killing or wounding several water buffaloes, and a bunch of ducks and chickens. It was unbelievable how mean and cruel these young soldiers were behaving.

I couldn't understand their behavior and told them to stop this crap. They looked at me, the new cherry, the FNG, and told me to shut up. One guy told me that I would feel the same way after I had been there as long as they had. I wanted to deck that guy, but it was a fight I could not win since all of them would kick my ass. They all had rifles in their hands, loaded, chambered and ready to fire. I had not brought my weapon with me, preferring to leave it at the base camp so I would not have to worry about it while I was painting. I also knew that they would lie about what happened. They gave me a look that told me they wouldn't take any shit from me. If I reported what I saw them doing, I knew I would be taking a certain risk physically; and of course, it would be their word against mine. I was pissed off and decided to complain and face the consequences anyway. I figured if I did not say anything, who would?

It was a very rude awakening for me that afternoon; I could see that not everyone wanted to do good things for the people of Vietnam. That was confirmed and driven home when I got back to the base camp. I tried to complain about what I had seen, but no one wanted to listen to me. The men told me to stop making trouble for myself and mind my own business. Someone told me that I was still too new to fully understand and judge these men; well, it has been over 35 years, and I still do not understand!

#

Tomahawks at work in an LZ.

Author's note: There is a time for action and a time for prayer and God's help. This was one of those times we needed prayers to help keep us from crashing. I strongly believe in the power of prayers!

To those not familiar with the use of the term Charlie, it was GI slang for the Viet Cong, from phonetic alphabet for VC (Victor Charlie). Sometimes we called him a respectful Mr. Charlie.

Answer to a Prayer

In March of 1967, there was a lot of action in Binh Duong Province, in particular, a place known as Ho Bo Woods. This still contained large elements of the politico-military forces of the Viet Cong's Region 4 Headquarters. This area was laced with tunnels and spider holes (camouflaged sniper holes that the VC used). There had been some heavy fighting in this area during the previous 15 months, with no end in sight. Basically, Charlie owned this piece of real estate. He made us pay dearly for every inch of ground we walked on or flew over. This was "Indian Country," and it was not a very good place to be flying alone on any kind of mission. In this area our troops had discovered a large underground complex that included a three-story hospital and offices for the officers, which were all buried under the forest. This was one of those bad places where I could feel the fear creep up my spine, and I could taste it in my mouth anytime I entered the area. It was a very nasty place to do business, and I never looked forward to flying missions into or around it.

On this one particular morning, we had an early start before sunrise. We had been airborne for an hour, but were having a very difficult time locating anything below us in the darkness. When daylight broke over the forest, we had to contend with a thick ground fog that covered everything as far as we could see. Below us looked all white, like a rolling cloud on the ground. We could not see the treetops in most places, so we could not tell if we were flying over an open area or trees. The few LZs (landing zones) inside Ho Bo Woods were small clearings where GIs had cut down the trees or blown them up with explosives, so even the LZs were no bed of roses. They all had tree stumps and fallen logs, which forced us to hover our chopper just a few feet off the ground, so that the troops had to jump out. We also had to throw out the supplies.

We had been flying support for some elements of the 25th Infantry Division on this day. We were all alone, mostly flying single-ship supply missions of fresh food and ammo for the ground troops. We had been concentrating so hard on watching out for Charlie that no one was watching our gas consumption. Needless to say, we had wasted lots of our fuel in a series of long searches, trying to locate the troops.

It was still very early in the morning. The part of the forest we had been flying over was now completely engulfed with heavy, thick fog. There was just no way we could carry on our present mission. We circled around to get our exact bearings and location. The pilots had become a little disoriented by the fog, which covered guiding ground references. The fog was not burning off, but it was slowly rising. It rose upward to around 100 feet or more, just enough so we could not see the treetops anymore. The good news was that no one could see us either, so we were safe from any ground fire.

The bad news was that our fuel warning light had come on with its audio alarm sounding off. The light flashed on the instrument panel as both pilots froze at once. Neither one had any real clue to our present location or where our own troops were below us. We did not have enough fuel to make it out of the fog-shrouded forest. We had no idea which way to turn the aircraft. All directions held a mystery. All the ground below us was hostile and forbidding. There was no right place to go. We were stuck in this twilight zone between certain death and the fog.

We had remaining only about five to ten minutes of fuel. None of us really knew for sure how much was supposed to be left when the fuel warning light came on. We did not know how much time we had before our aircraft would drop out of the sky into whatever waited for us below. If it were treetops, then our ship would crash and the rotor blades would thrash the trees and twist the body of the helicopter and those inside it. We knew what that would look like because we had seen one of our company ships do that same thing just the week before. That image played over and over inside my head.

The other possibility was that if we could crash land and survive, we would certainly be at a high risk for being captured or killed by enemy troops. It would be a long time before anyone could find and rescue us. The fog would hide our aircraft for hours, and no one would have any idea where we were because we did not even know for sure ourselves.

All these thoughts ran through our minds. Our hearts were pounding like long distance runners in a race we had just lost. I looked around, as I would normally do in this kind of situation, trying to figure out what I might need once we crashed. I grabbed my M-16 rifle and some magazine clips. I wasn't carrying any food or water. We did have lots of colored smoke grenades to use in case we were in need of a rescue attempt. But in this fog, no one would be able to see them.

The pilots had been in radio contact with our other company helicopters, but none of them were close by. That was assuming that our guess about where we were, was in fact, where we actually were. Even after we had given our mayday distress call, no one would be able to quickly respond.

Our fuel should have run out, and we knew we were running on sheer luck. We did not fully understand why we had not dropped out of the sky yet. The fog was endless in all directions. There was just no opening anywhere to be seen. I began to silently talk to God, asking for His divine help to find us someplace to land before we crashed into the forest below.

We were mentally ready for the worse kind of crash. Not knowing what we were falling into gave us no preparation or defense against the certain destruction that came when the rotor blades tore the aircraft apart.

Out of nowhere, just below us where we had already looked, there was a clear opening over a grassy meadow area—a perfect LZ to drop down into. We turned and lined up with the LZ just as the engine died, having consumed its last ounce of jet fuel. The helicopter was less than 25 feet from the ground, and the blades were still rotating with enough force that we did not drop very hard. There was no damage—a perfect landing, in fact.

I immediately jumped out of the ship as it hit, taking my weapon with me. Around the tree-lined meadow we saw movement everywhere. Our helicopter was completely surrounded. We were on the ground, ready to defend ourselves, but there was no way we were going to win this battle. We were completely outnumbered and surrounded. Any resistance on our part would have been a death warrant for sure, so we just held our position and waited.

Then we began to notice the uniforms they were wearing. They were elements of the 25th Infantry. By some unbelievable luck, we had dropped right on top of one of their small temporary camps. We couldn't have been more blessed if we had tried. Not only were we surrounded by our own troops, but they also had a supply of JP-4 jet fuel for our helicopter.

It was a strange experience and hard to explain. For example, why did this LZ just open up in the middle of so many square miles of solid fog? Why was there a clearing at this spot waiting for us? Why hadn't our helicopter run out of fuel before we saw this opening? Why had we not seen this opening before when we were looking in that same area?

It was a very lucky or blessed day, depending on how you viewed the events. Just good luck you might say, maybe? But then, perhaps other forces were at work. Maybe the power of a small silent prayer opened a big hole in the fog? I do not know for sure why it all happened as it did. I do know that we did not crash, and no one was killed or injured—and that was good enough for me. I do not need anyone to tell me that prayers do work—I believe.

#

Author's note: Sometimes you really have to listen to that inner voice and act very quickly. The trouble is getting other people to respond as well.

A Hellhole

I was still fairly new to Vietnam, or as they used to say, still an "FNG," when this took place. We happened to be in an area next to the Parrot's Beak. This is the part of Nam where Cambodia sticks out into South Vietnam. This also is where all of those trails from North Vietnam used to empty into the south. The weather was hot and dry, and our rotors kicked up a ton of dust every time we landed or took off. It made it lousy for those troops living in tents on the ground. But, it was not much better for the helicopter crews. In spite of the cooling air from the rotors blowing on me most of the day, I sat in my own pool of muddy sweat, my head boiling under the flight helmet.

This was one of my first weeks of flying combat missions in Nam. I was pushed right into the middle of Operation Cedar Falls. We had been conducting operations in and around a large mountain that overshadowed the whole flat area below. This was around the beginning of 1967, and I was only 20 years old. I was the crew chief/door gunner on a UH1-D model helicopter, better known as a Huey. The 128th Assault Helicopter Company, of which I was a member, was actively engaged in supporting the operation. Our company had been taking lots of fire from the ground, and there had been some damage to several of our unit's aircraft. But so far that week, none had been shot down.

On this particular day, we landed at a small forward base camp. It was being used to supply the forces in the area. Sitting parked inside the camp, there were six large flatbed trucks of ammo waiting to be unloaded. This was not a very secure area, as we soon found out. There were no fences or large bunkers, no watchtowers, just a few strands of barbed wire with a few men sitting behind a couple layers of sandbags.

We had landed there that morning to take a break, refuel the aircraft, and try to eat a meal if we could. We were about 100 yards from the flatbed trucks when we heard and felt a blast. We looked up and saw a sudden ball of fire, followed by many more explosions. A VC (Viet Cong) had penetrated the airfield and had thrown some kind of explosive devices on the beds of the trucks. They were all on fire and exploding.

The force of the blasts knocked us off our feet. Several of the trucks had large artillery shells on them. The explosion and fire caused hundreds of rounds to heat up, which then began randomly firing off from the bed of the truck. They were going in every conceivable direction: up, down, sideways, and right at us. It was a death zone as fire exploded everywhere. What made it even worse were the hundreds of cans of machine gun rounds that were getting hot and firing off in random directions, making every place dangerous.

Some of the artillery rounds were shooting straight up into the air and coming back down on the camp. The rounds were hitting the ground all around us. We could not take off in the helicopter since the sky was full of even greater dangers from the fire. We decided to make a run for it and take cover; my door gunner and I ran for a nearby hole that had been dug into the ground about 25 yards from the aircraft. We covered the distance in what seemed to take a lifetime. Machine gun rounds were zipping right past our heads as the ground shook from dozens of artillery explosions all around us. Dirt was flying in our faces. We could feel the heat of the fire on us as we jumped into the hole.

We were shaking and out of breath as we rolled to the bottom of the ditch and tried to cover up with our arms and hands. But even though I had found the safety of this hole, I felt an urging to get out of there. It was just an inner voice, a feeling, a sense that we should not be there! I felt that we needed to act with great haste. I told my gunner to get out and move as quickly as possible, and he thought I was out of my mind to even suggest that. He did not wish to leave, what seemed to him, a secure and safe hole. He did not want to venture out again into the open killing fields above the hole. He wanted to stay right where we were, which made great sense at the time.

I told him we had to move out of that hole and right now. He wasn't going to move, but I was determined to follow my inner feelings. I grabbed him by his uniform and pushed him up and out of the hole. He fought me every inch of the way, but I continued to push him. Finally, we were exposed to the open rounds.

I pointed in the direction of another hole, and off we half crawled and half ran. We hit the other hole and rolled into it. There were already two guys in this hole. They wondered why we were in there crowding them. It is one of those unwritten rules of combat that you do not put all your men in the same hole—this prevents one round from taking everyone out of commission. There we were with everyone yelling at me for being crazy. I was explaining myself when all of a sudden there was a flash of light, followed by a thundering force of energy that came right at us from the other hole. An artillery round had come down directly into our abandoned hole.

We peeked out from our new hole to see smoke and fire rising out of the enlarged hole that we had evacuated only moments before. The hole looked like an entrance to hell, with fire and smoke billowing out. Everyone became very quiet and just sat there, each in his own thoughts. We had come very close to cashing in our chips and we knew it. Just a matter of a few seconds had separated us from instant death or continued life.

My friend was no longer angry with me, but he had a puzzled look on his face. He asked me how I knew we should leave the hole. I did not know what to tell him. The feelings inside me were so overwhelming that I had no choice but to take action and follow my gut feelings.

As soon as we could move again, we ran back to the helicopter, which for some fortunate reason did not take any hits. We got it started and flew out of there while the smoke still curled up into the skies around the camp. The ammo had destroyed the trucks and a big part of the camp, but we were all okay and safe. We flew around the mountain and headed back to our airfield at Phu Loi. Inside the aircraft the crew was still a little shaken by the entire life-threatening experience. But I was feeling something else altogether—I was feeling alive and blessed by the unfolding of the events that afternoon. I knew that Someone had been definitely looking after me this day. There was no other explanation for any of it. Somebody up there loved me and I could feel it. I felt very much loved and at peace as we flew back to our base camp that night.

The mountain in the background is Nui Ba Den,
known locally as "Black Virgin Mountain."

Author's note: I could have been sent to jail for life for following my intuition—I had chosen to disobey a direct order in combat. Sometimes, you have to totally trust that voice within yourself—so much so, that you are willing to risk everything else. This was one of those times. If I were wrong, I would have a very high price to pay.

Life or Death Decision

In the spring of 1967, in an area about 35 miles northwest of Saigon, I had to make one of the biggest decisions of my life. We had been flying solo missions, mostly supply runs to small encampments of the 1st Infantry Division. The troops were there to slow down the movement of supplies that were coming directly from North Vietnam off the Ho Chi Minh Trail. There had been some fighting, but not nearly as bloody as we had expected it to be. Even though men were getting wounded and killed daily, this was considered a relative pause in the action between much bigger battles that loomed ahead for us.

Our intelligence reports indicated that we should be on the lookout for large movements of both supplies and troops coming into this sector. We had not seen any signs that this was true, but we had been keeping a watchful eye on anything that moved on the ground. We had not received any hostile fire during the morning operations.

My helicopter commander was a major who had just arrived from a tour of several years in Germany. He was a West Point graduate and was a strictly by-the-book style military leader. That was the way he had managed his duties in Germany. He was determined to continue those ways in the Nam. He appeared to me as a real "no nonsense" type of guy with very little sense of humor. When he gave an order, he expected a full 100 percent obedience by those he commanded. He did not want to foster any friendships between himself and us lower ranking souls in the unit. He was in charge, he was "the man," and for those of us who did not outrank him, we were there to support and obey his orders. That was the way things were going to be. We knew he wouldn't be open to any questions or suggestions, we had to do as he said; there was never going to be any debates about what he wanted us to do.

During his first couple of weeks in the Nam, the major was still trying to figure out how to find the LZs and how to read the maps of the area. He did not know the names of places we had to fly to, and he had no clue as to where these places were in relation to other places or to our base camp. Without a map in his hand, this guy wouldn't have any clue to where we were. (The "old guys" who had been there for a while could follow roads and rivers and head toward landmarks such as Black Virgin Mountain.) Yet, he asked very few questions, if any.

On this particular morning, we were flying higher in the sky (over 800 feet) than felt comfortable to me. We were not at our normal treetop-level altitude. The major had an aversion to flying too close to the ground. He did not yet realize the risks that flying at higher altitudes presented. Eventually he would learn—like all new pilots did—that flying at treetop level was actually much safer. We could sneak up on enemy troops well before they could see or hear us coming; this was the common procedure in Nam—fly low and fast. Keep your profile down close to the ground.

From our more lofty position in the sky, we could see much farther around the countryside. I think it may have been helpful for him in spotting landmarks for his navigation. We did have a greater view of all that was down below, but it also made us an easier target. We were not high enough to avoid small arms fire and not low enough to sneak up on anyone. We just kind of hung in the sky like a big fat, slow moving target.

We were flying just a click (a kilometer or 0.62 of a mile) outside of a small hamlet, when I spotted a group of about 30 people below us who appeared to be moving down the road in a military formation. They were all carrying what looked like some kind of weapon on their shoulders. There also was a man in the front who seemed to be acting as a leader for the group. They were all dressed in the typical black pajamas that the VC (and most everyone living in Nam) wore. Since this was so close to the Ho Chi Minh Trail, it certainly appeared that it could be a good-sized squad of VC (Viet Cong).

The major went into action right away giving orders. He immediately determined that they were VC troops—he had no doubts. He ordered me to fire my M-60 machine gun on the formation below. Now, my M-60 could fire 750 rounds of 7.62 mm of ammo a minute—it would have shredded that group of people in just a matter of a few seconds. I looked down at the formation and thought what he saw was correct, but then I froze. I couldn't pull the trigger on the machine gun. I could not get myself to squeeze off a single round. I was overcome with great apprehension and a feeling that something was not right.

I sat behind my M-60 doing nothing. The major was going crazy and yelling at me. He let me know that he had given me a direct order to fire. It was not optional. But I just sat there, knowing that something was not right with this picture. I told the major I was not going to fire. I had some heavy doubts about what we were seeing down on the road.

The major could not believe that I had actually questioned his orders. He was mad as hell. He told me that I had disobeyed a direct order in combat. That was a punishable offense. He let me know, in no uncertain terms, that he was going to bring me up on charges. Those charges could mean 20 years or more in a military prison at Leavenworth.

I told him that we needed to fly lower. I wanted him to make a pass over the group's formation so we could get a better identification. In the meantime, he had circled the aircraft so that the left door gunner was directly in line to fire his weapon on those on the ground. To my surprise, the door gunner also refused the order to shoot. He showed some exceptional courage by supporting my position. He fully understood what he had just done, and that took my breath away. He was certainly not looking for any trouble from the major, but there he was making a stand with me on this issue. It could have been viewed as a mutiny by the military court system. This was a very serious breach of military law, and we each could have been facing life sentences. I was in awe that he had such courage and conviction, and he was basing it on his belief in my feelings. I hoped to God that I was right, for both of our futures. That was a lot of weight on my shoulders.

The major was debating with the copilot, a young warrant officer from Texas, about calling in an air strike or at least some artillery. The young pilot, who had flown with us many times before, suggested that we take the aircraft down for a closer look. Finally, after what seemed to be a very long time (all of these conversations had happened in less than a minute), we dropped down from our rather higher and awkward altitude and made a descent toward the group of people on the ground. We had our M-60 machine guns at the ready position, aiming right at the heart of the group.

We came down to about 100 feet. We were unsure of what to expect and were ready for all hell to break loose as we passed off to the right side of them. The first clue we had that they might not be the enemy was the fact that they stayed on the road the whole time we were above them. They had not run into the cover of the surrounding jungle. The second big clue was that no one was firing at us as we passed by them at only 100 feet in the air.

As we flew across the road, it became painfully obvious to all of us who they were; this was just a group of school age children with their garden tools, marching in a formation to the community garden. The leader was a priest dressed all in black. My heart raced; I got all emotional and actually felt tears rolling down my face. I realized just how close we had come to killing all these young children.

I couldn't see the major's face, but I imagined that it turned pale. All of us onboard were visibly shaken by this event. The major had given direct orders to both his gunners to kill them all. He even wanted to order an air strike on this group of 30 children. Now, he said very little. I had chills running down my spine and noticed that my hands were shaking.

Why had I and my trusting door gunner both refused to fire? I have no answers. I went with my feelings, which at the time were so very clear and strong that I should not pull the trigger. I risked going to jail because I followed my feelings and not my orders. What if I had been wrong and they were really VC? I had risked the helicopter getting shot down and the life of every crew member—based only on my feelings. I quickly learned in Nam to never question my intuitive feelings. It seemed that those feelings were greatly heightened in combat and dangerous situations. In this case, it saved 30 young children and a priest from being killed. That would have been a major tragedy that I could never have lived with because it would have haunted me for the rest of my life.

The major and I became much better friends after that day. He actually learned to trust those working for him. He began to ask questions and rely on the combat-experienced men around him. He turned out to be a very good human being and a fine officer. He also proved many times over to be a brave and courageous pilot—someone whom I felt confident flying with and risking my own life for. I think we both learned something that day that forever changed the way we looked at life and ourselves.

#

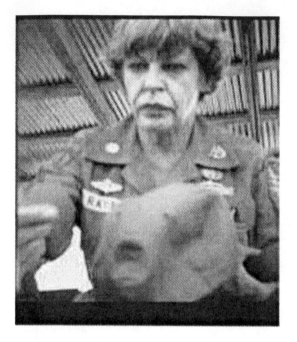

Martha Raye signing her autograph
with love, on a GIs hat.

Author's note: This story was first published in the book "Angels in Vietnam: Women Who Served" by Jan Hornung. I met Martha Raye in Phu Loi when she came to entertain our company. She was a super woman and loved by all of us guys!

Colonel Maggie—Nurse, Entertainer, and Honorary Green Beret

Almost everyone knows about all of Bob Hope's trips to Vietnam. He did his annual Christmas Shows for TV, which were recorded live at some of the safest bases in Vietnam. Hope and his crew were surrounded by TV cameras, reporters, and lots of tanks and protective armed troops. I was at his Christmas Day show back in 1966, just north of Saigon, and I enjoyed it very much. It was one of a few good memories that I have of my tour of duty. The highlight event of the year for me, however, was meeting Martha Raye, better known to the troops as Colonel Maggie.

I met her in Phu Loi, South Vietnam, in the early part of 1967. She came to our small airfield base camp without any fanfare. She just arrived and began causally talking to the guys. We, of course, knew of her from all of her old movies. I mentioned to her that I wanted a photo to show my mother, her biggest fan, and she turned that into a five-minute comedy routine about how only the really old folks remembered her. She teased me about that, and then she put her arms around me. She made fun of everything, including referring to herself as "The Big Mouth!" The guys in my unit, the 128th Assault Helicopter Company, were really impressed that she had come all the way out to see us. We never had any big-name entertainers come through our camp, so her visit was something very special to all of us.

Later that day, I got my chance to get up on stage (the top of a flatbed truck) and get my photo taken with her. I found her to be a very real person, and she gave me the feeling that she really cared about all of us. There were neither reporters nor TV cameras on her visit. She was there because we were there.

At that time, her reputation was rapidly growing among veterans. We heard many stories about her from the Special Forces units out in the boondocks. When we flew into almost any small SF camp, the guys who had met her spoke most highly of her. She was their hero for sure. She had been traveling to Vietnam (I am told that she paid her own way) and spent weeks, and sometimes up to six months at a time, in country. She kept this pace up for over nine years during the Vietnam War. She was not there just to entertain the troops, she also engaged in nursing work wherever it was needed. She spent most of her time out in the field or in the hospitals, and going to some of the most dangerous and remote locations in Nam.

She was not looking for any publicity or photo opportunities; she went where she knew the need was the greatest. She visited base camps where no other entertainers dared to go. She walked through the mud and rain and took the heat and mosquitoes all in stride. No one ever remembers her complaining about the food, weather, transportation, or life in general. She spent time at places that did not have hot showers, let alone places for women to use a restroom. She had to endure the same hardships as the GIs. Her job was to keep up our spirits and make us feel loved and appreciated. She didn't come to Nam for a visit, she came to work. That, for her, meant sometimes using her nursing skills to help with patients.

There were many stories going around about all the battles she had been in while in country. She did not try to shelter herself from harm's way. She refused over and over again to allow anyone to risk his life to protect her or to evacuate her to a safer place if she were subjected to an enemy attack. There is one story that made the rounds within the Special Forces units, but it somehow never made it into the newspapers or on the evening news at that time, that I can recall. I have some of the facts but not all of them. But this story reveals the real character of this wonderful woman warrior.

Colonel Maggie, who also was a trained RN before going into the entertainment field, went to entertain and visit a small Special Forces camp. (It could have been at Soc Trang around the early part of 1967.) I was told that she and a clarinet player had gone to the camp to entertain, but while they were there the NVA attacked the camp. Mortar rounds and small arms fire were incoming. It appeared that there was a full-scale assault on the base camp. It was uncertain if the camp would be able to hold off the assault. The camp medic was hit, and since Colonel Maggie was a nurse, she took over and began to assist with the treatment of the wounded who kept pouring into the aid station.

The camp was in great danger of being overrun for several hours. The higher-ups in the military tried to dispatch helicopters to the camp to evacuate the wounded and the entertainers. But a combination of bad weather and heavy fighting made that task a dangerous mission for the flight crews. All this time, Colonel Maggie was subjecting herself to the dangers of flying shrapnel and incoming automatic rifle rounds as she tended to the task she was trained for, treating the wounded. She remained calm and fully active in doing her work, even with all that action taking place just outside the aid station. She kept focused on treating the wounded and did not seek shelter or safety for herself.

She kept refusing any and all rescue missions. She spent hours putting her skills as a nurse to use treating patients and even assisting with surgery. She was in the operating room for 13 hours; she then went through the aid station talking with the wounded and making sure they were okay. It was said that she worked without sleep or rest until all the wounded were either treated or evacuated out on a Huey helicopter. She did not leave that camp until she was satisfied that all the wounded were taken care of.

This is just one of the many untold stories about Martha Raye— but ask enough Vietnam veterans about her, and you will find even more tales of Colonel Maggie. She finally received some long overdue honors before she died. They ranged from the *Jean Hersholt Humanitarian Academy Award* in 1968 for entertaining troops in Vietnam to the 1993 *Presidential Medal of Freedom* for her lifetime of dedication to America.

Colonel Maggie, Martha Raye, was an honorary member of the Special Forces. She received her prized Green Beret and the title of lieutenant colonel from President Lyndon B. Johnson himself.

Known as "Colonel Maggie of the Boondocks" by her many military friends, Martha Raye (born Margaret Teresa Yvonne Reed on August 27, 1916) died October 19, 1994. Raye is buried in the military cemetery at Fort Bragg, North Carolina, an exception to policy she requested in 1992.

#

Martha Raye at Phu Loi. I am behind her.

I am standing on the stage behind
Martha Raye.

Author's note: My mom was always fairly good at tuning into things, and this letter she sent me about her dreams was one of those amazing times she was right on.

My Mom's Dream Letter

My mother sometimes had the ability to see things beyond the normal range of understanding. She always went with her feelings and seemed to have that certain gift for knowing things ahead of time. It must be genetic since all of my family displays this ability to varying degrees. My mother made an impression on some of the guys I was stationed with in Nam because of a letter she wrote to me in the spring of 1967.

In her letter, she went into great detail about two dreams she had about me in Vietnam. At first reading one might dismiss them both as just an interesting imagination. There was such a parallel to what had taken place, however, that it was more than just a coincidence or a lucky guess. Let me explain the two dreams and how they both unfolded for me in real life.

Dream #1: My mom talked about her first dream in vivid details. She described seeing my helicopter flying along at treetop level with me sitting behind my machine gun and firing it at the jungle below. She saw all the soldiers sitting nervously on the floor and the canvas seat of my aircraft. She went on to describe the men and what they carried and what they looked like. She then went into detail about the LZ where we were going to land our Huey. She pointed out that there was a fire along the right side of the LZ where she saw trees burning. She saw tracers going from my aircraft to the tree line and tracers coming back toward the ship.

She went on to tell how the men jumped out of the Huey as it was touching down, not waiting for it to come to a full stop. She saw a young soldier carrying a machine gun, jump out and run forward. A guy carrying more ammo for the gun followed him. She talked about the surrounding jungle and trees and small details that made her sound as if she had been an eyewitness to all that she described.

105

I put down her letter after reading her first dream. I realized that what she had seen was exactly what had happened on the same day she wrote the letter. When she was dreaming about all of this, it was daytime in Nam. California is nearly 8,000 miles away, but more important, there is a 14-hour difference in time. Her details were so vivid and exact about that day, I thought I was reading an instant replay of the events that had taken place. I showed the letter to some of the guys who had flown the mission with me, and they agreed that it was an accurate account of the whole experience. It was as if she had been there flying with us on the combat assault. I was not really amazed by my mom's dream—I guess I had seen her predict too many events—but a couple of the guys thought it was very strange and spooky.

Dream#2: In describing her second dream, she stated that it was about something that had not taken place yet. She firmly believed that it would take place soon after I got this letter. She realized that the whole dream was a rather strange one, but she felt that all of it would happen just as she described it in her letter. In this dream, she saw two soldiers standing out on a dirt street in a small Vietnamese village. They both appeared to be intoxicated as they staggered around yelling insults at each other from about 100 feet apart. She went on to say that it looked like the opening credits for the old TV show *Gun Smoke*. The scene she was referring to showed two gunfighters engaged in a gunfight on the streets of Dodge City.

In her dream, the two soldiers were facing off for a gunfight with each other. They both had holsters around their waists from which they drew their weapons. She said that they fired at each other, both missed, and no one was hurt. She felt for sure that all this would happen, but why she had this particular dream and what relationship it had to me, she did not fully understand. She was just passing it along to me as a fact.

I read that part of the letter to some of my buddies and received a good round of laughs about my mom's prediction. So I told them, "If my mom says it will happen, then it will happen!" I challenged them to go with me to the village that afternoon and witness it for themselves. I strongly trusted my inner feelings and my mom's belief that it would take place. I wanted them along to witness the unfolding of events that were sure to take place that afternoon. However, I think they wanted to go just to prove I was wrong and have a good laugh if nothing happened.

We got a ride to the village in the back of a half-ton military truck and went to the local bar to have a few beers. I decided to sit outdoors so I would not miss any of the action that would surely take place that afternoon. After several hours of drinking and waiting, the guys started kidding me about my mom and the letter. I stood firm and said that it would happen. I had no doubts about it. We were about ready to leave to go back to the base camp, when we heard a couple of gun shots. At this time, we had gone back inside the bar to get a last beer, so we had missed the buildup to what happened. As soon as we heard the gun shots, we ran outside while everyone else in town was running inside for cover. By the time we got outside, it was all over. Someone told us that it was only two drunken soldiers shooting at each other. No one was killed or hurt.

My friends stood there in a collective frozen quiet, unable to say a word. They looked at me in disbelief at what had happened. We got on the truck and headed back to base camp. The guys were all spooked and did not want to talk about it again. The ride back was deathly quiet. No one spoke a word to me.

I will never understand why it all happened as my mother predicted, but I do accept it as reality and fact. It did happen, and my mom knew it would. Who knows why?

#

Author's note: There is nothing worse and more frightening than a mob of men, but it is even worse when they are supposed to be trained and disciplined soldiers. This was the most afraid I ever was in Vietnam—and not just for my own life but for everyone on my helicopter. To this very day, I still have some uneasiness with crowds of people.

Panic in the LZ

Working with any ARVN (Army of the Republic of Vietnam) troops was always a dangerous assignment because we could rarely count on their support when things got tough. We never knew how they would react to certain combat situations. One spring day in 1967, I was about to find out how they would react to being attacked.

It was a perfect day weather-wise in Nam—warm sunshine, no rain, and just a hint of a gentle wind. It made flying a lot more comfortable for me and my gunner. That was because we had the doors off the helicopter, and we were sitting facing the outside weather. There was always that breeze from our rotor and the forward air speed of the aircraft, but on some days there were heavy rains. It blew inside just enough to make us wet and chilled.

We were doing some rather easy hash and trash (resupply) missions up along the Cambodian border. We got a radio call asking us to go pick up several wounded ARVN troops in a remote LZ, not too far from where we were flying. The pilots changed course, and we headed to the LZ. The only thing we knew about the situation was that it was under mortar attack. They had a few wounded men that needed to be taken to a MASH unit; nothing too much out of the ordinary. It was almost a routine dust off (medical evacuation), so we were not expecting much trouble since the LZ was secured by 300 ARVN troops. The estimated attack force was just one VC mortar team, which was dropping rounds at random in the LZ. Our plan was to fly in at treetop level, undetected until the last few hundred yards. Then, we would drop down so they could load the wounded. It would only be a matter of a few seconds before we would lift out of there. We would certainly be out before the mortar team could zero in on us and place their rounds on our aircraft.

We pulled over the last few trees and quickly dropped down to where they had popped yellow smoke. We hit the ground hard for some reason; I guess we were in a hurry. A couple of medics began to load some wounded troops onboard. It was going very slowly. I looked out across the LZ, and I could not believe what I was seeing. Almost half of the ARVN troops had panicked. They were running for our little helicopter. Before I could do anything, several dozen of them were trying to get in our aircraft. They were pulling off the wounded to make more room for themselves. I turned to look at the other side of the ship. I could see my left door gunner trying to keep his own seat from being taken away.

Those ARVN soldiers had turned into a panicked herd of animals. They were stepping on each other and their own wounded men. They fought to get inside the small aircraft with us. All was beginning to fall apart in the LZ. The pilots were trying to pull up on the collective and get some lift off the ground. However, we had dozens of men inside and even more hanging onto the landing skids. They kept coming at us until we were completely engulfed with bodies of panicked, frightened men. It was an ugly sight; there seemed to be no way we could leave that LZ. We were like a large insect being devoured by an army of hungry ants!

Meanwhile, we had been on the ground long enough for the mortar team to zero in on our position. They started dropping rounds closer and closer. They had enough time to "walk" the rounds to the LZ, adjusting about 10 yards at a time. The rounds were hitting so close that we could feel the impact of the explosions as they shook our ship. Time was critical. We had to get out of there or get out of the helicopter before a round hit it.

The pilots were shouting on the intercom to shoot them or do whatever it took to get them out of the aircraft. My gunner and I were not about to shoot any of them; we began kicking and pushing them off as the ship struggled to rise off the ground. There were so many of them, and they just kept hanging on. We could see the fear in their eyes. Some had even pissed in their pants. These ARVN troops were going to stay in that helicopter even if it meant that all of us crashed into a treetop or were hit by a mortar round.

We were finally able to lift about two feet off the ground. The pilots swung the tail rotor around in a circle a few times to stop the advancement of other troops. As we turned our ship into a giant buzz saw, the troops fell down or jumped out of the way. Luckily, no one that we saw was cut up or killed by the turning blades of the tail rotor. We turned the aircraft around the other direction and chased away several more dozen men that were still trying to get onboard. In the meantime, my gunner and I had been shoving and throwing off as many of them as we could. It was a fight for our lives inside the back of the chopper. These guys were not going to get out without a fight. They were screaming, crying, and hitting us. I was hitting these guys as hard as I could. It was just us two gunners against a mob of 50 or more men trying to get into the aircraft. Some of them tried to pull us out and take our seats. Rifle butts and fists battered my flight helmet. It was hell in the back of the helicopter.

At one point, I saw my gunner swinging an ammo can at about a half dozen troops' heads in an attempt to fight them off. The pilots were crying out for us to shoot them, but that was something that neither of us felt was an option—after all, these guys were on "our side."

Finally, we were able to lift above the LZ to a height of about eight or nine feet. Several men were still hanging onto the skids, so we stomped as hard as we could on their fingers and kicked at them until they fell back to the ground. This effort allowed us to pull up a few more feet. We could feel the dirt from the mortar explosions that were now hitting almost directly under us. We headed across the LZ as rounds exploded behind us where we had been parked on the ground. That, of course, meant all those men were getting hit as well. We couldn't worry about them; we still had to get enough forward air speed to get over the tree line up ahead.

We still had an overflow crowd onboard. We needed the full length of the long LZ to get enough transitional lift to barely clear the treetops at the end. We were lucky that we did not have a full tank of fuel because we couldn't have carried any more weight and made it out. We cleared the trees by a mere foot or two at the most.

Back on the ground, the wounded were lying scattered about. They had been walked over and stomped on by their fellow troops. I checked inside the helicopter and was not surprised that not one of the original wounded men had made it out with us. We had risked our lives to evacuate their wounded, but not one of them was on his way to the MASH unit. In fact, they were still back in the LZ, and now they were more injured (some were possibly even killed) as a direct result of the massive panic in the LZ.

I looked around at these young South Vietnamese soldiers. I was totally disgusted by what I saw. They were huddled together, and some of them were crying. These men were of the same genetic race as the VC, who would fight us to the death. I did not understand how different they could be. It angered me to be there fighting "their war." I had no respect left for them or for the South Vietnamese in general after this day in the war. They showed me that they did not have what it was going to take to win the war.

My reasons for being there, to help the South Vietnamese stop the communist aggression, were totally shattered in one scary afternoon. I would never have the same zest and enthusiasm for the war effort again.

When we dropped off the South Vietnamese "deserters," we were asked to go back and get their wounded and killed; we declined the request. There was no way we would go back in that LZ ever again.

On a related note: I was never able to endure crowds again when I returned to the U.S. Waiting in lines for movies or wading through crowds at sporting events still makes me uncomfortable. It all brings back memories of the panic in that LZ.

#

Author's note: This is one of the biggest mysteries from my tour of duty in Nam. There are no explanations possible.

Spiritual Armor

In April of 1967 I was sitting around on standby. We were waiting for any action that would require more ground troops to be brought into an area where our guys had made enemy contact. The rest of my helicopter company was participating in what we called "eagle flights." Several of them would fly troops into suspected areas of enemy concentrations in hopes of making contact. Then, helicopters would quickly drop a backup force into the LZ to overwhelm the opposing forces. My ship was the command and control ship (C and C) and we had the ground commanders onboard.

We were supporting the ARVN (Army of the Republic of Vietnam) rangers out of the Phu Loi area. It was not a very large force, perhaps 150 men plus about six American advisors. They had been looking all morning for suspected VC (Viet Cong) elements hiding along the Saigon River across from Chu Chi; they had made no contact.

Late in the morning we got some frantic radio calls that they were under heavy fire. They needed help right away. We jumped into our helicopter and took off with the ARVN commanders onboard. We headed out as fast as we could to the hot (under fire) LZ. We could hear all the radio chatter going on between the helicopters. All nine of our ships had taken hits and had been damaged. The gunships were escorting them back to the base camp at Phu Loi. All of them made it safely back those few short miles, but it meant that there were no more gunships on station to protect our single aircraft when we landed there. Worse yet, there would be no one there to rescue us if we got into any trouble.

By the time we arrived in the sky above the LZ, there was a full engagement of hostility going on below us. The ARVN had stumbled upon a large group of NVA (North Vietnamese Army troops) who had infiltrated down from across the border in Cambodia. There was an estimated force of around 500 NVA fighting the smaller and outgunned ARVN rangers. The battle was not going well for us. That is when the ground commander decided that they needed to be closer to the action and wanted us to drop them off on the ground on the edge of this hot LZ.

As we began our descent and were about 20 feet above the ground, all hell broke loose. The sky filled with red and white tracers (red were NATO ammo and the white were from Chinese and Warsaw ammo). Each tracer round usually represented five rounds of shot ammo, every fifth round being a tracer.

On our own M-60 machine guns, the ammo belts came set up from supply with a tracer for every fifth round out of the ammo can, however, I had altered mine by making my own ammo belts for combat assaults. I had added solid tracers for the first 2,000–3,000 rounds, just to make the enemy think I had more firepower than I really had. Firing off these belts would really light up the sky and make it appear as if I were firing more rounds than I actually was. I was hoping to get a psychological edge over my enemy. I do not know if it worked or not, but it made it much easier to direct my aim and to make quick adjustments; and it did make me feel more powerful.

As we got lower, closer, and, unfortunately, slower, dozens of rounds from automatic weapons were pelting our ship. I could hear the pings, but mostly I could feel the bullets ripping holes in the metal walls. The sky was full of tracers. Yet, I had my orders not to fire back since there were friendly troops on the ground that we didn't want to hit with "friendly fire" (from our own guns). I sat and faced the wall of fire that came at me from all angles. Everything was directed at our small helicopter, which was being shredded apart by the impact of the heavy firepower.

When we hit the ground, the ARVN commanders scurried off like a bunch of rats leaving a sinking ship. One of them stopped and turned around to face me. He pulled his automatic weapon up to his shoulder and sighted in directly on me sitting behind my idle machine gun.

I was looking toward the rear of my helicopter, checking to see if we had anyone coming at us from that direction, just as he pulled off a short burst. My pilot later told me that the guy had put in a new ammo magazine and aimed his weapon right at my chest. There were about

18 rounds in the clip, and he fired them all in just a matter of a few quick moments.

I had slightly turned my head in time to see nothing more than a stream of light entering my body. I could feel the impact of something hitting me hard in the chest, directly in the heart, or what should have been my heart if I had not had a ceramic protective plate on my chest. The impact threw my whole body up against the wall of the transmission well. I sat there with no air left in my lungs since the punch to my chest sucked out my last breath. The brunt force of the hit also severed the radio cord to my flight helmet, so I sat there in total silence with fire and smoke whirling up from a large hole in my chest protector. For a few short moments, I had no fear even though I thought I was dead.

Just three days prior to this mission, I had agreed to test out a new ceramic chest protector. I had been wearing a flak vest, which could not really stop anything. Now, looking down at my two-day-old chest protector, with smoke still seeping out of a deep cavity over my heart, I was not sure if I were dead or alive. The power of the round had bruised my chest, but I saw no blood. I felt no sharp pains, but my neck really hurt from the whiplash when my body flew backward.

The pilot managed to pull the ship back into the air, about 10 or 12 feet above the ground, and we moved as far away from the LZ as we could. Due to the damage, our ship could not stay up for long. We were able to move only a few hundred yards past all the fighting before we involuntarily landed and skidded to a stop. Ignoring my own possible injuries, I rushed to help the aircraft commander get out. Then, I raced around and helped the copilot out of the other side of the helicopter. I looked back and saw the left door gunner and blood splattered everywhere. Red flowed across the nylon seat, onto the metal floor, and down the outside of the aircraft.

When I got to him (I was on the opposite side of the helicopter when I saw him) I could see that he was in major trouble. I saw blood running down his body. There were multiple holes in his neck, shoulders, and all over his back and butt. I could see that he was in a great deal of pain. I tried to do what I could as I thought about the NVA troops that would be coming after us within a few minutes. I knew time was important. I got him out of the helicopter, rendered some quick first aid, then put him on my shoulders and back and carried him to a safe place away from the helicopter.

The two pilots joined me, and we huddled at the edge of a clearing away from the downed Huey that sat like a big piece of Swiss cheese in a large mousetrap. I soon heard the familiar "whop, whop" sound of another Huey. I looked up in the sky and saw one of our B-model gunships coming down to land. I quickly dragged and lifted my gunner, running as best as I could to that gunship. I gently laid his body on the helicopter's floor and pushed his legs inside. My aircraft commander rushed past me and jumped onboard. I began to get on the aircraft, but they waved off the copilot and me, saying there was no more room for us—too much weight. We both stood there, speechless and bewildered.

As I watched in disbelief, the gunship flew away and disappeared beyond my sight, leaving us very close to the enemy that had just shot us down. The copilot, a captain, and I were more than just a little concerned about our safety. We knew we were only a football field or two away from 500 NVA troops. We also knew that we could not trust the ARVN forces either, since we had been shot at by one of their commanders.

I needed to take some kind of action and not just wait for the enemy to find us. I went back to my Huey and pulled off one of the M-60 machine guns from the gun mount on the side of the helicopter. I also took a few thousand rounds of ammo. I began the walk back toward the hot LZ where we had gotten shot up. I just didn't like the idea of waiting for someone to come after me. I would rather be the hunter than the hunted, so I put the gun on my hip and took the battle back to the enemy.

The captain was the only black helicopter pilot in our company at that time. There were so few black pilots in Nam that I often wondered if it was a cultural thing or racism. I had assumed that those who had been selected and graduated from flight school had to be super qualified—even more so than most of the other pilots. Now, for him to survive on the ground with me, he had to become a grunt. Unfortunately, all he had in his hand was a pistol. It looked really small, and he carried just a couple of ammo clips for it. We were not ready for any kind of a long battle by any stroke of the imagination. He was willing and brave, and I figured that was a lot. I decided to go

115

on the offensive and attack. I figured two Americans against 500 NVA were fair enough odds. I also was hoping that the ARVN rangers could handle some of them. I was not thinking too clearly, and my adrenaline was kicking into high gear. Looking back on this idea from the vantage point of old age, I do not think this was a bright idea at all.

There was a thick tree line along the shore of the river. I wanted to make sure that the NVA did not approach us from that covered position. I walked toward it with my M-60 blazing away from my hip. I was killing trees and knocking leaves and branches to the ground. I was a giant lawnmower rolling through the jungle. Birds and monkeys were flying and jumping—everything in my path was falling down and being blown away by the massive firepower from my machine gun. I was John Wayne in one of his old war movies. It all seemed surreal to me. I looked behind me, and sure enough, the captain was still with me, covering my rear end with his little handgun. What a brave man, and even more so for following me though the forest.

Little did I realize that after a few minutes and a few thousand rounds, my gun barrel would melt from the heat. It became red hot and was smoking, but the bad news was that it no longer worked! I pulled the trigger and heard silence. It was not the sound I wanted to hear after I had attacked the jungle with my weapon of mass destruction, cursing and ranting at the unseen enemy. I wondered if I had pissed off all of them. I looked down at my gun; the barrel had actually bent at an angle. I had never seen anything like that happen before.

I looked back at my captain. We both knew it was time for some intelligent E and E (escape and evasion). We moved out of the woods, looking for a place where we could become as invisible as possible. We spent the rest of that day (several more hours) trying not to get too far from the helicopter because that was where our rescue would eventually take place.

We had a lot of time to kill (no pun intended) while we waited for a ride back "home" to our base camp, or anywhere out of there. We finally saw a Huey coming to get us. I looked up into the sky only after I heard the sound of the engines and the old rotor blades popping. I finally saw the Huey pull over the treetops behind us. I now knew how we could sneak right up on old Charlie out in the boonies. We both ran quickly, not walked, to the Huey and were onboard before it fully settled its skids on the ground. I felt that we had overstayed our welcome, and it was time to go home.

Later, a Chinook helicopter hoisted our damaged Huey out of the crash site and carried it back to Phu Loi Airfield for repairs. When we examined it, we were struck with disbelief. There were 17 holes in the transmission-housing wall on the left side of the aircraft, behind where the door gunner sat. The bullets and fragments had exited here before entering the door gunner's body. We had expected to see the exit holes, but we also thought we would find 17 entry holes on the right side of the ship where I sat. In fact, if we took a straight line from where they exited and where they should have entered, they would have had to come directly through my body. The left door gunner and I were like silhouettes, our backs directly in line as we faced in opposite directions to fire our machine guns on the left and right sides. There was a transmission and a wall between us. On his wall there were 17 exit holes. Yet, on my side there was nothing, not one single hole. Nothing seemed to have entered from my side of the aircraft.

Common sense told us that something was wrong with this picture. We all knew that the gunfire had come from the right side of the ship. We all saw the sky, which had been aflame with tracer rounds heading toward where I was sitting. The facts of what had happened and what we were seeing did not make any sense.

No one could offer us an explanation of what had taken place. No one even had a theory. It was impossible for 17 exit holes to appear on one side of a wall without having entered the other side. The strange part is that there is a big transmission between the gunners' positions, and nothing should have gone through to his side from my direction. The exit holes were on a straight path from where my chest and body were on the other side.

An Army safety board investigated and was as puzzled as all of us who had lived through the experience. It was impossible that it could have happened as we saw it. But the holes were there. We saw what we saw. There were those 18 rounds fired directly at me—one entered my chest protector and the other 17 exited the far side of the aircraft without ever hitting me. It was as if they went through me. I can offer nothing more to explain this, except to believe that there must have been some kind of "spiritual armor" that protected me from harm's way on that fateful morning along the Saigon River.

#

Author's note: I am not sure who this woman could have been—a ghost, an angel, or my imagination—but it allowed me to relax and begin the mental and spiritual healing processes. After all I had been through in Nam to this point in time, I no longer feared anything. I knew and truly believed that Someone was looking after me.

Healing Hands

During an intensive period of combat in Vietnam in an operation code named "Operation Junction City," I discovered something I never expected to find. Let me begin with some background leading up to this moment.

My commanding officer (CO) brought me into his office one afternoon and strongly suggested that I take some time off, R and R (Rest and Relaxation), in country for a few days. He knew that I had been interested in going back to the north coastal city of Nha Trang. My CO knew that I had lived though some very dangerous and nightmarish flight missions the previous three weeks when I was shot down three times and had been injured. (I was recognized for those actions by being awarded the Distinguished Flying Cross. I also earned a handful of Air Medals, and a Purple Heart for a very minor hand wound.) In that same time period, I had almost been captured. My physical and emotional health was noticeably at a weak point. I was totally exhausted and had no more energy left to give.

To the credit of my CO, he recognized that it was time for me to take some time off and recharge myself. I did not fight the idea too hard. I had actually looked forward to flying up there and spending some lazy days on the beaches and swimming in the South China Sea. Early the next morning, I got on a helicopter heading north to the air base in Nha Trang. I took very little with me, choosing to travel light. I did not bring a weapon nor did I even give it any consideration.

I got a ride to the downtown area with a young Vietnamese man on his pedicab. He pedaled as fast as he could and took me to a nice but small hotel. It had no more than a half dozen rooms for rent. However, it was clean and had a peaceful feel to it. I wanted to keep away from the Army and spend some quality time living in the city with the people. That meant I was staying at a hotel that was at least three or four miles away from the closest military base. I was also the only American for several miles in either direction, and I must believe that I was the only GI dumb enough to stay overnight in the city without any kind of weapon.

This city was fairly safe, but it had VC living there, and the VC occasionally attacked the nearby bases. This was by no means a protected compound, and there was no security to stop anyone from capturing or killing me. It is strange, but those thoughts and questions come to me only now as I write this—at the time I felt invincible. Youth can do that to you.

The view from the window in my room afforded me a great look at the large Buddha up on the hillside at the edge of the city. I had seen it from the air when we had flown in that afternoon. It was huge. We had actually flown circles around it in our helicopter. We could see that it was also a temple. People were going under it into a large chapel-like area. The statue sat on top of the temple and served as the roof.

Looking in the other direction from my room, I could see the most wonderful rolling surf washing onto some of the world's finest beaches. As far as I could see, the white beaches spread across the shoreline, melting into the soft blue waters of the South China Sea. It struck me how this beauty was so much in contrast to the war torn part of the country where I had been living and fighting. What a welcome relief it was to be here in this great room with its soul-refreshing view; I was pleased with my choice. This was all very impressive stuff to my young self, and it sure as heck beat being back in the world I had just come from.

One of my concerns was getting some much needed rest and sleep while I was there. I really was very tired, but I was having a lot of trouble relaxing or falling asleep. And even though I had wanted to go out and explore the city, my energy was so low that I could barely walk. I felt I needed to sleep for an entire year, but I just couldn't get the old body and mind to shut down and rest. My mind was still fighting all those battles of the war that I thought I had left behind.

When I had checked into the hotel, I told the manager not to bother me with anything and not to send me any "girls" since I was not interested in having a prostitute in my room. All I really wanted to do, and was very much looking forward to doing, was sleep.

I lay there on the bed, half awake and thinking about home, when I heard a soft, muted knock on my hotel door. I got up and opened the door. There before me stood a beautiful part Asian, part French woman. She looked to be perhaps in her 20s, but she had an ageless look to her and could have been any age I imagined her to be. I noticed that she was somehow different, not normal. Her skin was a brilliant white; she seemed to almost glow. Light hung around her like a veil. It radiated from within her, not from the outside sunlight.

She stood there, not saying a word, and looking demurely at me with her eyes slightly cast downward. I told her that I was not interested in whatever she was offering. I did not want to pay for anything nor did I want any of her services. I told her to go away. I closed the door and walked back to my bed, leaving her standing in the hallway. I fell onto the bed face down with my head deeply buried in the pillow. I tried to relax and, I hoped, to sleep.

Suddenly, I felt the gentle pressure of two soft, feminine hands gently rubbing my back. I did not look up. I lay there, transfixed on the feeling of peace coming from within me. I did not move nor did I say anything to her. I just lay there while she rubbed all that tension, anger, and depression out of my body with her hands.

My mind and body completely relaxed. I was half drifting between being fully awake and in some kind of altered state. I just felt so loved but not at all in any sexual way. It was more like a spiritual uplifting; it was that same kind of feeling that I got when I used to fast for long periods of time—a light-headed, other-worldly floating, almost out-of-body experience. Yet, I was fully there. And so was she.

It occurred to me that I had left her standing outside in the hallway. How had she gotten inside my room? I rolled over to look at her eyes, but the light coming in through the windows blurred my vision so I could not fully see what her eyes looked like. I did see her soft, motherly smile as she rolled me back over to continue rubbing my back.

All my pains and tension were gone. I felt alive and well once again. I was really feeling so good about her being there, I rolled over once again. I wanted to see this woman who was giving me all this healing energy. Now my mind and body were stimulated by natural desires, and I had decided that I wanted to spend some time with her.

121

I wanted to take her around the city and to the beaches. When I turned over this time, there was no woman there. The room was quite empty except for me.

I quickly looked all around the room, checking all the possible hidden recesses. The door was still closed, as it had been when I had closed it earlier. I was alone in the room. I jumped out of the bed and raced into the hallway. I looked both directions, then I ran downstairs to the street. She was not to be found anywhere. When I asked the people outside the hotel which way she went, they told me that no one had been out of that door for hours. They also said that no one had come into the hotel either.

I went back to the manager and demanded to know whom she had sent to my room. The manager looked at me as if I were crazy. She said that no one was sent to my room. She stated that she had been watching the hotel all day long, and that if anyone had come or gone, she would have seen her. She asked if I had been on drugs or had been drinking. She did not understand what I was talking about.

Well, I was not drinking nor had I done any drugs. All I knew was that I had seen her and that she had touched me, and not just in a physical way.

I wandered back to my empty room. I felt so much love and peace within me that I did not worry about understanding what had happened in that room moments before. All I knew was that I felt a surge of joy and peace within myself. I was able to relax and sleep, forgetting about the battles of war. I went to sleep almost as soon as my head touched the pillow, and I was able to sleep like a baby. I have never slept that well in my whole life before or since.

When I woke up, I felt connected to the world once again. I was relaxed and at peace with myself. I went out to the beach and walked along the wet sand in the twilight. The warm waters touched my bare feet as I looked up at the stars in the early night skies. I felt extremely close to the divine that night. I could feel God's love filling me. I did not understand who that woman was then, nor do I today.

Who she was? What was she doing there? Who had sent her? How did she disappear without a trace? The answers I have not, but I do know that it was not a dream. Something very special happened to me that afternoon. It also was something that I could never fully explain to anyone else. I didn't think that anyone would ever understand- since I do not even know myself who she was. Until recently, I have only revealed this long held secret to a few friends.

Believe what you want—I will never know for sure who this woman was or why she came to me—but I know that I was "touched by my special angel." Even if no one ever believes this story, I know I will cherish that memory forever.

I spent several days in Nha Trang before returning to the heat of combat and the war. But I was forever changed by that "touch."

#

W.H. McDonald Jr.

Author's note: This poem has appeared in various publications including Jan Hornung's book "Angels in Vietnam: Women Who Served."

Carol, Has It Been a Hundred Years?

My tired
War-torn heart
And body
Want to stop
The reality of this dream.
I want to wake myself up
And roll over
And find you there.

Memories,
Of your flashing,
Sunshine smile,
And soft laughter,
Bring me a moment
Of sanity
In this insane place
Filled with dying
And
Lonesome young poets.

\#

June 1967
War Zone C, South Vietnam

124

Author's note: There are some events in life that hang with you for years and years afterward—this was one of those emotional experiences.

Out, Out, Damn Spot!

The 1st Infantry was involved with a big operation called "Operation Billings." They were inserting troops into some very hostile areas. The dense jungles held not only VC (Viet Cong) but also a large number of NVA (North Vietnamese Army) troops fresh from their trip down from the north. Our company was engaged in supporting this operation from the beginning. We had been landing in some very hot (under fire) LZs and had experienced lots of damage to our helicopters over the first several days of the operation. We had been coming back into those same LZs to resupply ammo and food, and to bring in replacement troops. We often left with wounded and dead, taking them back to the base camps or to the closest MASH (Mobile Air Surgical Hospital) units.

One day we received a frantic call for assistance from a group of about 100 men who were trapped and fighting for their lives in an LZ that was being fiercely defended by the enemy. There were NVA and VC units surrounding this group of men in the beleaguered LZ. In some places the LZ's perimeter had partially collapsed. There was hand to hand fighting on the edges of the clearing that was being used for our Hueys to land in.

We could tell from the voice of the radioman that they were in the thick of a firefight. We could hear the gunfire and explosions in the background as the guy yelled over his radio. They needed a dust off (medical evacuation) as soon as possible. As it turned out, we were the only available aircraft in the sector, so we turned around and raced to their location. We were not sure what we were going to find when we got there.

When we approached within close proximity to the LZ, we saw the yellow smoke that they popped to guide us to our pickup point. We could also see red and white tracers bouncing off the trees and the ground. Looking back at it now reminds me of battle scenes from the *Star Wars* movies where they are firing lasers at each other; the

125

tracers were lighting up the sky and the ground in much the same manner. There also were several explosions from enemy mortar rounds falling into the LZ. I assumed some of the explosions in this open meadow were from hand grenades. It was a living hell for those men inside that LZ. The smoke drifted through the broken trees that had fallen and were on fire. Men were running and moving in all directions. There seemed to be no organized plan of action—it was total chaos unfolding below us. No area in this lethal place looked secure or safe from the action.

We were flying at treetop level as we pulled into the LZ. This made us an easy target for the VC and NVA troops in the surrounding jungle. We could feel the belly of the helicopter taking hits. Tracer rounds also were flying through the open areas of the ship where we had taken off the doors. The ship rocked and bounced along the treetops. Intermittent, violent upheavals from ground explosions rocked our aircraft. I thought it was going to be torn apart by the pounding of the blasts. Every explosion caused our helicopter to rock and roll as if it were going to suddenly drop out of the sky and into the trees a few feet below us.

I had my machine gun fully at the ready but could not pick out any clear targets below. I could not fire since the good guys and bad guys were mixing it up in the LZ. There was no way to see who was whom. I had to sit there while the enemy took his potshots at us. It seemed to take hours to travel that last 100 yards to where our soldiers had popped smoke for us to land. By the time we set down, we could see hand-to-hand combat taking place a short distance from us. We were the biggest target in the LZ, and we could not hide anywhere. We needed to load the wounded and get out of there as fast as possible.

There were more explosions just yards away from us. I could feel the dirt and pieces of tree branches hitting my face and body. All around me, men were dropping. Their bodies were being ripped apart by automatic gunfire and mortar rounds. The green grass was turning red from all the flowing blood. I unplugged my communications line from my flight helmet and jumped off the ship as soon as we were parked on the ground. I ran about 20 yards to the medics who were dragging wounded men toward our ship. I grabbed someone's leg to help out. There were bullets hitting the ground all around us, and some were hitting the wounded men we were trying to evacuate. It was a miracle that all of us were not killed.

The pilots were yelling at me to hurry up and get back into the helicopter. Every second we were on the ground, we allowed enemy mortar teams to sight in on our ship. All it would take was about 30 seconds or less before they could get us in their range and drop a round or two on the helicopter. Getting out of the LZ as fast as possible was our key to survival.

To make matters even worse, the trees and the grass had caught on fire. We now had a raging forest fire engulfing the area. It was hot and the smoke made it hard to breathe. I kept going back to help load more bodies onto the floor of my Huey. There was nothing gentle in this act as we threw these men in the ship as fast as we could. Within about half a minute we had loaded six wounded soldiers on the floor and two more on the canvas seats.

By now, all hell had broken loose. The mortar rounds were landing just yards away, and we were the focus of attention for all of the automatic weapons' fire. There was a wall of tracers coming at us, which we had to fly through to get out of there. I jumped back onboard and looked at the medic who stood watching me as we began to hover and lift off. His eyes were full of tears that rolled down his face, turning his dirty cheeks muddy, as he raised his hand to wave goodbye and to somehow bless his men. It was the saddest goodbye in the world. He knew he was probably not going to make it out of there alive. He got his buddies on the ship and that must have given him some satisfaction at the time. Our eyes connected for a brief moment, and I raised my hand to bid him goodbye—but it was more than that. I knew and he knew that he might not be alive when I came back. I silently sent him my prayers. We were all in God's hands now.

The pilots pulled up on the collective stick and tried to rise out of the LZ as straight up as we could fly. However, the heat of the day, the height of the trees, and all the extra weight onboard forced us to fly directly over the fighting. We slowly gained enough altitude, we hoped, to clear the surrounding trees. We could see the tree line coming up at us, and it appeared that we were not going to clear it. We needed more room to get enough transitional lift to compensate for all the weight we were now trying to take out of this LZ. We continued toward the trees and somehow managed to clip only a few branches with our skids.

I looked back, trying to get a good shot at the enemy troops with my M-60. I was able to let off about 1,000 rounds into the outer jungle areas where I knew our troops were not engaged. I then was able to take a quick glance back at the LZ as we began to climb above the tree line. The medic with the sad eyes was running for his life. There were bodies falling everywhere I looked. This was the worst LZ I had ever seen in the war. I sat back for a minute to try to regain my composure, and I tried to take a very deep breath. I felt my heart racing and pounding in my chest, and I was having trouble catching my breath.

I remembered the troops that we had loaded on the ship. I set my gun down and looked at where they were lying on the floor and seats. What I saw made me feel sick. There were large pools of thick red blood flowing on the floor of the ship. Since the doors had been removed, the wind blew right through the aircraft. The rotor blades and air speed also made for a lot of wind at the speed we were traveling—and it made the blood fly all around the inside of the ship. Fresh warm blood was splashed on the walls, the windshields, our clothing and helmets, and all over my gloves and face. The pilots had trouble seeing since so much blood had splashed on the inside of the windshield. There also were severed body parts that had fallen off and were laying in the pools of blood on the floor.

I was absolutely stunned by the sight of all this, but I quickly realized that I needed to take some action to help these guys. There was no medic onboard and no medicine. I did not have the knowledge or the means to stop all the bleeding. I was helpless to do much except offer my prayers and some moral support. I went over to check on their condition, and I was angered to find that not one of them was still alive. All 8 men were dead. They had continued to take hits when we were lifting off. Their bodies were riddled with holes.

I became upset about risking all of our lives to bring back only dead bodies. I told the pilots so we could change our destination to the nearest camp. We did not need to fly to the MASH unit anymore.

I sat there looking at these young men. Most had their young, frightened eyes still open. We stared at each other while the ship continued to speed back to the closest camp. We needed to dump these bodies, clean the windshield, and go back to that LZ. We were the only lifeline, the only link with the outside world that they had. I sat there in a daze, thinking about what we had just been through. The eyes of the medic still haunted me, as did all of those dead men lying there next to me. I sat there with all of my clothing soaked in red blood, and I knew I would never forget this scene before me.

Suddenly, something caught my attention. I looked over at one of the young men lying there with his dead eyes wide open, staring directly at me. I could feel his presence. I could feel him reaching out somehow. I could feel all of them. It was as if they were still there with their bodies. They were confused and frightened and lonely. I could sense the sorrow of their thoughts and almost hear their cries. It was really spooky I did not know if I had cracked up and been caught in the horror of the moment by my own fears, or if I was really sensing the souls of these men. I sent up a prayer for all of them. My feelings were all locked and controlled. I looked at all these dead men and couldn't find it within me emotionally to even shed a single teardrop—and part of me really wanted to.

I went back to my position behind my machine gun and sat there gazing out at the vast landscape beyond. I felt such sorrow and waste. I felt so much pain within that I thought I would never be able to completely express it to anyone. No one would ever understand what had happened. No one would even want to hear about this experience. I felt terribly alone and isolated from the whole world.

We finally got to a nearby base camp and unloaded the dead. We took a short five-minute break to clean the windshield and wipe some of the pools of blood out of the ship. Then, we jumped back onboard and took off again—heading back to hell.

We were joined by some other aircraft from our company on the return trips, so we had some help for the rest of the day. We ended up flying about 15 hours into and out of this LZ, taking several dozen men, many of them dead, out of the LZ that day. We were able to save very few for the MASH unit. The LZ had been a disaster for those men. I felt bad that I was not able to give them better support. I often wondered if that medic ever made it out alive. His eyes still burned in my heart as we went back to our own base camp that night in the darkness.

We landed back at Phu Loi late at night. All I wanted to do was to get that blood-soaked clothing off and to take a shower. I wanted to get rid of the smell and feel of death that was on me and in my ship. When we were unloaded, we were informed that there was no more water available for a shower or to clean up the helicopter. Well, there was no way that I was not going to get cleaned up. My gunner and I decided to use some jet fuel, since that was the only available liquid to clean anything with. We washed out the entire inside of the helicopter and all the seats. It smelled bad and was a fire hazard for sure, but there was no way that we were going to let all that blood stay in our ship.

We took off all of our clothing on the fight line, then poured the jet fuel over our bodies to rinse the blood away. We washed our entire bodies with that stuff, including our private parts and our hair. We were careful about not being close to anyone who was smoking, or anything else that might cause a spark.

We walked back to our hooch naked save for our underwear, boots, and dog tags. We put on some clean underwear and climbed into bed smelling up the entire place for everyone else. We did not sleep at all. With the smell of the gas and the thoughts and images of that day still with us, we could not rest.

The next day, with the heat (the temperatures reaching over 95 degrees) along with the high humidity, our bodies began to redden and chafe. We were hurting and uncomfortable as our bodies exploded with a red rash from head to toe that looked as if we had been painted red. We both took a lot of kidding about how we looked and felt, but it was still better than going to bed with all that dried blood all over us.

When I went on R and R, I took a lot of enjoyment in taking long showers with warm, clean water. I just wanted to clean off the Nam and all that blood. Sometimes I still feel the need to wash away those blood stained memories—"out, out, damn spot!" But those Nam stains go very deep into the soul.

#

Spc. 5 Bill McDonald and
128th AHC secretary, a local hire.

Author's note: I was badly injured in this rocket attack but never reported my injuries to the Army. I was scheduled for R and R (rest and recreation) that morning, and I wanted to make sure that I left on the plane. Had I reported having been knocked unconscious and hurting my neck and back, I would have missed the reunion with my mother who was waiting for me in Japan. To this day I still feel the effects of that injury.

Rockets' Red Glare

It was a muggy night, which could have been said about almost every night I was in Vietnam, but this particular night it just seemed a little worse. I was tired but was feeling rather good about having survived another long week of being in country. My short timer's calendar was filling up; I was at about the halfway point in my tour of duty in Nam. I was ready for an R and R to Japan in just a few hours. I was very much looking forward to some relief from all the dirt and the muggy heat.

I was lying on my bunk around midnight, and my buddy Steve was still awake on his bunk above me. Everyone else had been long asleep. I was hyped up about leaving in the morning on a helicopter flight to Saigon (Tan Son Nhut Air Base). That was where I would hook up with my R and R flight to Japan. I was just lying there in my underwear, trying to stay cool and wishing away the hours. I began to hear thud-like sounds in the distance. These were not the same sounds as the normal and familiar nightly bursts of artillery fire that our base camp engaged in for hours each night. This had a whole different quality to it. I lay there listening and trying to place this new sound.

My buddy leaned over from the top bunk. He was hearing the same thing I was.

"Incoming!" he exclaimed aloud what we were both thinking.

Yes, these were the sounds of rockets and mortars coming in on top of our base camp. We shouted out to the others to wake up and get dressed. But just as everyone was beginning to roll out of their bunks, I felt myself being lifted through the air. I must have flown a full 15 feet before dropping headfirst onto the hard cement floor. I lost consciousness briefly, perhaps no more than 10 seconds. It was long enough that if I were a boxer in the ring I would have been declared a loser by a TKO, technical knockout.

The noise that accompanied that liftoff temporarily deafened me. It felt and sounded like a freight train running through our small wooden hooch. My head felt as if a thousand-pound weight had dropped on it. My vision was all fuzzy, and I could hardly stand up. I felt lightheaded as if I were floating on a cloud. A huge bump was forming on my head as I struggled to get my bearings. I yelled out for everyone to get into the bunkers, which were just outside the doors at each end of the hooch. That order, however, was already too late as everyone had beat it out of the building except for me and one new guy who was lying on the floor next to me. He was holding the back of his neck where he had blood oozing out of it. A small piece of sharp metal was sticking in a hole just below the hairline. He was okay, but he was concerned since he could not see the real nature of his wound. It was bleeding and running down the nape of his neck, but it wasn't a serious wound. That was his first or second week in the Nam—what a way to start off. He crawled out one end of the hooch as I checked to make sure that everyone else was out of there.

I stood up and almost fell back down. I was woozy and my legs had a difficult time staying directly under me as I staggered around hanging onto the bunk beds and footlockers. I looked at the rifle rack where we had our M-16s stored and locked in place. The barrels of all of them—every single one of them—were bent at a 90-degree angle. The pure force of that explosion had bent those steel rifle barrels. I had never witnessed that kind of brute energy before; I looked at the rack in disbelief. The gun rack had been just five feet in front of where I had been standing when the blast went off directly behind me. It had thrown me in the air, up and over the top of the rack. It hit home how powerful that explosion was. If the gun barrels could be damaged that badly, it was no wonder my head was feeling so bad. At least there wasn't any visible blood on me.

I was still in my undershorts and tee shirt. I did manage to grab my boots but no socks as I stumbled out of the door. I jumped into the sandbagged bunker right outside our door. I landed in about two feet of cold, muddy water. I was crowded in with a host of others trying to keep out of harm's way.

133

We had no weapons and most of us were not even dressed. We huddled together as more explosions rocked and jolted the camp. The whole earth shook each time one hit near us. One of the younger guys (about 18 years old) grabbed hold of me with both of his arms. He wrapped his shaking body as close to me as possible. I returned his hold so he would not panic or, worse yet, start to cry. I told him everything would be okay and that he needed to relax. I felt like his father, but I was only three years older than he was.

The explosions shook the sandbags on the metal top over our bunker. Sand and dirt cascaded down on us. I looked outside the bunker and saw that the sky was bright with red flames. Most of the rocket rounds had hit our airfield and a few helicopters were burning and exploding. I could see from the shadows cast by the fires that there were large holes in the earth right by our hooch. We had apparently taken some close hits from what turned out to be Russian-made rockets. That night we were hit with 250 mortars and rockets, according to the after-battle briefing.

I looked around quickly in the dark shelter and saw lots of large eyeballs looking back at me. I had to assert myself and take charge of the situation. I decided to go out and check the bunker at the other end of the hooch to see if the rest of the guys were okay. I quickly counted men in my bunker and then ran to the other one. I looked inside and took a quick roll call. Everyone was accounted for.

Then we heard someone yelling, something about the perimeter being breached by the VC. That meant that there were now enemy forces within our compound. We had no rifles, and our machine guns were down by the airfield, close to where the helicopters were burning. That location seemed to be the likely target of the VC as they penetrated our outer defenses and came inside. None of us were ready to go down to the flight line to check out our aircraft.

I decided to get out of the bunker and locate the first sergeant (see picture below). I thought he would need all the information available about what was happening. I ran over to his bunker, which was across the company area. I could still hear more rockets dropping inside the camp. When I appeared at the entry to the sergeant's bunker, I thought he was going to shoot me. He had his pistol right in my face. He had heard the same stories about VC inside the camp, and he was not taking any chances. I briefed him quickly, then went back and got

134

my door gunner and our clothing. I hated the thought of fighting a war in just our underwear! We ran for the airfield to get a couple of M-60s and to check out our helicopter. We found a couple of pilots on the way, and we went looking for a flyable aircraft. We mounted the guns in the darkness and did the quickest preflight inspection in history. We got ourselves airborne as fast as possible. The airfield was still burning as some helicopters had taken direct hits. It seemed Charlie knew exactly where we parked our birds each night.

We hovered just a short distance before the pilot pulled up on the collective and pushed the cyclic stick forward. We tried to scoot the hell off that runway as fast as we could to get out of the rocket fire. We headed out to the only spot in the dark sky where there were no tracers coming or going. We did not turn on any of our running lights since we were greatly concerned that we might be hit from our own troops as well as the VC.

We got on the radio and heard that help was on the way. "Puff, The Magic Dragon" had been summoned for duty. Puff was a converted old Douglas C-47 "Skytrain" (DC-3). In a matter of a few minutes, Puff laid out a blanket of fire across the surrounding jungle. That old aircraft devastated every living thing within its target zone with just a few bursts of fire.

We wanted to make sure we were not in Puff's killing zone, so we pulled up to an altitude above him. We watched as he flew around the outside borders of our camp, unloading hell on those below. It was a most impressive sight to watch as Puff rolled into action. It was as if we were watching the old movie *War of the Worlds* as a shower of fire created by the solid line of tracers came raining down. It did not last very long as the ground fighting quickly became quiet.

We landed and checked to see if our services were needed for any dust offs (medical evacuations). Once the night sky cleared and we were on the ground again, we found that the camp looked like hell. There were surprisingly few destroyed helicopters sitting on the pads. Most of the rounds had missed their intended targets. However, there was a lot of damage that needed to be repaired.

I went back to my hooch and found my bunk and locker. There were holes in my locker, which was next to my bed, and my record player and speakers were destroyed. There also were holes in some of my uniforms and hats that had been hanging in my locker. I had a rather odd feeling when I realized how close I had been standing to what was now all my damaged gear when the rockets hit us. It was about this moment that my head reminded me once again that I was in pain. Great pain!

I had a flight leaving for my R and R trip in about 15 minutes. I was not about to spoil that by reporting any injuries. I also was concerned that someone might notice that I was injured and cancel my R and R. I pulled my hat over the bump on my head and walked out toward the flight line to find a chopper to hop on. I wanted to get out of that potential cemetery as quickly as possible and while I was still in one piece.

The smoke was still rising slowly from small fires around the base camp as we pulled off the runway. I looked back at my hooch and saw my buddies waving to me as we passed overhead. I looked down and felt a little guilty about leaving them there. I did not know what the next night would bring for them. As we circled over the camp in the morning sunlight, I could still see several VC bodies lying across the barbed wire.

I was going to be in Japan sometime later that day. It felt unreal that I could be living in a world where such contrasts existed. It was almost like a parallel universe. My head was killing me. Nothing, however, was going to stop me from boarding my flight out of Nam. It was my time for an R and R, and I was more than ready to go!

#

First sergeant and Bill McDonald of 128th AHC.

Author's note: I hurt all the way to Japan due to my head injury. My mother was waiting for me at the Hilton Hotel, running up a bill that she had no money to pay. If not for that fact, I would have reported to a hospital in Japan. Seeing my mother was not a good experience for either one of us. It was a mistake to bring her to Japan, but it was her first and only trip outside of the United States. So, I do not regret giving that experience to her. I was not the greatest of company, however, and I had changed.

R and R in Japan

Getting on that big, safe civilian airplane that was going to take me away from the Nam, even if only for six days of freedom, was pure joy. I had just escaped a hell of a night without getting killed, and now I was on my way to Japan to have some fun and to meet my mother.

My mom had never been anywhere in her life. She had spent her entire life in the San Francisco Bay Area, except for a few trips to Reno (once to divorce my dad) and a couple of years living in Coos Bay, Oregon, when I was very young.

I bought her airline ticket and paid for her food and hotel. I thought it would be a nice gesture as well as an opportunity for us to do some bonding as mother and son. There had always been a lot of emotional distance between us. I knew that she really didn't jump up and down with glee about seeing me, but I knew that the trip would be too much for her to say no to. Since I had paid for everything, all she had to do was get on the plane and get herself across the ocean. I knew she was excited about going to Japan; I just wasn't so sure how excited she was about spending any time with me.

I sat back on the flight to Japan and engaged in a nice conversation with a grunt from the 1st Infantry Division who was very happy to get out of the boonies and get a hot shower and some warm meals. He and I had formed a great relationship by the time the plane landed, so he decided to spend his six days with me at the Hilton.

On this flight with us was a small group of civilian workers who were taking some time off from their overseas jobs for a little R and R (Rest and Recreation) themselves. These guys were working for government contractors and were getting paid some really big bucks. This rubbed me and my new friend the wrong way. We made a few rude remarks that were loud enough to be heard by a couple of them sitting across from us on the airplane. I think we got a bit self-righteous about how we were risking our lives for less than minimum wages and these guys were making a profit off of the war.

When we landed and got to the Hilton Hotel, these same two men were checking in next to us. Instead of being angry, they invited us to be their guests for a few nights on the town. They wanted to pick up the tab and show us a good time. Of course, we said yes. After all, we wanted to help them lessen their guilt. It just wouldn't have been right if we had said no.

My friend and I checked into a room next to my mother's. We took hot showers and ordered room service. I ordered two large, cold glasses of milk packed in ice; my buddy had a hamburger and fries sent up. We were in heaven for sure. I called my mom to see if she were in her room. She was, so I left to visit her while my buddy lay back on the clean sheets of his bed, eating his burger and fries with the biggest smile on his ketchup- and salt-stained lips I had ever seen.

I knocked on my mom's door and she opened it. We very briefly hugged. I tried to explain how I was doing. I didn't really know what I should tell her—I almost had been killed less than 20 hours before. I had been blown up into the air and thrown about 15 or 20 feet, had landed on my head, twisted my back, neck, and shoulders, and was now suffering immense pain. I didn't want to tell her about getting shot down a few weeks before or about getting wounded. I didn't want to tell her about all the guys who got killed or all the helicopter crashes. So, I stood there saying everything was okay and not to worry.

We invited her to dinner with us that night at the hotel. We all sat down and none of us had a clue of what to say. There just wasn't any way to tell her what we had been doing or what we would face when we returned to Nam at the end of the week. There were some long moments of uncomfortable silence followed by small talk. We asked her if she would like to go nightclubbing with us around the city. She declined, which was best for everyone.

The next few nights, our guilt-ridden friends from the airplane spent a small fortune entertaining the two of us. We went to the best nightclubs in the city with all the greatest entertainment. They even paid for women to sit at our table just to talk to us and dance with us. All the young women spoke very good English and knew a lot about Americans. They were not prostitutes but college- and university-educated women who were hostesses at these rich nightclubs. This is the story we were led to believe anyway. It seemed like a high school date with them all dressed up in American-style prom dresses. I drank lots of beer and almost forgot I was in pain. My head still hurt me though, and I was feeling dizzy and sleepy all the time. I was even throwing up everyday as well. It seemed that I had a head concussion that continued to bother me for weeks and months afterward.

Several days went by. We continued to party each night, and my mother stayed in her room. We tried to get her to go sightseeing with us in the daytime, but she said she was too tired and too old to walk around. Hell, she was only 47 years old! She acted and felt like an 80-year-old. She resisted all of our efforts to engage her in social activities with the two of us. She joined us for a few meals, and we had some light conversations, but she didn't want to do anything else with us.

By the time the week was just about up, I decided to check our hotel bills and my mom's, which I was paying for. I wanted to make sure that I had enough money. I almost fell over when I saw the room service charges that my mother had billed to her room tab. She had been ordering room service several times a day and had run up a huge bill. I was seriously concerned that I would not be able to pay both bills. I couldn't understand why my mom was doing this to me. I do not think she understood how little money I was making or how much I had with me. In any case, it rubbed me the wrong way, and it caused a slight rift between us.

When it came time to leave, she decided to stay on a couple of more weeks and go visit some old friends who were stationed in Japan. As we got on the bus to head back to the airport, she came out to the front of the hotel to say a cold goodbye. There were no signs of worry from her about my going back—maybe she was just hiding it from me—but I would have felt much better had I seen some concern on her part. I sat on the bus more depressed for having seen her on my R and R than I wanted to admit. It was one of those defining moments in my life when I knew that whatever there was between my mother and me, it wasn't about love. I felt emotionally orphaned and alone as the bus pulled away from the hotel. I could see her waving and then walking back inside the hotel lobby even before we were out of sight. My head was hurting, but it was my heart that was breaking. Nam was waiting for me, but I wasn't ready to return.

#

W.H. McDonald Jr.

R and R Flight to Japan

We flew over
The sea today
With its vast spiritual blue carpet
Spreading out
Below the horizon.

We flew away
From fear
Of death mongers
And killing fields,

Traveling far beyond
The war's reach
And the smell
Of blood.

We flew over that sea,
And she watched us
And held us
As we floated
Through the sky
Casting our small
Shadow
On her surface
Where she embraced us.

And
For those brief moments
We shared a oneness
And felt peace
And love.

#

Over the Sea of Japan
June 1967

Author's note: Listening to your higher self and knowing what will happen cannot always guarantee that you can or even should alter someone else's future. It is a tough call, when to say something and when to be quiet. In April of 1967, I had an experience that almost cost me my life, my freedom, my reputation, and perhaps, my own sanity.

Visions of Fire and Death

We were flying lots of combat assaults in and around War Zone C. We also were running a few missions into the jungles along the Cambodian frontier area. We had been inserting small units of men into places that were off of our Vietnam operational charts and maps. We were deep into Cambodia, dropping off guys that were not wearing any recognizable military uniforms. They carried weapons made in east European countries, and they did not appear to be wearing any dog tags or have unit identification patches. We were never told what they were doing or who they were. They appeared to be Americans, but we did not ask any questions because we knew if we had, we wouldn't have gotten any answers.

Around the base camp at Phu Loi, I started to feel uneasy about a particular helicopter, tail number 744. Whenever I walked by it on the flight line, I got chills and felt uneasy. I mentioned this to a couple of guys and was shocked when they told me they had the same feelings about the aircraft. Their feelings were not as strong as mine, but they did not feel right about this particular helicopter. They were concerned about having to fly in it. It seemed that several others also had picked up on this "feeling." There was just something about this chopper that made almost everyone uncomfortable.

One night, I got back to the base camp from flying all day in the Ho Bo Woods area. I'd had some hairy moments in a couple of hot LZs. I was really tired and emotionally drained of all my energy. This was not that unusual, since I had been flying about 12 hours that day. When I finished inspecting my own helicopter and making small repairs, I had to go see the captain about an assignment for the next day.

I found out after talking to him that I was scheduled to be the crew chief on 744 the next morning for a series of simple "hash and trash" runs (taking out food and ammo to troops in the field) to some Special Forces camps. It was an easy assignment. It was certainly less dangerous than what I had been doing all week. My own aircraft was due for some regularly scheduled maintenance the next day, so I was available to fly on any aircraft. The first sergeant asked me to check out 744 and perform an inspection on it so it would be ready in the morning.

I had an immediate sinking feeling in the pit of my stomach. I felt fearful as I approached the helicopter. When I reached out and touched the skin of the aircraft, I had an instant inner picture of something that I knew was going to happen the next day. I could somehow feel and see in my mind this helicopter crashed in the jungle and broken apart into pieces. I could see bodies of soldiers lying in the forest with the wreckage, all on fire and burning. The whole scene was of fire and death. I could somehow mentally feel the searing heat. I pulled my hand away from the helicopter, but the inner vision of death, destruction, and fire was still there. I knew for sure, without any doubts, what was going to happen to that aircraft the next day.

I sat down and tried to think about what to do. I had been given orders to fly on this aircraft. I could not just refuse to go; that was a punishable offense in the military. It was not just some paper punishment, but possible long-term jail time for refusing to obey an order in combat. I sat there and pondered what to do. I would be putting everything on the line by refusing to fly the next day, but I also knew that if I did fly, I would never return. It was not a matter of being afraid of a combat situation; I knew this was a fatal mission for everyone on it.

There was something wrong with that aircraft. I knew I had to find it. So, I spent several extra hours doing the daily inspection. I even asked for assistance from two or three other crew chiefs. I finally gave up and wrote in the logbook that the helicopter was unsafe to fly. I put a "red X" in the flight logbook, which meant that someone else had to officially check it out after I had. I was determined to ground this ship. I was hoping that someone would find what was wrong with it.

The guy doing the inspection asked me what was wrong and why I had grounded the helicopter. When I tried to explain why, it did not sound right. I came off sounding nuts. He checked the entire aircraft anyway and found it in perfect order. He couldn't find one thing wrong. He signed off on my "red X" entry, and the aircraft was once again ready to use for the next mission.

I was not satisfied with the situation. My feelings kept growing stronger the more I thought about it. I went to the CO and told him about my concern that something was terribly wrong with 744. I felt it was something wrong with the rotor blade system, but I couldn't provide any proof. He thought I was insane or over the edge. He gave me a direct order to be there the next day on that helicopter. I flatly told him no. I refused to fly on that ship. I told him to assign me to any other mission, on any other helicopter the next day and I would go. I would not, however, get into that helicopter no matter what the consequences of my actions.

The CO let me know that I was going to have to face charges and possible prosecution for my actions that night. He lectured me about what could happen to me. He warned me in no uncertain terms that I was disobeying a direct order in a combat zone. I could be facing military prison for a long period in my young life. But I knew what was going to happen. I had to go with my own feelings. I had to trust that what I felt was the correct path to take. I made the only choice I felt I could make.

I went back to my hooch and joined the rest of my flight squad. I told them all that had happened. They had already heard about "crazy Mac" and what I was saying. It seemed everyone knew what I had done and said. I expected some teasing or worse from them all. That was not the case. Some had feelings themselves, and a few others in the company believed me, based on previous experiences, at least enough to give me some benefit of the doubt on this. There was one new guy in the squad who did not share that view. He thought I was a nut case for sure. He thought I had been in too much combat and was now afraid for my life. His name was Al Durell, from Fair Oaks, California. He had just transferred in from Saigon, where he had left a desk job to volunteer as a door gunner.

Al was having no part of my insanity and was laughing at me behind my back. When I went over to him and got close, I could feel the heat of fire. I could sense death. I did not know how to tell anyone about this feeling I had, but I knew in my heart and mind that he was going to be killed the next day. I had to hold my emotions back as teardrops formed in the corners of my eyes. I looked him straight in the eye and told him that under no circumstances was he to go flying the next day. I went on to say that no matter what he did, he was not to get on helicopter 744. If he did go out, he would never come back. He would be killed.

Al told me that he thought I was nuts and wanted me to leave him alone. He also said that he had no assigned flight gear and had not had a flight physical yet, since he had just arrived. Therefore, he was not even on flight status. He was not scheduled to go out on anything, let alone my dreaded aircraft 744. He told me to stay away from him.

I turned around and walked back to my own bunk bed, which was just across the aisle from his. I looked back one more time. I told him that if he were asked to fly tomorrow because they were short of flight crews, that he was not to go. I got back a blank stare. He walked outside to get away from me. I could feel the tension in the hooch. I was either going to be proven wrong the next day and have to face possible jail time, or I would be proven right, which meant others would be killed. I really did not know which I would rather have happen; I had a difficult time getting any sleep that night.

The morning came and I was already tired. I dragged myself out of bed and had to face all my buddies. I guess they were just as concerned about what would happen that day as I was. I gathered my flight equipment and walked down to the flight line where I had been given another assignment. I would be flying combat missions, but it felt a lot safer than getting into 744. As we took off, the sun was just peeking over the treetops. We pulled around and I could see that old 744 was still grounded. It was not going anywhere.

We flew about 12 hours that day and had seen very little combat, just a few rounds exchanged in one hot LZ. Our gunships had quickly attacked the area, so none of our helicopters were shot down or damaged. Coming back to base camp we were all relaxed. I still had some concerns about my feelings of death and fire; they would not go away. I did not understand why I was feeling like I was. Helicopter 744 was not flying any missions that day. It was on the ground when we had left that morning.

As we pulled around and made our approach to land at Phu Loi, I could see an empty space where 744 should have been parked. My heart began to pound, and I felt fear inside. I already knew that it had crashed somewhere. It was too late to help them, too late to save anyone. I knew this already.

We landed. I got out and ran for the flight office to check on the status of 744. I found out that 744 and her crew were overdue by about two hours. No one had heard anything from them since they had picked up some soldiers from an isolated LZ to take them to another area. No one had arrived at the destination area. Now 744 was presumed missing and down. I was pissed off and stormed out of the office looking for the CO. When I saw him, I asked him why he had let that helicopter go out on a mission. He told me not to overreact and that he was in charge. He did not have to justify his actions to me, he said. They had needed another helicopter, and he had gathered a crew that afternoon and sent it off. They had only one door gunner, and the new guy, Al, had volunteered. They could not find a crew chief since that was my original assignment, and they had left with an empty seat.

No one knew exactly where 744 might be. There were no radio calls to give any indication or clue as to where a search might be effective. It was several hours past the time they were supposed to be back at the base camp before any kind of a rescue effort was put together. Finally, the unit sent out a rescue helicopter, and I volunteered to go along. We took off in the vague direction of where we thought 744 might be. There were hundreds of square miles of jungle to look over, and it was now dark. As luck would have it, we traveled as if we were honing in on a beacon of light. We began to see a flicker of light miles away in the dense jungle. From our high position in the sky, we were able to see a greater distance than if we had flown our normally lower altitude.

As we approached the light, it became evident that it was a fire. The jungle was on fire. We flew over the top of the main burnt area. We looked down and saw broken twisted metal and bodies thrown at random all over the jungle floor. We hovered over the treetops, just out of reach of the flames, trying to see if there was any movement at all. There was none. I volunteered to go down a rope to the ground and personally check out the site for any survivors, but the pilot did not want to endanger the ship or me. It was just too risky, and we did not really know if there were any VC waiting for us below. We

147

circled around the crash site several times, hoping that we would see something move.

The scene below us was horrible. All the bodies were burnt and charred. We could see shapes, but that was the only clue that these were in fact once human beings. These were the same images I had already seen in my mind the night before. I felt sick about it all. I was mad because no one had done anything to stop or prevent this from happening. The trip back from the crash site was deathly quiet. No one spoke a word about my predictions or what they had seen.

We relayed what had happened to the base camp. When we arrived, everyone knew the fate of the crew of 744. We did not know what had happened, but we knew that they were all dead.

It did not take long before the military justice system kicked into action. An accident investigation team from Army Headquarters in Saigon came to our camp. They had gone out to the crash site looking for the reasons that it exploded into a fireball. They could not find anything at that time. They did not find any logical reason, other than possible pilot error, for the helicopter to have crashed and burned. They did have one other idea—that I must have had something to do with it. They took me into a room with a light over the top of my head, just like in the movies about police interrogation. They kept asking me how I knew for sure it was going to crash and burn before it did. I kept telling them my same story over and over again, but they did not believe me. They found it impossible to accept the fact that someone could know about things in advance. They tried to get me to confess that I had done something that caused the crash and the deaths of those men. I never moved from my original statements. They became rude and told me that they knew I had done something, but they could not prove it yet.

The investigation team had checked with all the maintenance crews. They found out that I could never have gone near helicopter 744 after I had turned it over to the other mechanics to check out. There was no way that I could have done anything, but that was not good enough for the Army. When the investigators left, they refused to let me off the hook. They said they would be watching me, and that I had better not do anything like this again. Some 35 years later, I finally was able to read the final accident summary—it was a trunnion bearing which caused the main rotor to lose control.

#

Footnote:

Helicopter UH-1D 64-13744—Date of Accident 04/06/1967
Incident number: 670406221ACD; Accident Case Number: 670406221
Number killed in accident: 7 total: 3 crew members, 4 passengers

Accident Summary:
The trunnion bearing on the rotating part of the swash plate came out in flight causing loss of control to one main rotor blade. Suspect the trunnion retaining bolts were improperly torqued, allowing the assembly to move in and out, wearing the bolt's shanks until there was no retaining shoulder. The aircraft fell from cruise altitude. Turbine wheel blade failure.

The following is the crew and passenger information for this incident:

Name: **CPT Richard Eric Newton**—Aircraft Commander
Age at death: 37.3
Date of Birth: 12/07/1929
Home City: Columbus, OH
The Wall location: 17E-113
Call sign: Tomahawk 26
Started Tour: 01/09/1967
Length of service: 16 years
Married
Race: Caucasian
Religion: Protestant—no denominational preference

Name: **WO1 James Leo Darcy**—Pilot
Age at death: 22.1
Date of Birth: 02/28/1945
Home City: Helena, MT
The Wall location: 17E–111
Started Tour: 01/11/1967
Length of service: 1 year
Single

Race: Caucasian
Religion: Roman Catholic

Name: **SP4 Alger Edgar Durell Jr.**—Door Gunner
Age at death: 20.5
Date of Birth: 10/06/1946
Home City: Fair Oaks, CA
The Wall location: 17E-110
MOS: 11B20—Infantryman
Started Tour: 09/24/1966
Length of service: 1 year
Single
Race: Caucasian
Religion: unknown

Name: **SP5 Richard Monroe Dykes**—Passenger
Age at death: 27.0
Date of Birth: 04/10/1940
Home City: San Jose, CA
1st Infantry Division
The Wall location: 17E–110
MOS: 63C20—General Vehicle Repairman
Started Tour: 07/29/1966
Length of service: 6 years
Married
Race: Caucasian
Religion: Protestant—no denominational preference

Name: **MSG Vincente Medina-Torres**—Passenger
Age at death: 42.2
Date of Birth: 01/22/1925
Home City: San Juan, PR
1st Infantry Division
The Wall location: 17E–112
MOS: 13B50—Cannon Crew member
Started Tour: 08/26/1966
Length of service: 22 years
Married

Race: Caucasian
Religion: Roman Catholic

Name: **SFC Henry Edward Patenaude**—Passenger
Age at death: 37.4
Date of Birth: 10/27/1929
Home City: North Cambridge, MA
1st Infantry Division
The Wall location: 17E–113
MOS: 82C40—Field Artillery Surveyor
Started Tour: 09/12/1966
Length of service: 18 years
Married
Race: Caucasian
Religion: Roman Catholic

Name: **SP5 Conrad Earl Poole**—Passenger
Age at death: 25.2
Date of Birth: 02/01/1942
Home City: Oneonta, AL
1st Infantry Division
The Wall location: 17E–114
MOS: 13E20—Cannon Fire Direction Specialist
Started Tour: 06/25/1966
Length of service: 6 years
Single
Race: Caucasian
Religion: Methodist (Evangelical United Brethren)

W.H. McDonald Jr.

Author's note: Written in a mood of frustration on January 16, 1967, in Hobo Woods, South Vietnam.

I Learned About War Last Night

I learned about war
Last night
And I killed you.
You looked through your eyes
Last night
And you saw me.

You and I
Are only government pawns
Upon a voyage
That could only have been rehearsed
In nightmares.

My breast-fed-friend,
By whose design
Have we fallen prey?

#

Author's note: This story shows you that not everything is so serious. There is a little humor and fun even in war zones.

The First Unofficial Bombing Raid of Cambodia

The day began with a short briefing in flight operations. Normally, I would be on the flight line waiting with my ship. This day's mission, however, was different because we were carrying men into an area that looked like Cambodia on the map. I was told that we were going to take a small group of men on a single-ship mission to grid coordinates such and such.

When I looked at where that was on the map, I blurted out something about that being in the Parrot's Beak, inside of Cambodia. The two pilots glared at me and stated once again that we were going to grid coordinates such and such. I restated the obvious, and they told me for the last time that we were heading to those grid coordinates and any mention of Cambodia was to be forgotten.

We gathered our gear and loaded the chopper. We did a thorough preflight inspection and lifted off just as the sun was rising over the tops of the surrounding jungle around Phu Loi. We pulled the Huey up and into the morning sunrise. I always loved flying that time of the day. Sunrise in Vietnam with all the haze made for some beautiful colors in the early morning skies, and also at sunset.

We went to a small base camp close to the border between Vietnam and Cambodia and picked up a group of men wearing an assortment of unidentifiable uniforms. No one had anything that would label them as American or even NATO. They were on some kind of secret mission and their nationalities were purposely disguised. They also had weapons from eastern block countries, AK-47s and such. These guys did not talk at all. Their conversations were nonexistent and there were no smiles. These six men that we were taking to those grid coordinates were all business.

We flew to the grid coordinates at a high altitude. I was used to flying most of our missions at treetop level or even lower at times, but on this mission we were up about as high as I have ever flown in a helicopter in Vietnam. When we got close to the grid coordinates of the LZ, we began a steep dive and cruised into the LZ just above the

153

treetops from about two miles out. I had my M-60 at the ready, but the jungle was so thick I couldn't even see the ground under the trees, let alone any VC or NVA who might be taking some shots at us. I could feel the tension of my passengers the closer we got.

All of a sudden we sprang upon a clear opening just big enough for our ship to touch down and take off again. It was a tight fit, but it was the only opening in the jungle for miles in either direction. We quickly dropped down into the LZ. The landing was not very soft as we slightly bounced. The men were off before the Huey had even stopped sliding forward on the ground. I gave the pilots the okay to take off. Without any hesitation, they were trying to get out of there as fast as they could. We barely cleared the treetops as the pilot pulled the collective throttle up and began heading back to get supplies for these men.

The good news was that the LZ was cold (no enemy fire). Our concern, however, was that we not attract too much attention because we had to go back there again with more supplies. The possibility of having a hot LZ increased the more times we kept landing in it.

We went back to where we had originally picked up the men, and we took on a full load of supplies of ammo, c-rations, medical supplies, and for some strange reason, two cases of toilet paper.

It was a long and boring flight back to the LZ at grid coordinates such and such. I was actually getting sleepy and was having trouble staying awake. I began to look at the cases of toilet paper and wondered what one roll would look like if I threw it out from 6,000 feet. I was wondering if it would unwind and stretch out to its full length. So, I decided to solve this personal mystery. I opened one of the cases and removed one roll for my airborne experiment over the jungle of Cambodia.

I pulled about six feet of it from the roll to get it started. I then tossed it straight out of my helicopter into the sky. It began to unravel immediately. I am not sure how long a roll of classic American-made soft toilet paper is, but within a few seconds that entire roll was floating like paper fireworks slowly onto the tops of the triple-canopy jungle below me. In fact, it looked so neat, and I was so bored, that I decided to throw another roll. Well, one good thing led to another, and by the time we had almost gotten to the LZ to unload the supplies, one of the cases of toilet paper was totally empty. So, I decided to drop that "cardboard bomb" overboard to join the toilet paper. I did not want to have an empty box show up in the LZ.

The LZ proved to be uneventfully safe, and we were able to successfully unload everything quickly and leave right away. We pulled back up to 6,000 feet, so we had a great view of the entire area below us for miles. All of a sudden, I heard one of the pilots yelling at me about what he was seeing.

"Mac, what in the hell is all that white crap over the tops of the jungle?"

"It almost appears to look like someone toilet-papered the jungle tops. Is that possible?" the other pilot added.

Of course, I was now caught red-handed, so I had to tell the truth.

"Yes, Sir, that sure looks like toilet paper to me also. We must have had a case fall out when we hit some air turbulence. I assume that all those rolls just popped out of the box and unraveled themselves across the tops of the jungle. Yep, that is what it looks like to me, Sir."

One of the pilots began to yell at me, but I detected a slight laughing sound from the other one or both.

"Mac, this was a classified mission into Cambodia where we are not supposed to be. Now you've bombed Cambodian territory with American toilet paper! It's spread out for miles on the tops of their jungle. Everyone will know we were here!"

"But sir, we are not in Cambodia, we are only in grid coordinates such and such," I replied.

There was a long silence. Then I heard, even over the sound of all the helicopter noise, the crew, including my left door gunner, laughing.

"Okay Mac, if you say the case fell out, then that is what the official report will say. In the meantime, let's pray for some good heavy rainfall to wash all the evidence of our 'bombing raid' away," one of the pilots said.

Thus ended the first unofficial bombing raid of Cambodia in 1967. Of course, it wasn't Cambodia, it was only grid coordinates such and such! And I swear that the box must have really fallen out. That is my story and I am sticking to it. If I tell you anymore, I will have to kill you!

#

Author's note: Sometimes God looks after and protects the ignorant and the stupid, as is evidenced by my adventure out on patrol as a point man. Looking back, it all seems rather funny now, but at the time we were not laughing. Not laughing at all!

Walking Pointless

In the late summer of 1967, I was almost through with my tour of duty in Vietnam. I was down to less than 90 days, and I was beginning to see and feel that there really might be "a light at the end of the tunnel" for me personally.

I was back from a short day of flying and was one of the first crew chiefs back to the company area. I had just finished pulling maintenance on my Huey and was about to clean up when one of the officers in our company contacted me. He informed me that since I was the only Spec-5 (Pay rank equal to that of a sergeant) around, he needed me to organize a small patrol of volunteers. He wanted us to go into the jungle a couple of miles outside our base camp at Phu Loi to do a search and recovery mission to look for a lost weapon that fell out of a chopper on its approach to the runway. Someplace within two miles of the end of the runway there was a loaded weapon laying in the jungle that they did not want Charlie to find and use.

Thus was born the first and only Tomahawk Short-Range Reconnaissance and Recovery Patrol. I, being the highest-ranking enlisted guy they could find, was tasked with the leadership of this ragtag group of volunteers. My first task at hand was to find enough guys willing to go outside the safety of the base camp to walk through the jungle with me as their leader.

I managed to gather a very diverse group of men that included a cook, a couple of motor pool mechanics, an off-duty administrative clerk, an avionics repair technician, four helicopter mechanics, another off-duty crew chief, and one actual 11Bravo, infantry-trained door gunner. We made up the Tomahawks own version of the dirty dozen.

We must have looked strange walking out of the compound past the razor-sharp rolls of barbed wire that surrounded our camp. A couple of the guys didn't even bother to put on a shirt, going bare-

156

chested with their dog tags dangling and bouncing together, making lots of noise. The cook still looked as if he were working in the kitchen; he had food stains on his clothing and was wearing a camouflaged steel helmet with the words "Kill for Peace" written on it. The others wore whatever they were wearing at the time I asked them to volunteer. One guy was wearing cut-off fatigues with his bleached-white hairy knees exposed. Only a couple of the guys bothered to take along a flack jacket, and everyone had on a different kind of hat. We looked like crap, but we felt like a dozen John Waynes ready to assault the beaches of some South Pacific island. We were certainly not going to be sneaking up on anyone, but I felt that was good. It was as if we were walking on a trail in the American Southwest where the guide tells you it is best to make a lot of noise in order to scare off any rattlesnakes. Anyway, that was my mindset. I never claimed to be a good military thinker.

At least we took some real firepower with us. We all had our M-16s. One guy even had an M-79 grenade launcher that he had found on one of our missions. He had never fired one before, but he was willing to learn if the situation presented itself. We took four ammo magazines for each of our M-16s and nothing else. We did not have a radio, so if we somehow managed to make any enemy contact, we were all alone. I did think to bring a red smoke grenade to mark the enemy's location, if we did need a gunship to help us.

One of the guys brought along an AM radio. He had an earplug in one ear listening to some rock and roll music on the Armed Forces Radio Network out of Saigon. We could hear him singing to himself as we walked along through the bushes and trees. Several of the men were smoking cigarettes, and one guy had a cigar in his mouth. If I remember correctly, I was the one blowing smoke and looking every bit the part of my comic book hero, Sergeant Rock of Easy Company. I looked mean and nasty and was leading this group as their point man. It was my job to check for tripwires, booby traps, land mines, and the enemy. Should we happen upon any of them I would be the first to sound the alert or drop dead, whichever happened first. I was moving along at a good pace as if I were just strolling through the Golden Gate Park in the summertime. The guys were talking away and laughing. We were all enjoying the walk. None of us had ever been on a patrol. Only one of us had any infantry training. We were not going to sneak up on anyone, not this day or anytime. If the enemy were out there, they would know we were coming.

Most of the guys had volunteered to go for the excitement and to get out of the base camp for a couple of hours. They wanted to do something that they could write home about in their letters to their friends, and I am sure there were some really enhanced versions of what we did that day on patrol. I would love to read some of their accounts in their old letters.

We had marched more or less two miles from our camp, and we were alone in the jungle. We really didn't know how far two miles was, but we thought since we had walked about an hour through the jungle, it must have been about two miles. Of course, if we were walking faster than two miles per hour we could have been twice that distance from our camp. It occurred to us that we could get in some big trouble out there, and if that did happen it would be difficult to get any help at all. Having no radio gave us very few options if we happened to make any enemy contact. We were on our own and would have to take care of ourselves. By this time our thoughts became a little more serious. The talking stopped, and even the guy with the radio in his ear turned it off so he could fully listen for any noises. The party attitude that we started with suddenly became much more serious. We realized that we were in the middle of "Indian" country. We were very much all alone, and we would have to count on our own abilities to survive. That was a sobering thought for us. We were now ready for war.

I led the group across an open field, which was not the right thing to do in the first place, but it looked much easier than going around through all the dense trees and brush. When the group was about halfway across the field, my door gunner asked a very simple question, "Mac, why do you think there is a plowed field in the middle of the jungle?"

The question immediately froze me as I looked around and saw what he was talking about, the ground looked turned over. Grass was bent and partially under the dirt as if it had been dug up and replaced like divots at the golf course. I began to think of all the logical reasons the ground might look like that, but all my answers came back the same—it was a freaking minefield. We had walked into the middle of a field loaded with land mines! Worse than that, now I needed to get us out without getting anyone killed.

We all just stood there. No one dared to move an inch. I told everyone what I thought it was, but all of them had already figured it out and knew the mess we were now in. The patrol was now standing in the middle of a very dangerous place, and no one was laughing or joking anymore. All we wanted to do was to get ourselves out of there and go back to the comfort and safety of our base camp. Yep, the party was over, so let us all go home now!

Slowly we turned around and moved "step by step, inch by inch," following each other back on the same exact path that we took into the field. Everyone put his next step in the old footprints ahead of him, thus insuring that everyone behind the leader did not step anywhere he had not already stepped.

It had taken us less than 10 seconds to walk halfway across this open field but almost a lifetime to get ourselves out. No one was in any hurry to rush out of the field. No one wanted to walk in the wrong place, so it was a slow and deliberate walk back to the cover of the jungle. Since I was the first one into the minefield, I was the last one out. I felt as if I had sweated off 10 pounds of ugly fat in 10 minutes. We were all drenching wet.

I decided that we would sit back and wait about 30 minutes before walking back to the base camp. We were not going to find any weapons out there on this day or any day, and we knew it. All we were doing was risking injury or death. No one argued about the logic of that decision. I think everyone was happy to call it a done deal and return back in one piece.

We found our way back through the trees and brush to the barbed wire perimeter of our camp. As we emerged from the cover of the jungle, we walked more quickly and with greater purpose in our steps. When we got inside the wire, no one said anything. We certainly learned that walking on patrol was not as much fun as we had thought it would be. I reported back to the officer that we couldn't find the lost weapon. He didn't ask any questions, so I went back to my bunk and lay down for a late afternoon nap. I was wide-awake and wired but very thankful that I wouldn't be leading any more patrols while I was there. No one else ever volunteered for any patrols again that I know of. I know I sure as heck didn't.

#

Author's note: Sometimes I hate to be right—it even spooks me. I learned that sometimes my efforts to avert something bad from happening to others may, in fact, become the direct link for that karmic event.

The Mummy

One day during the summer of 1967, after returning from many long hours of flying combat assaults in the area known as War Zone C, I had a most unusual and hard-to-explain experience. I had landed safely at our base camp in Phu Loi where I spent the next hour performing postflight maintenance on my helicopter. All was normal up to this point in the day except for one small hole in the tail section caused by a single round, probably from an AK-47 Russian assault rifle. I had assumed that it was a Russian weapon, even though we had seen Chinese AK-47s in the area as well. Picking up a bullet hole in the helicopter was not that unusual. I had picked up hits before during the long days of combat assaults. I normally never heard or felt a thing at the time and rarely, if ever, even noticed any gunfire directed at me. It was just one of those "gifts" we found when we stopped to refuel or had a chance to look over the body of the helicopter, as I was doing that night.

Normally when I worked on my helicopter on the flight line at night, I was concerned about my flashlight becoming a target for snipers. When I first became a crew chief I was not too bright and used to hold the light under my chin so I could free both my hands. Basically that made my head a nice target in the darkness of night. But on this night something else was bothering and worrying me.

What made this night different were the feelings I was beginning to have. I knew something was wrong, but I could not put my finger on it right away. I was sitting alone in the dark. The door gunner had long gone to clean the M-60s and to get dinner. I sat there looking at the star-studded night sky. Every so often there were a few tracers at the edges of the camp, some incoming and some outgoing rounds. After being in Nam for over half a year, I was used to seeing this each night. I was lonely and wondered if that was what I was feeling. Nothing made me feel comfortable or at peace. There was an inner

160

turmoil telling me something was not right. I also could feel it in the air.

I finally put away my tools and grabbed my M-16 rifle. I started to walk slowly back to the 2nd Flight Platoon's hooch. I was thinking about how good it would feel to lie on my bunk and close my eyes. I was really exhausted. I could have used and enjoyed a warm shower, but at this hour of night I knew there wasn't any more water. It is hard for most people to understand how tired we got from sitting behind an M-60 machine gun all day while flying over the jungle. Even though we were just sitting there, we were supposed to be alert and looking for the enemy. We had to remain awake to protect our helicopter from being shot down. If we fell asleep or were daydreaming, we could very well get ourselves and our crew killed. So we spent the entire day, in this case 15 hours long, on the edge trying to stay alert for those few moments of terror when we were under attack.

It never failed, however, that on some of those hot, humid, long days, I dozed off occasionally while sitting behind my gun. Maybe that was one reason I found a new bullet hole in my helicopter's tail; I never heard or felt a thing. In any case, I needed some sleep. I normally started my day about an hour before sunrise. It ended only after I had repaired the helicopter after we returned to the base camp. Then, I could leave the flight line and get something to eat or go to sleep. This night I didn't finish until 10 p.m.

As I walked into the hooch, that nagging feeling got worse. Something was really wrong. I felt I was close to whatever or whoever it was. I put my M-16 in the rifle rack and threw my flight gear onto my bunk. I had my back turned to a group of young men (but then we were all very young men), and I could feel something that made me sick inside. It was a chilling and painful feeling. There are no words to describe it. I noticed that it got worse when one of the guys got closer to me. I sat down on my bunk, thinking about what I was feeling and trying to understand what it meant.

I turned around and saw a guy standing next to his bunk bed. I was staring at him when he noticed me. I got up and walked over to him. I was beginning to feel a dread within myself. I knew for sure that something was going to happen to this man. Something was shadowing him. I felt it. I did not know what to say to him, so I just blurted it out.

"You're in great danger, and I'm not going to let you fly on any combat missions the rest of the week. I am taking you off flight duty for a few days. I want you to spend the time in the base camp where you will be safer."

"Are you nuts? Have you been here so long that you have flipped over the edge or something?" That was all he replied that is printable, the rest was sprinkled with many four-letter words and phrases. I could hardly blame him for his response.

The other men all stopped talking and stared at me. I really think that they thought I had flown one too many missions and was mentally and emotionally unstable. The hooch got really quiet for a few minutes; then, they went outside to get a beer and talk. I was left alone and wondering about what I had just told this guy. I did not know where it came from or why, but I knew for sure that something was going to happen to him the next day. I was in charge of scheduling the gunners and crew chiefs, so I made sure that his name was taken off the morning flight roster.

When I went to bed that night I could hear the guys talking about me. I knew that they had told some of the officers. Sleep did not come easily even though I was in great need of it. I lay there thinking about what I had said. I trusted my feelings and decided to stick by my words. I would make sure that this guy was out of harm's way. The next morning before taking off on my flight, I left orders that he have the day off. I did not want him to have even a remote chance of being in combat.

When I got to my helicopter, one of the pilots asked me about what he had heard. I said that I truly believed that this guy was in great danger that day. The pilots winked at each other and smiled. Everyone thought I was ready for a rubber-walled room in a stateside asylum. The thought of that makes me laugh a little now. It's the "Catch-22;" if they thought you were nuts, then you went home; but if you were sane, then you had to stay and fight in an insane war. I guess that makes sense to someone.

We took off early in the morning as the sun was still peeking over the palm trees and streaking through the patches of fog. I looked back at the company area as we pulled up to about 50 feet, and I could see the guy standing there looking up at me. He was still mad at me, and of course, no doubt thought I was nuttier than a fruitcake. As I looked back, I could feel the shadows closing in on him. I did not understand that feeling since I had taken him out of harm's way and given him a free day to relax around the camp.

We had been flying several hours that morning, carrying supplies to an isolated Special Forces camp in the hills. We had not seen much action, as it was a rather quiet day in Nam. Then, we got a call to return to our base camp to pick up a dust off (medical evacuation). We were to pick up a wounded troop and drop him at the 3rd Field Hospital in Saigon, about 15 minutes from our camp.

We headed back as fast as we could. We did not have a clue as to why there was a casualty at the base camp when there hadn't been any attacks reported that day. We landed at the medical unit where they carried a stretcher to our Huey. On it lay a man with bandages all over his head and face. He looked like a mummy, and I could not see who he was. I helped load him onto the floor of the helicopter and we took off.

In the air, one of the pilots asked me to look at the man's dog tags. I pulled them out from the inside of his shirt and slowly turned them over in my hand. I already knew who it was before I read the tags. It was the guy I had warned to be safe, the same guy I had tried to save from injury, the same guy I had failed to protect with my warnings. I told the pilots who it was. For the rest of the ride it stayed quiet except for the noise of the turbine engine and rotor blades. No one spoke a word to me or to each other.

When we returned to base camp we found out that the guy had found a Soviet rocket launcher that someone had brought back to the company area as a war souvenir. He had been playing with it when it accidentally went off in his face.

The rest of the men in the company did not want to talk to me for several days after that. No one understood what I had felt or what I had tried to do. I did not even understand it myself. I learned something that day. Sometimes another person's fate is truly in his own hands, even if I tried to forewarn him. I did not feel good about what had happened. I felt I had failed him. Looking back, I know it was all in God's hands, and in this case, there was nothing I could have done to change it.

#

W.H. McDonald Jr.

Helicopter Blues

The morning sun,
Silhouetted by images
Of distant helicopters,
Rising and falling
Across the emotionless skies.

Countless rotor blades
Pushing and cutting and hacking
Their way over
The jungles and rivers below,
Taking young virgin warriors
To places where they do not want to go.

Rising and falling
And casting fleeting shadows
On the face of Vietnam below,

They forever keep moving,
pushing across the horizon
In search of death.

Taking
no one
where they wish
to go.

#

June 17, 1967
Somewhere over the Delta, South Vietnam

164

Author's note: There eventually was a light at the end of that proverbial tunnel. I was looking at the final hours of my tour in Nam, and yet I was still flying combat assaults. My last scheduled mission almost became my last flight anywhere.

My Last Combat Mission

Three days before I was scheduled to leave Vietnam, I was ordered to fly one more time. It was a simple single-ship mission, but we expected to possibly draw some enemy fire. It was not going to be a milk run or a hash and trash sortie. This one involved moving small units of men around looking for enemy contact. In other words, we would be out looking for trouble.

I was not feeling that good about going. After all, why should I be taking any risks just 72 hours before I would be leaving that war zone forever? I was uneasy, but I considered that it might be because of my status as a short timer and nothing more. I couldn't relax at all. Something just didn't feel right about my own aircraft or the mission. Old 576 checked out okay, but I still had a feeling of doom about this day. That Huey had served me well throughout my entire tour, but it felt like the end of the road for the both of us. I guess it was like having to say goodbye to an old girlfriend. I would miss this beat-up and wounded metal warrior long after I left country. At least my last mission was going to be on my own chopper. It seemed a fitting and special way to end the relationship.

I got up very early, over an hour before sunrise, to preflight the aircraft in the early morning darkness. I held my flashlight close to my body. I always tried to shield it from being seen by any lurking snipers. One never knew if there was anyone on the other side of the barbed wire who was watching for an easy target before crawling back into a tunnel before the sun came out.

My thoughts were reflective that morning. I was thinking back to my first few weeks in country and all that had followed. It was certainly a year filled with adventure, fear, love, hate, pain, fellowship, laughs, honor, horror, death, and bloody memories of places and people I would never forget. I had even celebrated my 21st birthday in Phu Loi with a three-hour pass. All I had time to do was to get myself drunk at a bar. Not the dream I'd had for my big 21st party bash.

I had lost some friends that past year, but I never really grieved. I wondered about that. Had I let my emotions die in this place? Was I really that cold and emotionless. More important, would I remain that way after I left "the Nam?" I was not afraid about any possible combat that morning. I was more concerned about going home and what I was going to be like when I got there. I was not the same boy who left Travis Air Force Base back in October of 1966 with my high school friend Mike Harrison. We both flew over on the same flight to Vietnam. I wondered if I would meet up with him and share a "freedom flight" back home together. Had he changed too? Would we still be friends?

I sat on top of my Huey watching the sunrise peeking over the surrounding jungle. I loved this time of the day. I had the whole flight line to myself that morning. There was plenty of time for personal thoughts and daydreaming before my pilots showed up. I just wanted to enjoy all my last moments of being a Huey crew chief. I wanted to get in touch with all I had learned and experienced. I didn't even go to the mess hall that morning for any food. I just wanted to savor being a part of history and of my unit. I knew there was something very special here that no one else, except those I had served with, could or would ever understand. These men I flew with were my brothers, my friends, my comrades! No matter where I might go in life, there would always be that bond that would never be severed. It was like a spiritual tattoo on my heart—I would forever be a Tomahawk warrior! I was proud of the guys I flew with and loved them dearly. Even if I could not cry for them when they died, I really did care about them.

My pilots finally showed up and did a short preflight inspection and kidded me about being a short timer. I untied the rotor blades and sat down on my old worn out and familiar canvas seat behind my M-60 machine gun. We were ready to fly. We got our clearance from Phu Loi Tower and taxied out onto the long runway. We began to build up speed and enter translational lift. The Huey was ready to jump into the sky and clear the jungle ahead of us, but when the AC pulled up on the collective, all hell broke loose. The engine made a loud banging sound like a small explosion. We lost power, dropped about five feet back down onto the runway, and slid forward several yards because of our forward airspeed. The engine was suddenly engulfed in flames as smoke filled the inside of the cabin. I jumped out of my seat and quickly ran to unlock the aircraft commander's door to help him out of the ship. (Our Hueys had heavy metal and ceramic armored plates that slid out from the sides of the pilots' seats. The bulky extensions were difficult for the pilots to reach to unlock and slide back. The door gunner and crew chief had the responsibility to open the pilots' doors and slide the armored plates out of the way so they could get out of the aircraft. In a crash this was even more important because of fire.)

After helping the AC, I grabbed the fire extinguisher that was strapped on the floor next to his seat. I completely emptied it as I suppressed the flames and put out the fire.

My door gunner had quickly done the same thing for the copilot. He and the pilots got a safe distance from the helicopter while I fought the fire. We stood looking at the burned engine compartment and the precious few yards of runway that were left between us and crashing into the surrounding jungle. If that engine had caught fire just three or four seconds later, we would have been at a higher altitude and over trees that we would have certainly dropped into. The difference between getting ourselves killed or seriously injured was only a matter of three or four seconds in the timing of that engine fire. I stood there thinking these thoughts and looking at the helicopter as a couple of airfield fire trucks pulled up to assist.

I dropped the fire extinguisher on the flight line and headed back to the company area. I felt relieved and exhausted. There is nothing like an adrenaline rush to drain all the energy out of you when it is all over. I walked slowly back down the runway. I turned back to see the crew still at the helicopter talking to the guys on the fire trucks. I had come so close to buying the farm on my last mission, it gave me chills to think about it.

I knew my luck was still with me, even on my last flight. No matter what, I vowed this was going to remain my last flying mission in Vietnam. There was no way that I was going to volunteer for anything more. The only flying time I was looking forward to was on my Freedom Bird flight home, which was leaving in less than 72 hours! God had seen me through my entire tour; my only concern now was for my high school friend Mike.

The night before leaving for home, I went to a holding company to get orders for my return flight. While walking around a building, I ran into Mike. God, it was so good to see him healthy and alive. We hugged each other but didn't say much. I was relieved to see and touch him again. I had promised his wife, Donna, that I would look after him and bring him home alive, which had been impossible for me to do since we had gotten separated during our third week in country.

Mike looked as tired as I was, but having orders to go home seemed to inject more energy into both of us. He was so happy about going home and seeing his wife again. I was just happy to be getting the hell out of the jungle alive and in one piece. I knew there wasn't going to be anyone anxiously waiting for my return home, so it was all rather bittersweet and a little terrifying. I was envious of Mike and some of the guys who were going home to be reunited with their loved ones. What would I find when I returned home? I didn't even know if I had a place to stay while on leave. I was beginning to feel very much alone.

#

Author's note: The harsh realities of the Vietnam war era in America only added to the readjustment problems of veterans coming home. I was no different. I was not treated as a returning hero. Americans turned their backs on all of us. We felt betrayed and unloved by our own nation. It was a most difficult transition for all of us. For many years following my tour of duty, I never shared my stories, medals, or photos. No one cared enough to even ask about them. It was as if we veterans were supposed to feel ashamed of what we had done, hiding our experiences from everyone, even our families. No one really understood us, and no one really wanted to. Movies and TV portrayed veterans as crazy PTSD (Post Traumatic Stress Disorder) killers. Not the image I had of myself, but it was one that America believed! My welcome home still makes me angry and depressed even after all these years. That is why when we meet other Vietnam Veterans, we always say to each other, "Welcome Home!"

There Was no Band Playing

When we got on the airplane leaving Vietnam, it was surreal. No one wanted to get too excited until we knew for a fact that we were up in the air and actually leaving Vietnamese soil. There was a collective, loud shout when the wheels left the runway; then, everyone kind of kicked back into their own little worlds. There was some small talk and a few tried to hit on the flight stewardesses, who were not very friendly to us.

I was sitting next to Mike just as we had on our flight a year ago to Vietnam. We exchanged some conversation, but nothing important or that I remember. Then, we each drifted off and sat there without saying anything. It is rather odd, looking back now, but neither of us exchanged any war stories or talked about what had happened to us on our tour of duty during the past year.

The other guys became quieter the closer we got to home and the farther we got from Nam. No one was talking as we approached the coast of California. I guess we were in our own worlds of thoughts. The announcement finally came over the intercom that we would be landing soon. I was thinking how nice it would be for a small cheering crowd to greet us as we got off the airplane, or at least an

Army band playing to welcome us back home. Neither of my wishes came true.

When we walked down the ramp, some of the guys, including me, stopped to kiss the ground. There were no bands playing, and there was no one to greet us except for several jeeploads of MPs. They were waiting to march us off into a hangar to search us for drugs and weapons. They were not the least bit friendly as they patted down some of the guys at random. We were not very happy about this kind of welcome. Some of us got pissed off at the treatment and began to complain loudly about it. The MPs got really nasty with us, and it began to look as if they might use force to get our cooperation. I thought for a while that we might have a small riot between the returning heroes and the military police. It was an ugly welcome. I was greatly disappointed by the whole tone of our return home. We were then herded onto buses heading to the Oakland Army Base; the group was very quiet. We were a little pissed off by our reception and by the way the MPs had treated us. I looked around the bus and saw a couple of guys trying to hide their wet, angry eyes. We were all deflated by the reception we had received. Instead of feeling joyous, as returning heroes should feel, we felt like criminals whom society was reluctantly allowing to return through the back door of America.

It stayed quiet on the bus for the whole trip. We were angry, dirty, tired, and hungry. We looked out of the windows and saw people giving us the "finger" and dirty stares from their passing cars on the freeway. It just did not seem right. What had we done to deserve that kind of treatment? I thought that if they knew what we had just gone through, they might treat us better or at least differently. I wanted to believe that they did not represent the rest of the country. After all, we were driving through Berkeley; maybe the rest of the country would treat us better.

When we arrived at the Oakland Army Base, the treatment was not much friendlier. It was a cold and foggy day, which matched our mood at this point. We were, however, not used to such cold weather, having just come from the hot rain forests of Nam. The Army personnel at Oakland herded us around like cattle. They never interviewed anyone—not one single question about how we felt or if anyone was having troubles emotionally or physically. They just went about issuing everyone a new uniform. It did not matter if we had orders for a new duty station or if we were getting discharged, they treated us all the same.

Once we got our papers, we were on our own. They provided no buses or other transportation to any of the airports or bus stations. There were neither airline tickets nor instructions to help us to get to our homes or to new assignments. (I had 30 days leave before I had to report to Fort Benning, Georgia.) After having waited and endured six hours on a hard wooden bench, they offered us a free steak dinner in the mess hall and said goodbye. I do not believe anyone went to eat the free steak dinner. Mike and I walked to the front gate where Karen and Donna had left us the year before. We found a waiting cab and piled in for a ride across the Bay Bridge. There were no special rates for returning veterans. I remember that the cabby charged us a bundle to cross over the bridge. I had the cab drop me off at my aunt's house in San Francisco. My mother was staying there after her divorce from my stepdad. Mike and his buddy went on to Sunnyvale and stayed with Donna's folks. I wish I had gone with them.

I knocked on my aunt's door and waited for a few minutes. I was looking forward to this moment. I had this wonderful Hollywood image of being warmly greeted and hugged upon my return from the war. The moment, however, did not live up to my expectations. The door opened, and I was standing face to face with my mother. She gave me a quick hug, not much more than a second or two of actual touching followed by a slight push away. It was very difficult to stand there without showing what I was really feeling at that moment, but I managed a smile.

I was depressed about the whole homecoming welcome, not just from my mother but from everyone I had met on my return. I was trying not to show how much I was hurt, pissed off, and disappointed. As always, I suppressed my anger and refused to show or share with anyone what I was truly feeling.

None of us really knew what to say to each other. I wanted to tell them about what had happened to me and how I felt. I wanted to share some of my experiences so they would understand. I took out my color slides from Vietnam to show them what it looked like over there. Within less than 10 minutes, my aunt and mother said that they were tired and were going to bed. It was still well before 8 p.m., and I had been in their home less than a half-hour. I was hurt that they didn't want to spend time with me.

I felt rejected and decided to celebrate by myself in the city. After getting a house key, I took the streetcar to Broadway. I wanted to go to some of the clubs and see the city at night. I didn't want to spend my first night back from Nam all alone. I wanted to share what I was feeling, but I couldn't find anyone at the bars who wanted to listen to me. All I really wanted after being away for that year in hell was to get a hug from someone who cared about me. I felt that no one gave a damn that I had come home alive!

One major mistake that I made that first night home was in wearing my uniform around the city. I found out that was not a good idea. People made me feel uncomfortable everywhere I went. A group of young, unwashed hippies followed me down the street, yelling and taunting me. They kept chanting a question, "How many babies did you kill?" One good-looking young girl came toward me. I thought she might say something nice, but she spit directly on my service ribbons on my uniform. Her spit dripped and rolled off my Distinguished Flying Cross, Bronze Star, and Purple Heart ribbons! It took all my inner strength not to physically kick their butts. They had no idea in the world what it had been like. They were judging me as if I had just pulled a tour of duty for the devil himself. I could understand their being against the war; hell, even I was against war. I could not, however, understand why people were so cruel and mean-spirited to us veterans. We were the pawns of a policy we did not write. We had not declared war on anyone.

What really struck me as rather ironic was that this was October 1967, just a few weeks after the ending of the famous hippy "summer of love" that was celebrated right there in that very city. Where was the love for me and other veterans? It seemed that whole loving spirit was a bunch of bull crap!

I had a difficult time that night; to say that I was lonely would be an understatement. I wanted to go someplace, any place, where people would welcome me home. I went to a bunch of clubs and wandered around for a couple of hours. I didn't even get drunk. I only had a drink or two. I finally got a cab to go back to my aunt's place. After listening to my tale about the hippies, the cab driver turned off his meter flag and only charged me for a couple of miles. That was the sole act of kindness that anyone had shown me on my first day back home. It was just a small gesture, but it still has an impact on me today. It taught me to believe that even small acts of compassion are always remembered and can alter someone's outlook on life. I got out of the cab and stood in the cold San Francisco night air, unsure of what I wanted to do. My big night out on the town was a bust. Spending my first night in America alone physically and emotionally was not what I had planned on or felt I deserved. I wondered how Mike was being welcomed home.

I went to bed that night in clean sheets and with no fears about being attacked by the VC, but it was not a good night's sleep. I was too upset about the way the whole return-home reunion had turned out. I couldn't handle all this unexpected rejection. I began to question my whole relationship with my family. I was dying to be appreciated, yet I got so little back from any of them. I felt like an empty pocket with nothing but my own cold hands inside. It hurt me deeply. I was left spiritually wounded and emotionally bleeding. I felt more alone than I had ever been in my entire life. I couldn't even shed a tear, I was dry inside. All my emotions were dead. I was without any outward expression. I had lost a part of my soul, and I wondered if I would ever find it again. I looked forward only to leaving home once again.

The next day I told my mother and aunt that I was going to Sunnyvale to stay with my little sister, Marsha, and her husband. That way I could visit some old friends and be back in the old hometown. I thought that might make me feel better about things. My mother did not show any disappointment at my leaving less than 12 hours after coming home to visit her. She may have felt something within herself, but she kept it a secret from me. My aunt didn't offer me a ride in her big Caddie, so I left on a bus for Sunnyvale that morning.

I had to walk from the bus station with my duffel bag to Marsha's place, which was about five miles across town. I had learned that no one really wanted to hear my story about Nam or any details about the war, so I said little about it. I quickly realized that no one really gave a damn.

I met my new nephew, Billy, whom Marsha had named after me. He was a beautiful baby, and he looked healthy and happy. I was honored that Marsha had named her first-born after me.

Except for the bed, I was able to relax at her apartment. Marsha had gotten the bed I was using from my older sister, who had been recently living the hippy lifestyle. The mattress had bugs in it that gave me massive bites all over my body. I had to go to the medical unit at Moffett Navel Air Station to get medication. I had gone all that time living in bad conditions in Nam, only to come home and get my whole body infected by some kind of bedbugs from my sister's hand-me-down mattress.

After the bug incident subsided, I went to visit Carol's mother. She was pleased to see me back, and we talked a long time. Of course, I asked about Carol and how she was doing at Cal. Her mother told me how well she had done in her studies, but I really wanted only to hear that she missed me. I also visited Mike and Donna. They were in love and enjoying being together. I did not spend much time visiting them so that they could enjoy their moments together without having me as company.

Almost all of my friends were away at college or had moved away, so I had few people to visit. I couldn't resist going to Berkeley to see Carol, but it was not a very good visit. I felt out of place and awkward being there. I think she was happy to see me leave. She was no doubt concerned that I might say something like, "I love you." There was a wall between us that hurt me. I left feeling more depressed and lonely than before.

I was home only a few days, and already I wanted to get away from my family and friends. Even though I had 30 days scheduled leave to take, I wanted to leave before Thanksgiving Day. I just couldn't leave fast enough as far as I was concerned. I felt so much emotional pain that I needed to get some distance between me and a place that I no longer belonged to or understood.

I purchased a used 1965 Mustang convertible. I did not have much money for the trip back to Fort Benning, Georgia, as I had used most of it for the down payment. I pulled an ad off of a community bulletin board in San Francisco. The ad was from a young man seeking a ride home to Florida, and he would help pay for gas. I picked him up at his place in the city. He was only 17 years old, and he had a friend with him who was about his age. They piled in the back of my car as I hesitated about taking them. They were dirty looking with long hair, and they wore tie-dyed shirts and love beads. I was going to tell them to get out of the car when they told me that they were runaways who wanted to return home to Florida. They had come to San Francisco for all that free love stuff going on in the summer of '67, and now they were stuck there. I felt sorry for them, and it was too late for me to get someone else to help with gas money.

I began to drive south on US 101 when I got to thinking that maybe I should check out these guys. I pulled into a gas station and told them if they had any drugs, I wanted them to flush it down the toilet. I made them go through all their stuff. They did end up pulling out several joints of pot. I then asked them for gas money, and they told me they had only five dollars between them. I got pissed off because they not only had no gas money, they had no money for food or a place to sleep. They also had lied to me about the money when I had answered their ad. I took their five dollars for the first tank of gas. They were not making friends with me at all. I had a feeling that bad times were ahead for them and me.

I was making good time on old Route 66, just moving along across the country. When I got to Texas, I decided to watch my speed. I was very cautious about my driving because of my past troubles with Texas law enforcement. When we hit the town of Pecos, I was going five miles below the speed limit. As I cruised down the main street of town, I noticed that people were looking at my car with its California plates and the two longhaired hippies. I began to feel uneasy about this town. All I wanted to do was drive though it and get out of there. When I stopped at a light at the far end of town, some cowboy-types got out of their pickup truck behind me. They walked around and stood in front of my car. They were carrying rifles that they had taken from a gun rack in the back window of their pickup. They motioned for me to pull over to the side of the road. I did not like what was happening. Since it was broad daylight, I hoped the police might rescue me.

I looked in my mirror and was relieved to see a police car coming up the street. I sat inside my Mustang and waited. The policeman, complete with cowboy boots, cowboy hat, and gun in hand, walked up to my car window. I started to get out of my car, and he kicked the door shut on my foot and arm. I got pissed off and asked him what in the heck he was doing.

175

He called me "boy" and told me to shut my mouth and slowly get out of the car. He had me put my hands on the hood of the car and asked me who I was. I told him I had just got back from Nam and was taking these hitchhikers home to their parents. He had me lie on the hot street with my arms stretched out over my head. He kicked me a few times and got a big laugh from the crowd of Texans that were now gathered around my car watching all the entertainment. The policeman then grabbed the kid in the front seat by his long hair and pulled him out of the car. He threw him onto the ground and called him "girl." He made a bunch of derogatory remarks about those two young hippies, calling them "queers" and "fags." He pulled out the other kid, too. He had all three of us lying on the hot street. He kicked and worked over the two hippies with a nightstick. He then took all the stuff out of the car. He threw it all out on the street to look for, I assume, drugs or weapons. He found nothing. I was very glad that I had already searched the boys; otherwise, they would have been in a Texas jail for 20 years to life, according to the drug law at that time.

I started to protest all this. The policeman told me to get myself out of there and not to look back or ask any questions. He was keeping the hippies and letting me go. He said it was because he saw my uniform with all its medals and awards on it. He wanted to treat me right, since I was a hero. I quickly gathered up my stuff and jumped into my car. I drove off looking in my rearview mirror to watch the crowd around the young men. I looked up and saw a billboard on the way down the road that said, "SUPPORT OUR BOYS IN VIETNAM." Now I know the kind of support Texans gave their "boys," and I was never so grateful to leave a state in my life. I fear to think what the fate of those boys was after I left them behind with a mob of rednecks. There was nothing I could do. Who was I going to call, the police?

I left Texas as fast as I dared to drive. God knows that I didn't want any more redneck sheriffs pulling me over to welcome me to their fine state. I drove for several hours without stopping until I saw a man hitchhiking along the highway. It was Thanksgiving Day 1967—what better reason was there to pick him up? Besides, I was lonely for company and for someone to share a meal with, even if I had to buy both meals. I found out that he was unemployed and had been looking for jobs out of state. He was now trying to make it home for the holidays. He was still several hundred miles from his home. We pulled into a diner for lunch. I wanted to buy him a Thanksgiving meal, but this place only had chicken. So, I bought him that, and we had a great meal together. We each were happy about spending time with someone other than ourselves. I took him as far as I could and said goodbye. I knew my family back in California was having a big meal with all the trimmings. Nevertheless, I had fully enjoyed my meal and the companionship it afforded me at that old greasy roadside diner. I did miss my family and friends; but I did not want the pain of being with them. I finished the trip and reported in several weeks early to Fort Benning, Georgia, ready for duty.

#

Author's note: Looking back, this is probably a very funny story. At the time, I was a fully embarrassed young man. But now, I can laugh about it.

All Washed Up in Georgia

In the winter of 1967, I was stationed at Fort Benning, Georgia, fresh from the battlefields of South Vietnam. All I had wanted to do was to serve my last 11 months and get out of the Army. The new helicopter company that I was assigned to had only one functional Huey and an old surplus chopper from the Korean War. There were over 200 other Vietnam veteran crew chiefs in this stateside aviation company, all serving out their enlisted time as I was. We were just more war surplus, kind of being stored out of the way. There was no real use for any of us, but the Army was going to hang onto us in case there was some national emergency. None of us were ever going to go back to Vietnam—we were all too short (time left in Army) for that. Worse yet, we all had a bad attitude about military life. Being old veterans, none of us gave a hoot for authority or stateside discipline. Finding something to keep us busy was the only real challenge for the career officers of the unit.

When I went to my new unit, I was faced with the grim prospect of some potentially fierce competition if I wanted to fly in order to keep my flight pay status. There was only one crew chief position, and all 200 plus of those veteran crew chiefs wanted it. For some reason, known only to God, I was assigned to the one and only Huey that they had, which was being used as a medical evacuation helicopter. It was an old Huey model, but it flew, and it sure beat hanging around the company policing up cigarette butts all day.

The duty required me to stay in the hangar area to receive any phone calls that might come in requesting us to medically evacuate someone. Almost everyday went by with no phone calls and no visitors. I slept on a foldout cot, and someone in a jeep brought my meals from the company mess hall. My 48-hour shifts included weekends. After a shift, I would come back to the company area, shower and change, go to the PX if I needed any personal items; then,

I went back to standby in the hot and muggy old hangar, waiting for a mission.

If I got a mission, I was to immediately call the pilots at home. They would drive out to the airfield where I would have the ship serviced and ready to go. I was lucky if the pilots even kicked the skids and walked around the aircraft to inspect it. They more or less expected me to have as much of the preflight inspection done as possible without starting up the engines. They were very trusting. Had they realized how little confidence I had in my own abilities, they might have had some very scary thoughts about not checking it over better themselves. The key, however, was to get into the air and to the medical extraction LZ (landing zone) as soon as possible. It could be a life or death situation, but it usually was not.

One afternoon we got a call from a Special Forces training camp up on a hilltop in Tennessee. Seems some young sergeant had a gas-fueled camping lantern explode in his face. He needed to be evacuated to a hospital as soon as possible for the treatment of his burns. We were the quickest option since the sergeant and his unit were several miles out in a wilderness area that had no access roads. We were still many miles away, so we got the old bird up and headed north, pushing it for all the speed it could generate.

When we got to the LZ, it reminded me of Vietnam. They even had to cut out a small area of trees for us to land. It was almost dark when I loaded him onto the ship and headed back to Georgia. We dropped him off at the closest hospital and proceeded to the Atlanta Airport to get some much-needed fuel. We called the control tower and got permission to land next to several large fixed-wing civilian aircraft. We were instructed to wait there for a large fuel truck that would deliver our fuel.

Up on the second floor of the adjacent building was a large windowed wall. This was where people waited to board or to meet people coming off of the airlines. It afforded them a great view of the airfield as well. It seemed that our Army helicopter was attracting lots of attention. I saw a sea of faces watching us shut down on the tarmac. Seeing that I had an audience watching, I strutted around my helicopter, checking stuff and thinking I looked really cool. I had on my flight jacket and helmet, and I looked like the tough aviator warrior that I was. I could not help but notice that there were several

179

young, very good-looking women waving at us through the windows. I, of course, waved back in a manly and macho way. After we refueled, the pilots said they wanted to walk around the airport to find hot coffee and food. That idea sounded good to me as well.

The fuel truck arrived to give us a full load of JP-4 jet fuel. I figured they would pump it for us, but the guy just pointed to the hose and motioned for me to do it myself. Now, I had never pumped gas from this big of a truck with the high-speed pumps that it used to fill large airliners. I had always been used to the very slow pumps on the Army trucks. I was used to taking the handle with one hand and just squeezing off several gallons a minute. I reached up and took the handle of the nozzle with one hand and put it in the gas-refueling hole of the Huey, which is just about head high on me. The guy in the truck turned on the pump, and that is when all hell broke loose.

I was trying to hold a tiger by the tail. That hose was pumping hundreds of gallons of jet fuel out faster than I had ever seen. It pulled me onto the ground and began to snake around the surface of the airfield with me hanging onto it. The fuel was shooting up and onto everything around me, including the truck, the helicopter, and myself. Finally, after what seemed like hours, he turned off the pump and the hose and I went limp. I saw an ocean of liquid all around me. I was sitting in a sea of highly flammable jet fuel.

I glanced up at the windows and could see that I was the center of everyone's attention. I wanted to hide and go away and die. I looked at my two pilots who were still strapped in their seats looking at me and the potential dangers. Then, I heard the sounds of fire trucks pulling up next to us.

The firemen pulled several hoses next to me and sprayed me with a fire-retardant foam, which in a few short seconds covered me from head to foot. They proceeded to spray off that with ice cold water. I was still standing, but as the seconds dragged by, I felt smaller and smaller. There was no place for me to hide. I knew eventually that I also had to get back into the helicopter and face the joking from my crew. Finally, they had washed me and everything else around me, and I was permitted to move.

I slowly got back into the helicopter, all cold and wet but more embarrassed than anything else. I did not look back up at the window area of the airport. I quickly closed the doors and we took off. The pilots decided to forget about getting any coffee or food, but they certainly didn't forget me. Sitting there all soaking wet and chilled, I didn't wish to spend any more time in Atlanta. Frankly, I just didn't give a damn!

#

Author's note: I decided to add this short story to show the transition between my life in the Army and my coming home. I came home with no money, no job, and if it weren't for my good friend Karen and her family's generosity, I would have been sleeping in my car.

I Am Back, But No One is Home

I got out of the Army November 7, 1968, and took my Ford Mustang convertible on a race cross-country to get back to California. I missed my family and my friends. I left Fort Benning, Georgia, and headed west, stopping only to sleep and get gas. In Mississippi, a drunken lawyer hit the front of my car while I was stopped at a red light and waiting well behind the crosswalk line. He drove his car across two lanes of the intersection and plowed right into me. He got out of his car, staggered over to my car, reached into his pocket, and pulled out a roll of hundred dollar bills. He peeled off four of them and told me to get in my car and drive away, which I did, based on how I felt about the southern legal system and their local police forces.

When I drove through Texas, I made sure that I followed all the laws and stayed on the major highways. I didn't have any car problems until I got to Los Angeles and stopped at an Army friend's house. I dropped off his record player and some items that he couldn't carry back by plane later that month when he got out of the Army. It turned out to be a good break because his parents allowed me to spend some time there while my car was getting repaired. I used the hundred dollar bills to pay for the repairs and some new tires for the car.

When I got on the road again, I was broke and had just enough money for gas to continue my trip home. I wasn't worried because I had been buying a $25 U.S. savings bond each month in the Army. I knew I had 36 bonds waiting for me to cash in that my mother was holding for me.

I pulled in to Sunnyvale, my old hometown, in the late afternoon. The first thing I found out was that my entire family had all moved to different places. My mother had gotten back together with my stepdad, and they had moved out of town to another city. I wasn't sure where my sisters were living, but I thought I knew where my brother might be. I decided to stop in at my old friend Karen's house and see her and her parents. I told them about my situation, and they offered to let me stay there for as long as I needed to. I was really pleased that they were so kind to me. I took them up on the offer and used their house as a base camp for the next couple of months until I could locate my family, get a job, and look up my old friends.

I found out where my parents were living and went to see them at an old converted motel in the town of Milpitas. I told them that I needed my bonds. My mother informed me she had cashed them all in and spent the money. They also told me that they didn't have any room for me to stay there with them. I was totally broke and not welcome to stay in their home—not what I would call by any measure, a great visit to see my parents.

I now realized that I was totally on my own to begin my new life after the Army and Vietnam!

#

Bill and his Mustang in 1968.

W.H. McDonald Jr.

Part 3

After Nam 1969–2002

The McDonald Family, 1974
"War: first, one hopes to win; then one expects the enemy
to lose; then, one is satisfied that he too is suffering; in the
end, one is surprised that everyone has lost."
Karl Kraus (1874–1936), Austrian satirist

Author's note: When I got out of the service and finally settled back in the San Francisco Bay Area, I made a point to visit my ex girlfriend, Carol. She had always been on my mind during the years I was away in the Army. As a 9-year-old child when I was in the hospital, some seven years before I ever met Carol, I had already dreamed that I would marry her. So, I never entertained any doubts that we would get back together. I only needed for her to realize that I was the right guy for her. She was reluctant to even date me, but I persisted and never took no for a final answer.

This story is the accumulation of the efforts on my part to convince Carol that we were truly meant to be together. I love telling this story because it demonstrates the magic and power of love. This was one of those once-in-a-lifetime, perfect moments when you know that God loves lovers! This was my moment, and I made the most of it.

Christmas Lights and Love

The day I got engaged was a very special day in my life. I had been waiting to officially ask Carol to become my wife. I wanted her to say yes, so the timing of when I asked her was very important to me. I had hinted around before, and she always gave me negative replies. It was going to take a small miracle to get her to say yes. I knew I had a long road ahead of me on this one.

Getting her to accept the engagement had me concerned. I knew that I had to ask her at the right time and in the right place, or it was just not going to happen. On pure faith, I went down and bought the wedding and engagement rings. This was my first step toward making it happen. My plan was to carry the engagement ring with me every time I visited her. This way, if I could sense the perfect time and place, I would present the ring, kneel down and ask her to marry me.

I brought the ring with me on that cold night, December 10, 1969, when I went to her apartment on Twin Peaks in San Francisco. The place had a view to kill for from the kitchen window, with its panorama of city lights.

I knocked on the door and her roommate, Beverly, let me in. I looked at Carol who was stringing Christmas tree lights. She glanced at me and said something about the lights not working. The two of

187

them had been trying to get them to work all afternoon. No matter what they did—changing bulbs, checking each individual light over and over—the result was always the same, no lights. These were the kind of lights that if one bulb was out or not in correctly and snug, then all the lights on the string did not work. In this case, there were six strings connected together of 100 lights each. All 600 lights were not working.

I listened as she explained the problem to me and asked if I thought I could fix them. I knew this was my perfect time. All I had to do was to zap the right bulb. When the lights blinked on in all their holiday glory, I would ask her to marry me! Now, all I had to do was to perform this feat of magic.

I told her that I knew I could fix it, and I would. I stood in front of the Christmas tree and rubbed my hands together. In my mind I had already said a small prayer for some divine intervention to help me fix the tree and to get Carol to say yes. I figured it was just as easy for God to create two miracles this night as one. I looked Carol right in the eye and said, with all the confidence I could muster, that I certainly could fix her tree lights.

I reached out and gently touched one lone, little light bulb on one of the strings of lights. I slightly twisted it, and the entire tree lit up. All six strings of lights were on and every single bulb was working— all 600 of them!

Her and her roommate's faces glowed as they stood transfixed on this small miracle of the lights. I turned around, looking as if this were exactly what I had expected to happen, which I had, and I reached deep into my pocket. I knew at that moment I was not going to get a better sign that this was the right time and the right place to ask Carol to be my wife.

I got down on one knee and asked her to marry me. She said yes. Later, she said that if I were really this lucky, she wanted some of that luck to rub off on her too.

Well, the rest is history. We got married within three weeks and still remain married today. Now, whenever I see a Christmas tree with its lights shining brightly, I always remember those miracles, one small and one big on a cold December night in 1969 when I became the luckiest man alive!

The miracle of lights.

Footprint

Sometimes,
Someone says something
That lays a footprint
On the surface of my memory,
Much like those
That were fossilized on the moon
By lonesome
Astronauts.

When I awoke
This morning
And saw you standing
Silhouetted against the dawn's
Morning light,
I heard you whisper my name.

It sounded like
The music one hears
Only within seashells
Or dreams.

It sounded
Like love.

It sounded
Like us.

#

Bill and Carol in front of SCUBA store, 1971, Walnut Creek, California.

Author's note: I was lucky that I did not kill one of these guys. My adrenaline was cooking, and I was in no mood to take prisoners!

Three Unwise Men

I got a phone call early one morning while I was managing a scuba diving store in Walnut Creek. It was about two in the morning when the police called to say there was a false alarm going off at the shop. They needed me to go down and turn it off. The official on the phone said that an officer had checked out the shop and everything was okay.

I got up from my warm, comfortable bed and drove 15 miles to the store. When I got there, the police were already gone. I had to go into the dark store alone. I looked around inside the building and noticed that one window was completely broken out. All the glass was laying shattered on the floor. I was already inside the building by the time I saw this. The lights were still off when I went to the phone and dialed the police department. I also saw evidence that someone had been robbing the place. The glass display case for the large diving knives no longer held any knives.

While I was on the phone I heard what sounded like several people breathing. It was coming from behind the desk where I was standing. I informed the cops of the situation; then, I saw three large young men facing me with huge diving knifes in their hands. I dropped the phone. My adrenaline pumped as I faced a combat situation three years after my Vietnam tour of duty. I was ready to defend myself and do whatever I had to. For a few terrible moments I felt like I did when I was in Vietnam. These guys had no idea what they were going to be up against that early morning.

In a flash, I managed to say the quickest prayer of my life: "God, help me!" From that point on, everything seemed to be in slow motion, but I knew it was happening very fast. I trusted that God would help me.

I had decided, in those briefest of moments, to attack all of them. The idea was totally insane, but I knew it was the "right" thing to do and I followed my feelings.

I jumped out in front of them, blocking their only escape route. I yelled at the top of my lungs as I had seen in those old Kung Fu movies. I must have sounded and looked crazy. This was totally unexpected and it startled them. They panicked as they tried to get past me. I rushed toward them, knocking down all of them. I jumped on the first one I could grab and rolled over on top of him. The other two watched as I took the knife out of his hand and stuck it into his mouth and down his throat a couple of inches. If he had moved or tried to talk he would have gagged on the knife blade. He was lucky that this knife was from the store's display case. I made sure that we had only dull knives on display to keep our customers from accidentally cutting themselves when handling them. I do not think he knew this. All he understood was at that moment he had a crazy guy on top of him with a long knife blade poking down his throat. He was scared and began to shake violently. I looked at the other two guys and told them that I would not hesitate to cut their friend's throat if they tried to jump me to rescue him. They leaped over the glass display case and hit the floor running, leaving me on top of their friend with the knife blade still in his mouth. Using his dropped flashlight, I hit him as hard as I could on his head. I wanted to make sure that he did not get back up and harm me. I was concerned since he was about a foot taller and some 50 or more pounds heavier than I was.

The young man just lay there staring wide-eyed at me, wondering if I was going to hit him again or kill him. For a brief moment, I also wondered about that. I took a deep breath and knew that the fight was out of him. All I wanted to do then was just to hold him for the police.

The phone I had dropped was still connected to the police department. They had heard the yelling and fighting and thought the men were killing me. They eventually came and caught the other two guys.

I did learn something from that early morning encounter. Some might label my actions as just an adrenaline rush or luck, but I believe that God had protected me! There is no doubt about that, but more important, He also protected those young men from me. It was God's love that calmed me down in my moment of self-protective rage. No one was killed or badly injured. Thank God!

W.H. McDonald Jr.

Author's footnote: These young men, 18–20 years old, were from wealthy families. Their parents were doctors and lawyers. It took almost a year to come to trial. When it did, they each had the best lawyers that their parent's money could buy. They all got off with only probation. I figured they all got off with their lives as well.

What is interesting is that at the trial they talked about the guys as though they were mere children and not responsible. Their average age was 19 years old, the same as many combat soldiers in Vietnam. I was only 24 years old when this happened!

#

Author's note: I worked for more than four years as a scuba diving instructor in northern California. This could have been a life-ending event. I thank God that I was able to remain as clearheaded as I did because it saved all of our lives.

· SCUBA Dive into the Darkness

One weekend when I was a young scuba diving instructor, I planned a deep dive with two other instructors. We made plans to do a bounce dive to only 200 feet, then slowly come back up. That was the plan, and that was what we should have done. The key to good scuba diving safety is always to stick with your original dive plans. Once you are that deep, your mind is not thinking clearly enough to be making those kinds of life and death decisions. There is an effect called "Martinis Law" that states for every 30 feet a diver descends, it affects his mind the same as if he had drunk a double martini on an empty stomach. In other words, the diver gets high from the nitrogen in the compressed air that he is breathing. It gets more profound the deeper he goes because he is breathing in more dense air and the amount of nitrogen increases. This is called nitrogen narcoses. Most divers begin to have some problems at 125 to 150 feet. This dive was going to take us to the 200-foot level, so we needed to follow our dive plan right to the letter since our judgment would be greatly impaired at that depth.

The other two divers had on double tanks. Each tank had 72 cubic feet of compressed air. I was going with one single tank and would share air with both of them on the way back up if needed, so there was plenty of air for everyone. In order to do this efficiently, they each had an extra second stage regulator attached, so all I had to do was to grab this and breathe while coming back up. There would be no passing a regulator back and forth between us.

The dive took place off the shore of Mission Beach, California, where just a short distance from the shore the ocean bottom drops off 1,500 feet down a canyon wall. When we dove over the edge of this wall, it dropped into total darkness; it was very surreal and inviting in a spiritual way. I followed both of them as they rolled over the edge. We began to drop off into the darker depths of the canyon, using our underwater lights to guide us. We left a trail of silt and dirt kicked up by our fins and the movement of our bodies down the walls of the canyon. When we looked back up, we could not see anything except the cloud of debris that we had churned up behind us. We continued downward, our lights shining toward a bottom we were never going to see.

At 150 feet I was feeling slightly light-headed and could tell I was under the effects of the nitrogen. My two friends were still pushing downward as fast as possible. Our wetsuits were by now totally compressed, preventing the neoprene (rubber) from providing us any more buoyancy. Without the buoyancy, we would fall like rocks into the darkness below. (The normal wet suit has so much buoyancy that the diver has to wear a weight belt to drop below the surface of the water. In my case, I had to add 20 pounds of lead weights to my belt so that I could go under water. The deeper one dives, the less weight needed. The diver begins to fall faster toward the bottom because the wet suit rubber compresses. To prevent this, divers now can use a buoyancy compensator vest that they blow air into to compensate for the lost lift from their wet suits. I had an expensive vest with a small air bottle attached to it. All I had to do was release some air from the bottle into the vest as I went deeper. Coming up, I had to release air from the vest as it expanded, making me rise faster to the surface; too fast and I risked getting the bends! The rate of rise should be no faster than one foot per second or about the speed a diver's exhaust bubbles make when first exhaled from the regulator. The rule is to never go up faster than your bubbles travel toward the surface.) The wet suit rubber was so thinly compressed by all the pressure, that it was no longer affording me any protection from the cold northern California waters. I was chilled to the bone.

I looked at my depth gauge and saw we were approaching the 200-foot mark and should be stopping. When I looked at my two friends, all I saw were their fins creating a murky vortex as they continued their descent past the agreed upon 200-foot level. They just kept on pushing downward into the darkness. My one tank of air was running low. I realized that I had two choices: I could begin my ascent to the surface right then, and take my chances on having enough air supply to make it a slow, safe ascent; or I could go after them and stop them. Once I committed to either action, there would be no second chance. If I chased them down, I needed to convince them to resurface with me in order to share their air supply. I needed all their extra air to allow me time to surface slowly and make a small decompression stop at around the 20-foot level. If I were to resurface without making a stop, I would be impaired for life or perhaps even die from the effects of the bends (release of nitrogen bubbles in the body's tissues due to a too rapid ascent from a compressed atmosphere). If I chased them and could not get them to resurface, all of us would continue to drop into the 1,500-foot canyon's darkness to our certain death.

I had to make a very quick decision using a mind that could not be fully trusted. If I stopped at this moment, I had a fair chance at resurfacing on my own, and I knew that if they were mentally out of control, they were heading for certain death. I knew I could catch up to them, but I was unsure of my own mental abilities. It might be possible that my own mind was in such a state that all of us would be going to the bottom of the ocean.

If I caught up with them, I would need to turn them around immediately and head back to the surface so I had access to their extra air supply. I had way too much to think about in my impaired state of mind and so little time to make such a life or death decision.

I took a slow, deep breath and relaxed. I mentally tried to focus enough to say a short prayer. I knew I was not in control of myself or the situation. I needed all the help from God that He could give me. In that brief calmness and quiet, I knew that I could not leave my friends. I had no choice but to surrender myself into God's hands, so I raced after the disappearing fins ahead of me. My thoughts were of their safety.

I was not sure how I was going to catch these two guys and get them heading back to the surface. I was still trying to catch up with them when I looked at my depth gauge again. My heart was pounding, and I was having a hard time trying to read the depth on the gauge. I finally saw it—250 feet! I reached out to try to grab them, but they kept sinking deeper into the darkness. Finally, I was within a few inches of them and was able to grab one of them by the arm. He turned around with a wild-eyed look. He was having the time of his life. I put my depth gauge right up against his facemask to show him that we had now gone below 280 feet. How far below I could not tell since the gauge needle was stuck on the maximum level. We could have been below the 300-foot level; there was no way of knowing as we kept dropping like three rocks, heading toward the dark bottom of the ocean.

I took hold of both of their arms and inflated my vest with the last of the air in the attached bottle. It did not make much difference to my buoyancy. I began to kick with all my strength, pulling them both with me. They were not fully engaged in helping me in this effort, so we were making slow progress. We were going upward, blinded by the clouds of silt and mud that we had stirred up on our descent. We could not see anything, including each other. The only way I knew we were going up was by watching my bubbles floating slightly above us when I exhaled.

When we hit the 190-foot level, I could feel my head clearing slightly; I also had no air left. I sucked the last breath off my regulator and dropped it out of my mouth. I reached over and alternately began to use their spare regulators while slowly rising. They both seemed to come around about the 150-foot level. Their eyes gave me the indication that their minds were now functioning and engaged in what we were doing. We all managed to continue upward. We made as long a decompression stop as we could manage, using up all but the last few breaths of air, before making that final ascent to the surface.

When we got back to shore, I was mad at my friends for changing the dive plans while at the 200-foot level. The odd thing about nitrogen narcoses is that it makes the diver feel totally safe. They never felt any danger. They did not even realize or admit to how close they had been to killing all three of us. They thought they were okay and believed that they had been in complete control of the situation. They never accepted that they were in any way a danger to themselves or to me. They did not even realize that I had risked my life to rescue them.

I walked away knowing that if it were not for God's loving hand there was no way the three of us would have survived that dive. No one goes to those kinds of depths with such basic scuba gear as we had and survives. I knew that God rescued us, even if my diving buddies did not. I have to wonder how many times and in how many different ways God's loving hands have saved many others from dangers of which we are not even aware.

Bill teaching a SCUBA class in Monterey Bay, California.

Author's note: I made my wife question her own reality and scared the heck out of her in the process. Love is the most powerful force in the universe; it can move mountains and even walk through walls! Read this, and you determine if it was just a shared dream or something much more.

Shared Dream or Reality Check?

When we first got married and were living in Danville, California, a unique experience shook up my wife's sense of reality and changed the chemistry between us forever.

It happened one hot summer night just after I had finished my normal meditation time. I went upstairs to go to bed. My wife, however, stayed downstairs to sleep on the sofa where the temperature was about 20 degrees cooler than the upstairs. She was upset and worried about our son's health problems, my job security, and life in general.

I lay down to sleep, but I kept thinking about her sleeping on the sofa downstairs alone and worried. I kept drifting in and out of a sleep state, which was not like any sleep I had ever had before. I seemed to be floating in and out of my physical body. I felt light and at peace.

I looked around the room and noticed that the view was different. I was now fully awake and very much aware of my surroundings, but somehow, I was looking down at my body lying on the bed. I was actually floating in the air, or at least that me that was not my body. I was now up against the ceiling, and I realized that I was having another out-of-body experience. I saw a silver cord between myself on the bed and my conscious self that was on the ceiling. We were attached, but I could roam as freely as I wanted. I seemed to move toward whatever I was thinking about.

I drifted downward toward the wall above the stairway and actually drifted right through it. I continued to float down the stairs, hovered across the front room, and sat down on one end of the sofa next to Carol.

She immediately sat up, and we just looked at each other for a short while. I was sitting there in my out-of-body state and she was there in her physical body. I must have looked a little transparent to

200

her, but she was seeing me. The sofa rose off the floor a couple of feet and floated freely around the room. I think Carol realized that there was something not altogether right about this picture. Her eyes widened.

"Don't worry. I will always be there for you, whenever you really need me!" I said as I reached out to her.

Then, she panicked and became fearful of what she was witnessing. The whole sense of the experience then began to vanish. It was as if someone had sucked me into a large vacuum cleaner. I was dragged away and zapped right back into my body on the bed. I landed like a ton of bricks. I felt as if I had gained a million pounds in an instant. I opened my eyes and could remember every detail of what had happened. I knew that this was no dream. It really did happen to us.

I waited until breakfast to ask Carol if she remembered anything from the night before. Normally, she never remembers her dreams, but this morning she stated that she had a "nightmare." Before she could relate her nightmare experience, I told her the story of what had actually happened that night. She stared at me and listened in a total daze. My story of the night before matched her so-called nightmare down to the last detail.

She was blown away at first, and did not want to think it was possible. My knowing her nightmare made her realize that something had indeed happened. She wanted to believe that perhaps it was just some kind of a shared dream, that maybe all I had done was to pick up on her thoughts or the dream itself. Over time, however, she came to accept at least the possibility that it may have been much more than a shared dream. It was just too real. Whatever it was, she understood that it was an experience that expanded our relationship in ways that many couples never know in a lifetime.

The fact was that we did experience the same event. She tried with her most logical mind to sell herself on the idea that it must have been a dream that we both had together at the same time. Whatever happened is not really as important as the feeling I had from the experience. I know that Carol was my "dream lover," and in that state (whatever it was) I had let her know that I would always be there for her. And I plan on keeping that promise! Nothing else really matters!

Carol and Bill, Napa Valley Wine Train, 1995.

Author's note: The joys of loving someone and having her love you back!

Security Blanket

I have sewn you into
The fabric of my heart.

It beats as if we were one.

I look at you,
So quiet on the outside,
And wonder if you are
Dancing joyfully on the inside,
Like I am.

I know I can hardly contain myself
From smiling all the time.

When I unwrap myself
From you in the morning
It is like abandoning
My security blanket.

It is hard to let go.

#

Author's note: I actually suffered throughout this workday and couldn't shake the feelings of suffocation.

Suffocating While Delivering the Mail

I worked for a few years as a letter carrier; in fact, I was once the Vice President of the Oakland Chapter of the National Association of Letter Carriers. I was a lousy union official by my own admission. I just didn't have my whole heart into all the grievances and complaints. Of course, once I was promoted into management, I also found that I wasn't really that enthusiastic about that side of the fence either. Neither side wanted the truth or fairness; both wanted to have it their way.

I was working at an office in San Jose, and I was delivering the mail just off 1st Street out in a new industrial development area. There was a lot of construction going on in the area on the surrounding streets where they had dug trenches to lay pipes on the side of the roads.

I was out early on my deliveries and making good time when I began to feel really lousy. I couldn't catch my breath. I felt as if I were suffocating. I had to stop several times to try to breathe. I wondered what was wrong.

I fought this for at least 25 minutes; then, it was gone and I was okay. I wondered if I should go see a doctor to have myself checked out. By the time I got back to the office and punched off the clock, I was totally normal. So, I drove home.

When I got home from work, I greeted the family and turned on the local news to a story that caused me to jump up and give it all of my attention. The story was about a construction worker trapped by a cave-in of dirt in the trench he was working in just one block from where, and at the same time, I had my suffocating attack. It seems that perhaps I was somehow empathetically connected with this man and his experience. The news story related that the man died. I knew there was nothing I could have done to help, but I felt bad anyway.

#

Author's note: Sometimes we discover that our world is not really what it seems to be at all; we are actually a part of something much bigger, more beautiful, and more loving. I discovered that I am never alone and have never been alone. I was a part of something that I have no way to even comprehend let along explain to others. Something happened on a summer night in 1972 that altered my own sense of who and what I was. I do not drink or take any drugs. That would be the easiest explanation if I had been intoxicated, but I was cold sober. The only thing different was that I had spent several long hours in a deep meditation prior to going to bed. This was not a dream, although I am beginning to wonder if life itself is but a dream.

A Ride Inside a Rainbow

I am only able to remember the briefest pieces of information from the most enlightening spiritual encounter of my entire lifetime. Significant and life changing would be understatements to what transpired this one night. This was not a dream experience; this was in the truest sense, a spiritual journey of my soul. All my notions about reality and the purpose of life were shattered as I crossed from my physical world into a world of spirit. I have been cosmically altered by this event. There is a part of me that realizes that life really is but a dream.

The evening began normally enough for me. I had a long meditation and was feeling very peaceful and relaxed as I went upstairs to go to bed. I was still feeling rested and rather blissful from my meditation. As I lay there on my bed, I turned my attention to a photograph of my guru smiling at me from my bedside table. I was particularly focused on his eyes as my whole attention seemed to be drawn into the photo.

All of a sudden, I was no longer lying on the bed, but my body was. It was as if the real me had been vacuumed right out of my body and my spirit had no weight. I was soaring beyond that material body that was still in bed. I was transported to a place (if that is the right word) where there was no time; music, colors, thoughts, and love all became one.

I am at a loss as to how to even begin to describe this once-in-a-lifetime experience. This was not like my normal out-of-body experience; there was no attached cord or body floating around in some void of space. Words cannot fully capture the feelings or the colors and the sounds, but I will do my best to take you along on this inner journey.

I was being pulled along through what might best be described as space, the universe, but it wasn't like anything I had ever seen in any movie. I was going faster than light, zipping along through a vast heavenly universe of some kind. I was moving (and this is even harder yet to explain) inside of, or more accurately, as a part of a rainbow of colors. I could sense that I was a part of this traveling rainbow of souls. Moreover, I was not just one of the souls, I was *one* with them. I felt there was no separation. We were *all one*.

I was being told things that I could not remember when I woke up back in my body, but I do remember having been told something about who they were, who I was, and the meaning and purpose of what was happening. All of that information remains locked someplace in my inner self.

I do remember the incredible love I was feeling. I have never felt anything like that again! The whole experience was bathed and enraptured in a deep feeling of love. I felt love in ways that no one in a body ever has. I was love and love was the universe, and everything that surrounded this group of traveling colors was made of and reflected love. There were no boundaries for this love; it was without any borders and was everywhere and within everything.

We kept zipping along as we passed slower moving colors. It was like a scene from a *Star Trek* movie where they go into warp drive, and all those lights and colors zip past them as they move faster than light. While we were moving beyond warp speeds and moving as fast as "thoughts" (this is the only word that comes to me to compare the speed), we were moving and flowing with the music of the universe.

There was a musical sound that the universe around us was making. It was a part of us just as the love was. It was a sound that moved us along on our journey.

I never felt alone or as an individual; I always felt as *one* with this group of souls. It was as if I were a part of their family, but again, there wasn't any separation. It wasn't being a part of anything; it was being *one* with everything, and that was a big difference. I knew that we were all *one,* and I knew that we also were *one* with everything we saw and thought about. We felt no separation from anything around us, not with the colors or even the music we heard—it was all just *one*.

I could understand all of this while experiencing it, even though I cannot fully explain it. I saw and felt things that have no words or ways to convey their meaning back in the material world. I was with this group of "travelers" (the only term that seems to work to describe them) for what seemed to be an ageless amount of time. It felt like forever since time didn't seem to exist in this universe of colors and music.

Even though I am unable to remember everything I was told, it seems I was allowed to remember the journey itself and the love I felt while traveling with "my family" of travelers. I knew at some level that I was always a part of this "family," and that they have always been a part of me. I am not even sure how that would work or what that really might mean, but that was the feeling that I remembered as it was imparted to me.

While traveling in this rainbow I felt none of the restrictions that I have with my body. In fact, I had no body of any kind. I could not see myself, but felt that I was a part of the colors I was with. I also remember being happy beyond what I ever considered happiness to be. It was a blissful happiness that wrapped its presence all around me in a rainbow cocoon of love and joy. Yes, joy may be a better word than happy to convey what I was feeling. I was totally at peace with everything. There were no negative feelings within or around me—no fears, anger, or worry. I also felt a "knowing," a sense that we had some function or purpose for being a group. Whatever that "mission" was, I have no memory of what I was told or what I learned. It seems that my memory of what happened allows me to remember only certain elements of it.

I did not want to return to my flesh and bone body lying on my bed in the material world that I had been allowed to escape from. I felt I was being asked to return to prison. I felt a release of energy and began to slowly slide down until I slipped into my unconscious body.

I opened my eyes and began sobbing. I was overwhelmed with my loss of having to leave and return to the physical me. I also felt very heavy in my body, as I was no longer just a color that was free of all restrictions. Carol rolled over and asked what was wrong with me.

I couldn't begin to tell her all I had experienced, but I tried the best I could. While I was on this journey, it felt like years, decades, perhaps even centuries. When I "woke up" in my body, I felt I had been gone a mere few minutes. The clock, however, showed that it had been over an hour of earth time. Obviously, time was totally meaningless to this situation and experience.

Carol had no way of knowing what I was feeling at all the various levels of my being. I was both joyful and blissful, but a part of me was now lonely for "my family" that I had reunited with and then had to leave. I knew that what I had experienced was real, but why it happened and how it happened I was unable to explain. I did come away with the following impressions and beliefs even though I cannot recall any conversations or communications:

- I was a part of a family of color and light and of music and sound.
- I have always been a part of this family and always will be.
- I had traveled with this group at the speed of thought.
- I felt as *one* with this "family," but this family was *one* with everything including the music and the colors and the light around us.
- Love was everything! There was nothing else in the universe. Light and colors and music were expressions of love.
- I felt no stress, worry, pain, anger or negative feelings while "traveling" in this rainbow of beings.
- I felt that there was some purpose to this "family unit," some mission or something that this group (team, family, etc.) had. I felt I was told about it, but I have no memories. I have an awareness of this but nothing more.
- Time was meaningless in the universe that I been in. It seemed like forever; there was neither beginning nor end to it. It just was.
- I was loved beyond any measure of what anyone might imagine. Love was what this whole journey was about.

Love traveled with us and was a part of us and surrounded us. Love was everything including the music and the light and the colors. Love was the only thing in the universe. Everything else was just a reflection and a manifestation of that love.

- I came away realizing that we can never be alone. We have a "family" looking after us and helping us to evolve and progress spiritually on our journey.
- I felt that I was given certain information about events and things that when needed, I will remember.
- I know all that happened was not a dream, and that I was never asleep. I was fully conscious at all times. In fact, I was more fully awake and conscious than I have ever been.

I still reflect on this one supernatural voyage as a turning point in my life. I know now that I am never alone and that there are unseen forces and energies that are at work in our lives helping us. I know this happened to me. I have to believe very strongly that this same thing has happened to others as well. I believe that some people have chosen to keep these kinds of experiences to themselves to avoid being judged as strange or insane. Others may have allowed their own minds to convince them that it was all just a dream and not real.

#

W.H. McDonald Jr.

Author's note: This has happened twice that I can remember: once shortly after my "ride in a rainbow" experience, and once again about 30 years later when I was writing a poem about that original "ride" experience. In my heart, I know that they must somehow all be connected. What the light spheres represented, I do not know. Here is a short account of what happened.

Spheres of Bright Light

I was sitting in my meditation room relaxing and just enjoying the peace that I get after a long meditation. My mind was totally blank; I wasn't thinking about anything. All of a sudden, I was aware of someone watching me. I also noticed that the room was lighting up. I looked up to my left and saw a sphere-shaped object of light, almost like a miniature sun, dancing and flowing just out of reach above me. The light it emitted was so bright and so white it should have blinded me, but it didn't.

I looked directly at it, wondering what it could be or mean. It moved around slightly, and it never lost any of its brightness. I was fascinated by it, as it was almost hypnotic. I stared at it and felt chills running up and down my spine. I felt loved and at peace watching it.

After a brief period of time (I am assuming that it was very brief, a minute or two, but I did not have a clock to reference) it exploded into a huge burst of sparkling lights like fireworks on the Fourth of July. There was a sound so loud that I thought the entire neighborhood would wake up and come over to find out what happened. As it turned out, no one ever heard any sound except me.

The sparks from this energy of light spread to the entire room, filling it with light for a brief few moments before it was over. I sat there wondering what had happened and what it might mean.

I was trying to recall this experience about 30 years later to write a poem about it when I looked directly up from my keyboard and saw that same ball of light hovering over the top of my head. I was elated to have it back. I watched it once again as I had done so some three decades before. I tried to focus on it to see if I could learn something more about it. It danced around in the space above me in a dazzling display of light. Then, once again it exploded into a light show of white sparks.

The sound that it made almost knocked me out of my chair. I knew someone had to have heard this explosion. I ran downstairs to see the reaction of my family who was watching TV at the time. Once again, no one heard anything, and they looked at me strangely for having asked them if they had heard an explosion.

I am not sure what to make of these spheres or balls of light. They were identical in size, shape, and intensity of light. Both events ended in the same way with a large explosion and spreading of the light to the entire room. This light also surrounded me briefly as it dissipated and disappeared completely. Each time I felt loved and in great awe, but there seemed to be no messages or any material evidence that anything had ever taken place. It was just one more mystery in my long journey that I hope to one day understand.

#

Author's note: Sometimes things are not always what they appear to be, or in this case, what actually happened. Sometimes it just might be possible that we are the answer to someone's prayers.

Out of the Mouths of Children

I was on a family outing with some old friends and their two children, enjoying a rafting trip down the American River not too far from Sacramento. We had been rafting under a hot summer sun, and we pulled over to a beach to rest and have lunch. That is when we heard shouting and saw some activity on the beach up the river.

Our friend Beverly, who had been walking ahead of me, was quickly on the scene where two young men had pulled a 17-year-old boy from the river. The young man was not breathing. His face was white and bluish as he lay motionless on the ground. He looked like a dead person.

A group of young people with their heads bowed had gathered around him. No one was moving to do anything to help revive the drowned boy whose time was running out very quickly.

Beverly, who had just completed a Red Cross CPR class, was getting ready to jump in and help. She was willing to do what she had been trained to do, but she was not totally confident since she had never done this in a real situation before. I told her to step aside and allow me. I had been a professional lifeguard in my last year in the U.S. Army. I had some real-life experiences and also had taken the class several times over the years. I knew I could help. I knelt down and took the young man's head in my hands.

By this time, he looked very much dead. He must have been lying on the beach for several minutes in this condition. He looked as bad as I have ever seen someone who wasn't drowned beyond saving. I began mouth-to-mouth resuscitation. I could feel his chest swell up and rise each time I pushed my air into his lungs.

In my mind, I kept wondering why all these young people were not doing anything and why they had just left their friend lying on the sandy beach. I looked around and saw all these able-bodied teenagers still standing there with their heads bowed. I was getting angry with them as I continued to force my air into this young victim's lungs.

Finally, after what seemed several minutes, he coughed violently, shooting a stream of vomit right into my mouth and up my nose. I gagged, but only briefly stopped to clear my own mouth and nose. He then began to violently vomit several more times, so I turned him over on his side to allow him to clear out his lungs. At least a full cup of water came running out of his mouth as he gasped and sat up.

He began getting his color back as he continued to cough and spit. When he was fully alert, he stood up. All of his friends came over to hug him. He was still kind of in a daze, but he was very much alive, no thanks to all of his friends. I was a little annoyed by their lack of action, and I told them so. They looked at me as I told them that I thought they should have been doing something besides just bowing their heads.

"We were doing something, we were praying to Jesus to send us someone who knew what he was doing to come and save him," one young man said.

"Well, what good did that do?" I arrogantly muttered back to him.

"You came, didn't you? And you knew what to do! Can't you see, you were the answer to our prayers."

I stood there silently for several moments trying to collect myself. How could I not see that these teenagers had actually done something? I was there at the right time and the right place, and I knew what I was doing. I left feeling both humbled and blessed at the same time. My only thought was that of a passage I had read in the Bible: "Those whose glory above the heavens is chanted by the mouth of babes and infants." Psalms 8:1-2.

#

Author's note: That dreaded midnight call that all parents worry about—thank God my daughter, Daya, listened to my feelings before that night began.

The Midnight Phone Call

There is one thing that most parents dread above all else—that emergency phone call at midnight from one of the children. But let me start at the beginning of that fateful night when my daughter was a sophomore in high school and just beginning to drive.

I was sitting on the sofa watching the local news, which was showing footage of a car accident with major injuries. There were lights and emergency vehicles everywhere on the television screen when my daughter, Daya, asked me about borrowing the family car. She wanted to use my little four-wheel drive convertible to take her friends around on this Friday night.

Her words and her request hit me emotionally like a ton of cement bricks. I normally allowed her to use the car, but tonight it did not feel right. I had visions of her in the back of an ambulance with car wreckage across the darkened roadway. I could not get that mental image off my mind as I sternly relied, "No!" to her request.

She pleaded with me to reconsider. I stood firmly by my intentions not to let her be the driver of any car that night. She said her best friend could drive. So, I told her that she could go out, but under certain conditions that she would have to agree to. First, she was to make sure that her own seat belt was fastened. Second, she must tell whoever went with her to fasten their seat belts as well. I told her that was most important; she must insist they do this. I told her that I did not want to get a phone call from one of her friends at midnight, telling me that she was involved in a bad accident like the one I was watching on the television screen.

She thought I was overreacting to the news story, but I told her I felt this was much stronger than that, and she must assure me that she would do as I had asked her to do. She said she would, so I let her go out.

I felt very uncomfortable about her being out that night. I was strongly concerned, and I knew it had to do with a car crash. I did not want to worry my wife about it; after all, I could be overreacting as my daughter had said.

My wife and I were in bed when that dreaded midnight phone call came. In fact, it was right at midnight when the phone jangled us awake. I jumped out of bed, knowing already that the caller would tell me about an accident involving my daughter. Now the only questions were was she safe, where had it happened, and had she followed my instructions?

I picked up the phone and heard a boy's voice telling me that my daughter was sitting in the back of an ambulance out on a country road. He went on to say that he could not get close enough to talk to her because the street was blocked off. He said that there were half a dozen emergency vehicles and even a medical evacuation helicopter sitting on the road next to the car wreckage.

My wife looked at me and asked about the phone call. I told her to go back to sleep, that I needed to go help our daughter who had been in an accident. "Nothing to worry about," I told her, even though I knew it was much worse than we realized. I got dressed and was out the door on my way to the accident scene within a few short minutes after hanging up the phone.

When I approached the road she was on, there was no way to drive close to where she and all the equipment were. There were red lights flashing and rotating all over the country roadside. I looked down the road and saw her best friend's car, upside down and mangled on the side of the road. My heart was hurting because I knew the other passengers must be badly injured.

I walked to one of the ambulances parked on the roadside and heard my daughter talking loudly. She was upset and was talking very fast. She saw me and began to cry a little while telling me that she had made sure that her seat belt was tightly fastened. When she told her friends to do the same, they had laughed at her. They wouldn't put them on even after she warned them her dad had told her to make sure they used them.

I looked around at the damaged car and saw lots of blood and broken windows. I saw where one of the 14-year-old girls had been thrown face first through a side window, landing some 50 feet away after breaking through three strands of barbed wire fencing, also with her face. Her neck and back were broken. She would never again be able to move her arms or legs; she would be a captive of a wheelchair the rest of her natural days. Her face, once a most beautiful vision of her youth, was ripped and torn in several directions.

Another 14-year-old girl passenger did not get ejected from the car, but was tossed around inside as it rolled over three times. Her head was battered as if she had been inside a dryer being tossed up and down. She was still unconscious when I saw her. It took a full three weeks for her to wake up again.

The driver, my daughter's best friend, had been changing music tapes and was not looking at the road. When she looked up and saw that she was going off the road, she overreacted with the steering wheel and flipped the car. She was able to grip the steering wheel tightly to keep from being tossed around. Other than some bruises and bumps, she was okay physically. It was the emotional and spiritual damage that would take their toll on her later when she realized what she had caused to happen. Even though it was an accident, she put lots of guilt and blame on herself.

My daughter told me that her seat belt had held her even when the car was rolling over. She was hanging upside down when the vehicle came to rest on its rooftop. She saw that the other girls were hurt and tried to help them, but there was nothing she could do for any of them.

I took her to the hospital and got her checked out before bringing her home about four hours after getting that midnight phone call. My poor wife was worried, but grateful that our daughter was okay.

The next day, huge front-page photos of the car crash were all over the local newspaper. The crash looked terrible on the front page; then, it hit me. I realized the photos were the very images I had in my own mind the day before.

Had my daughter not listened to my demand for her to buckle her seat belt, she would have ended up like her young friends. If the others had listened to her that night, their lives could have been spared so much pain. But they had not listened.

I had known that something was going to happen that night. I had tried to do what I thought was the right thing. Once again, I found it is difficult to alter other people's destinies. My daughter did listen to me, and I feel blessed that I was able to warn her. I was beginning to believe that there was a very special bond between my daughter and me, and that she has some very special guardian angels looking after her.

Author's footnote: My daughter reminded me of something else that happened on that night that she felt was important and should be mentioned.

Right after the car crashed and rolled to a stop upside down on the side of the road, the neighbor who lived at the closest farmhouse reported the accident. She then came outside where she met a man standing along the road who claimed to be the young driver's father. He was waiting along the roadside for the emergency crews to do their jobs. The man spoke softly to her, trying to calm her down. She stood there watching transfixed in horror at the upside-down vehicle. Dust and smoke hung around the crash site like a misty fog in the cold night air. Rock and roll music could still be heard coming from inside the wrecked car along with the screams of the two young girls still inside.

The man claiming to be the driver's father remained until the emergency crews had finally arrived and all the girls were being treated. The neighbor woman said that she wasn't sure when the driver's dad had left the accident scene. Several others stated that they had seen or talked to him as well.

The witnesses told the young driver that her father had been there checking on her to make sure she was okay. When the driver responded with a blank stare, they went on to correctly describe him. That would be strange enough by itself, but the fact was that her father was living in Florida some 3,000 miles away at the time of this accident.

#

Author's note: I foresaw trouble for my daughter, Daya. Even though I warned her, she needed to experience this event herself.

The Party Warning Not Heeded

My daughter, Daya, and I have had many unusual experiences involving each other. This one began as a quiet, normal weekend night for my teenage daughter.

I was sitting on the sofa when she asked me if she could go to a party that night. She told me that it was in a good neighborhood, she knew the people giving the party, and their parents would be home. By all indications, this was going to be a quiet, safe, and sane party. But I had that old feeling that not everything was right. I told her about my feelings and that she could go, but she had to promise me that she would leave the party by 11 p.m. I felt if she stayed longer, something was going to happen to her or her car. I wasn't clear on what I was sensing, but I felt it would be unsafe for her to be at the party after that time. I told her I didn't want her having to call me to say something was wrong and that she needed my help.

"Am I going to get into a car crash or something?" she asked me.

"No," I replied. I felt that her car was in some kind of danger but did not tell her that. I reminded her again about leaving early to avoid danger. She gave me that look that teenagers throw at their parents, and she left the house.

After dinner, I felt uneasy about the party, but I needed to learn about allowing my daughter to live her own life and to experience her own karma. I just didn't want her to get hurt in the process. It was always hard for me to know if I should force myself into her life when I had these feelings. I did warn her this time, but I wondered if she had really listened.

It was about 15 minutes before midnight when my sad daughter called, asking for my help. She told me that a gang had vandalized her car, and she needed my help to get it back home.

The nice neighborhood party was visited by a local gang who were upset about not being invited or allowed into the party. The gang members fired a couple of rounds into the air. Then, they proceeded down the street with baseball bats, smashing the windows and

218

windshields of the 20 or more cars parked there. They had knocked off mirrors and dented hoods and doors. By the time the police arrived, the punks were long gone and the street was littered with broken glass and mirrors.

When I got there, I found that my daughter had not left the party at or before 11 p.m. as I had suggested. The gang had shown up about 10 minutes after 11 p.m.; that was when everything happened. I reminded her that had she left when I told her to, she would not now be looking at her brand new Honda with its entire back window smashed out and her side mirror broken off. There also were dents and dings to the body of the car. Inside, it was full of broken glass. I had to spend several minutes clearing the glass off the front seat so I could drive it home. I gave her my truck to drive and had her follow me.

She was quiet, and I didn't feel that a lecture would be any more effective than her seeing what happened when she failed to heed my warning. I could not spend my entire life warning her about events and dangers; this was something that she needed to develop and to handle herself. I felt that up to this point in our relationship I had in some ways enabled her by telling her too much. I vowed from that time forward to step back and let her get in tune with her own intuitive abilities, which I knew she had. We both learned a lesson that night.

#

Daya, age 2, in Daddy's Army boots.

Author's note: There has always been a special bond between my daughter, Daya, and me. This story is another one of those very special moments that we have shared.

Amazing Grace

It was during the summer of 1994 that a most wonderful and unexplainable experience took place in the lives of my daughter, Daya, and me. It all began when I went to Los Angeles for a church convocation. I was staying at a hotel in the downtown area and was attending the classes and meetings in the same hotel.

One afternoon, between events, my old friend Bob invited me out to lunch. He wanted to take me to a local Indian restaurant that was only a short walk from the hotel. We had a great lunch and some good conversation. We left the restaurant and began our walk back to the hotel.

We walked through the downtown area where many homeless people hung around the streets. As we stepped around one corner, a man with a wild look on his face jumped up in front of us. He thrust a filthy finger at Bob as he shouted out a date, including the month and the year. My friend stood frozen as their eyes met. I asked Bob what that date meant to him. He turned to me and said that it was his birthday, right down to the year.

We were both dumbfounded as to why, or how, a homeless man could possibly have known that kind of information. The man had looked just like all the other homeless men we saw around us, except for that strange look in his eyes. We turned and walked across the street to get away from the homeless man who had shocked us with his sudden insight. He did not follow us as we made it safely to the other side of the street.

Just outside the metro station steps, we came upon an old black man. He was standing with a tarnished saxophone in his weathered hands. The beat-up old instrument case lay open on the sidewalk with its precious few collection of coins. I felt an odd compulsion, so I approached him. I asked him if he accepted requests for music. He said he did, so I asked him if he could play my favorite hymn,

"Amazing Grace." He gave me an odd little smile, nodded, and said he would give it a try.

He lifted his dull saxophone up to his chapped lips and began to softly play. As the music flowed, people walking by on the street stopped. They slowed their cars and rolled down the windows to better hear. The music that spilled from this man's sax was unlike anything I had ever heard before.

Bob and I just stood there. Tears formed in my eyes. The music was so sweet and peaceful. The old man was playing this traditional spiritual hymn in a jazz style that sounded utterly perfect. The strangest thing about his music, however, was the effect it had on all those people who had just moments before been running around in their business suits and mentally engaged in worldly affairs. Even the other homeless men seemed to be transported beyond this street corner serenade. It was as if we were all together in some chapel, instead of on a busy LA city street. I noticed that people coming up from the Metro station stairs had stopped to listen. No one was moving. All of us were transfixed by the music coming out of this old man's saxophone.

When I looked at the musician, I noticed that a change had come over him as he played that song. His once dirty, street-hardened face and hands now appeared much softer. His eyes sparkled with a moist, far away look. He held that instrument tenderly, lovingly, as if it were his child. As he finished the song, he had a glow about him; he seemed radiant. A soft light seemed to come from him.

I quietly put a donation in his case. It felt as if I were putting the donation in the collection basket at my church on Sunday. He had a small, knowing smile across his ebony face. I asked him to play it again for me as I walked back to the hotel down the street. Once again he put that sax to his lips and began another sweet rendition of "Amazing Grace" in his soft jazz style.

Bob and I reluctantly headed back to the hotel. The sounds of his sax followed us and seemed to bounce off the tall office buildings that surrounded us. That song had not only transformed both of us, but I noticed that other listeners seemed to be as emotionally moved as we were.

When I boarded the plane to return home to Sacramento, I could still see that old man's face etched in my mind. The sound of his music was still playing within me. I sat on the plane, completely at peace with myself and the world. The memories of the song caused tingles up and down my spine, almost as if I were in love or being loved.

Now, here is the rest of the story...

When I returned home, my daughter came to visit me. As I began to tell her the story of the old man and the song, she stopped me. She asked me if it had happened that past Thursday. I replied, "Yes, it had." She asked if it had taken place about one in the afternoon. I replied that it had. She then told me about her experience with her boyfriend, at that same day and time in Sacramento while I was still in LA.

She and her boyfriend had been driving around town, and she was trying to find some music on his car radio. As she was turning the dial, she happened upon the sounds of a saxophone playing the hymn "Amazing Grace." She went on to explain that it had sounded very different from anything she had ever heard before. She said it sounded kind of like jazz. The song was so moving that they pulled off the road so they could listen to it with their full attention. They had both listened to the hymn in awed silence, just sitting there in the parked car.

I was moved by her story. I found it wonderfully strange that a radio station could have been playing that same song, at the same time as my street musician was playing it for me in LA. Also, both versions of the song were played by a sax and both had that soft jazz sound to them. The reactions of my daughter and her boyfriend were just as emotional as Bob and I had felt in LA.

I needed to take my daughter to pick up her car that same morning after we exchanged stories about what had happened to each of us. When I turned the key over to start my pickup truck, the radio came on playing "Amazing Grace." It was not the same version, but it brought us a moment of reflection over all that had happened. I suddenly had a wave of blissful love engulf me as the impact of what had happened sunk in.

We both looked at each other, and we felt bonded together forever. I do not know how any father and daughter could ever feel any closer than we did at that moment. We will never be able to fully understand what happened, but we will always cherish the memory of that hymn "Amazing Grace." Now, whenever I hear that song being played or sung, I feel such inner bliss because I know that God really does love us; and he blesses us in so many ways.

> "Amazing grace! How sweet the sound
> That saved a wretch like me!
> I once was lost, but now am found,
> Was blind, but now I see."

#

Author's note: Another wonderful spiritual moment shared with my daughter, Daya.

If You Build It—They Will Come

I built a new meditation room in the attic space above my garage. It had a pull-down ladder and a skylight that opened up for fresh air. I had tiled a small area next to a small altar and added a carpet to cover the rest of the small sanctuary. It held only two chairs comfortably, one for me and one for my guest, who was normally just my tabby cat who sat as long as I was up there.

I wanted to show it to my daughter, Daya, so I invited her over to see it. She kidded me about it because I used the phrase "if you build it they will come" from the movie *Field of Dreams*. I told her that now that I had built it, "they," angels or spiritual beings, would come.

We were alone in my house while my wife was out shopping. My wife had locked up the house before she drove out of the garage. She had closed the garage door after she pulled out, leaving my daughter and me alone. She knew we would be up in the attic space, so she had secured the rest of the house out of habit.

Daya and I were sitting in my newly-built meditation room when we heard the sounds of people walking to the door that leads to the garage from inside the house. We both got quiet and looked down the hole of the pull-down ladder. We heard the door open and saw light shining from inside the house onto the floor of the dark garage. Daya and I both knew that no one else was in the house, so she thought that we might have an intruder. I reminded her once again of what I had been saying, "If you build it, they will come." She quickly climbed down the ladder and rushed into the house, hoping to find whoever it was that had opened the door and made all the noise. She ran around inside the house for several minutes, checking under beds and looking in all the rooms while I was enjoying it all and laughing.

She finally came back and was baffled that all the doors were still locked from the inside, and that no one was inside the house. She and I looked at each other and wondered about what I had been saying. I did build it, but did they come?

#

Author's note: The connection with my daughter has remained strong all these years, but I have continued telling her less and less. I wanted her to develop and trust her own intuitive feelings, which I already knew she had. She did not disappoint me this one night, but she caused me some concerns at the beginning of our phone conversation.

My Daughter's Near Accident

Both of my children have inherited my psychic abilities in differing degrees, and each uses them in his and her own way. My daughter, Daya, was finally beginning to develop a stronger trust in her own feelings as she grew older. This became clearer to me with this life-and-death experience that happened to her several years back.

She was driving from Sacramento to Fairfield on Highway 80. She was just leaving West Sacramento when she began having the sense that something was going to happen. It became much stronger the closer she got to the town of Davis. She was becoming more concerned and more alerted to the possibility that something was going to happen that night. The feelings finally became so overwhelming that she slowed her car a little.

Then it happened. On the other side of the divided highway, which she couldn't see because of the bushes planted between the east and west traffic lanes, a car hit a pickup truck. The impact sent the truck airborne over the highway divider. It had flipped upside down in the air and was heading right into the opposite traffic lane, straight for my daughter's vehicle. As the unseen truck was veering toward her, she had just taken her foot off the gas to slow her car. Then, she saw the upside-down pickup on a collision course with her. The truck rolled over and dropped on the highway just several feet in front of her car. The momentum allowed it to slide into the other lane, thus leaving her a clear pathway past the totaled-out truck.

Her heart was pounding as she saw all this unfolding before her eyes. Had she not followed her intuitive feelings to slow down at that exact moment, the truck would have landed on top of her car.

I was home, feeling very uneasy about the night and my daughter. I didn't know what kind of danger she was in, but I felt there was something happening. I sent a silent prayer her way as I lay in bed not knowing what was taking place. Then, I got her phone call, another of those midnight calls I dreaded getting from my daughter.

"I didn't do anything to kill him. He was dead already!" She was upset, and these first words out of her mouth were not what I would call the most reassuring that a parent wants to hear.

She commanded my full attention as she answered my detailed questions. My heart beat a little faster, in time with my daughter's rapid, breathless account of the graphic details of this man's death. She related how she could see the man's face in the cab of his pickup truck as he flew over the road. Then, she described how she found his body. It was one exceptionally scary night and one too-close encounter with death for her.

One of the first people to stop and help her at the scene of the accident was an off duty California Highway Patrol officer, a friend of my son's and someone she knew to give her emotional support.

My daughter had saved her own life by listening to her inner voice. Learning to trust our intuitive feelings is a matter of great faith. That night she passed her first major test of her faith in that ability!

#

My daughter, Daya, on her wedding day, June 2002.

Author's note: This turned out to be a scary event for me to have been involved with. It felt like a doorway between the forces of good and evil may have opened. I wasn't even sure that I believed what my little sister told me, but she had asked me to help her. She honestly believed in what was happening to her and her family. I had no choice but to do what I could, even if it meant having to perform an exorcism.

An Exorcism

There was always a solid bond between my little sister, Marsha, and me as we grew up in our abusive and dysfunctional family. She has been through much turmoil in her life, and I have always had a soft spot for her in my heart.

When we were small, I remember playing mind-reading games with each other. One of us thought of a short sentence or phrase (Mary had a little lamb; twinkle, twinkle, little star; happy birthday; etc.) repeating it over and over in our minds. The other had three guesses as to what it was. Believe it or not, this was not too big a challenge for either of us. We also played a mental card game where she or I looked at a playing card from the deck, and then sent a mental picture of it to the other. The idea was to correctly guess not only the suit but also the exact card (four of clubs, jack of spades, etc.) We did not count if as correct unless we got both the suit and value of the card right. This was limited to one guess only, and there were times when we got between 20 and 30 cards correct out of a deck of 52!

Marsha had always been able to count on me when she needed to. So, when she asked me to help her with a problem, I felt I had to try to do something even though it was well beyond anything with which I had ever gotten involved.

My sister had many good reasons to believe that there was a powerful, negative force in her life that was causing her and her family problems. She presented me with a long list that made her feel this was the case. I listened open-mindedly and asked her if she had been to a Catholic priest to have them do an exorcism.

She told me the history of how she had first approached one priest and told him all the details of the strange happenings. He said he would help her. The following week she found out that he had quit the priesthood altogether and left town. He left no messages or reasons for not getting back to her.

The next priest she contacted heard her story and felt that it was a case for an exorcism. The following week when she had not heard from him, she went to the church and found out that he had died of a heart attack.

She was now coming to me to use whatever methods and abilities I had to rid her family of this evil energy. She was fearful of what could happen, considering what had happened to the two priests she had recruited. She was desperate for help of any kind. I knew that I needed to do something, even if it was only some psychological mumbo jumbo. She needed a strong spiritual and emotional anchor to hold her life together. She was the most afraid I had ever seen her. She was beyond scared.

She gave me a long list of improbable happenings that included a child's doll that spontaneously burst into flames and reports that one of her children was seeing "bad people" in the house.

She then dropped a bombshell on me when she told me about a possible connection with people associated with Papa Bray, a name from my past when I had lived in Hawaii. That made my blood freeze. This caused me to think that perhaps this was not just some mental or emotional experience from which her family was suffering. My sister went on to tell me about the relationship my mother had forged with Papa Bray after I had left the islands in 1964. My mother had dropped in to meet with him on her way back from meeting me on R and R in Japan back in 1967. My mother and a group of Papa's followers had apparently formed a secret group or society in California and Nevada. My sister tried to explain this to me but my head was spinning. No one ever told me any of this information while my mother was alive.

I decided that I needed some more information as well as some help with how to go about this so-called "exorcism." I knew something about these kinds of supernatural forces, but I wasn't an expert. I was willing to try, so I decided to visit and pick the mind of a Catholic priest I knew. He told me all he knew of the process and gave me a large container of holy water. He also wrote some prayers for me to give to Marsha for her to use.

I left his place and was driving back to Elk Grove. It was a normal drive all the way to the outskirts of town. However, when I got off the freeway and was driving down an old country road heading to my house, I encountered a heavy blanket of thick fog. This was strange because the entire rest of the valley was clear that night. I drove into the fog and it became difficult for me to see farther than a few feet ahead. I saw a dead dog on the road and drove around it. A few yards ahead, I saw a dead rat lying out on the asphalt road.

I kept driving through the soup-like fog, and I encountered another dead animal on the road, a cat. A few yards later it was a black bird, then a squirrel, a skunk, a raccoon, an opossum, and a string of another dozen or more dead animals lying on the road as I drove through the fog.

I remembered that Marsha's car had broken down on this same stretch of road the week before. She said that she had driven into a blanket of fog like the one I was now in, and her car had stopped running for no reason that she could find. She said it was an uncomfortable and frightening experience. She was finally able to get her car running, and she drove out of the fog.

Now, I was in this same area, and I was seeing more dead animals on the road than I had ever seen in my whole life in one place. I was feeling uneasy even though I did have a gallon of holy water in my vehicle, which didn't do that much for my courage. Everything inside of this fog-shrouded road was cold and eerie. I got concerned when the next dead animal I saw ahead of me was my beloved and favorite symbol of my own spiritual energy, an owl! I had to ask myself if I had ever seen a dead owl on a road. That was a strange sight in itself, but combined with the several dozen other dead animals that I had encountered in only about a mile of foggy road, it had me wondering what kinds of power were at work. I had gone into this only halfheartedly believing my sister. I also thought that she had emotionally created a good percentage of what had happened to her. As I drove through the fog, I wasn't so sure anymore. The abundance of dead animals was convincing me something terribly evil was afoot.

I got to Marsha's apartment and unloaded everything that I thought I would need to change the situation for her. I had my gallon of holy water, the written prayers, incense, and some holy pictures to put around her apartment. I had no clue what I was doing, but I put together a ceremony and combined what I had been given from the priest and from what I remembered from my studies under that old kahuna, Papa Bray. I was going down unfamiliar territory and making it up as I went along. My theory was simple—good overcomes evil! So, I concentrated all energies and prayers against whatever possible force was causing so much destruction in Marsha's life.

I used what few tools I had—incense, candles, holy water, prayers, chants, holy pictures, and some religious symbols—along with the power that comes from deep meditation. I really didn't know what I was doing. I was strictly making it up as I went along. I was trusting that I might stumble across something that would work. I remembered watching Papa Bray using chanting as a weapon against evil. He had told me about the great powers that come from the vibrations of sound. I used a form of chanting along with my prayers. I did the best I could and trusted that something would work. I finished my ceremony and chanting and then instructed Marsha to liberally use the holy water I had given her. She was to splash it on all her windows and doors for the following 40 days. She also was to burn the incense and to maintain a daily routine of meditation and prayer. I was exhausted and stumbled out of the house to go home.

After I finished my meditation at my house, I looked outside into the darkness of my backyard. I could actually feel a protective energy surrounding my home and protecting my family. I also could sense that something evil was just outside that layer of protection. I went to bed, concerned about everything that had happened. I also wondered about the priest who had helped me. After all, of the last two priests who had offered to help Marsha, one left the church and the other died, both within a week of consenting to help her.

By the end of the week I got a phone call from the priest. He was in a hospital in Mountain View. It seems his superiors thought he was breaking down emotionally, and they had committed him for observation and evaluation. When he talked to me on the phone, he had a slurred voice from the drugs they had given him. All his talk about reincarnation and such had them concerned about his emotional and mental health. If he wanted to remain a Catholic priest, he had to submit himself to this evaluation process.

Now the score card showed three Catholic priests' careers had ended or been interrupted.

That was the worst of it for everyone involved. My sister's life began to change for the better. I was confused at all that had transpired. I really do not know what happened or why. It is one of those many strange mysteries of my life.

#

Author's note: It is not every day that a stranger tells you that she has been dreaming about you since she was a small child. This was not just any child; she was a beautiful "ebony angel" who came into my life to teach me something.

Ebony Angel

It was around 1991 when a series of events took place that got my attention. The events had me rethinking some of my beliefs about children and about making judgments. One night, as I was getting ready to go to bed, the phone rang well past 10 o'clock. None of my friends would dare call me at that hour, as they knew I was normally in bed earlier. But on this night, for whatever reasons, I was still up and dressed.

I answered the phone and an older woman spoke to me. She was from the local foster group home where I had mentored a 17-year-old boy the year before. The woman, a professionally-trained social worker who had been working for the foster care organization for decades, was calling to ask me for advice. That was strange since we had never met, and she only knew about me from the boy.

I had never before been called by this agency for any advice. They had a full staff of social workers and counselors and certainly didn't need any input from someone as unqualified as I must have seemed to them. So there really wasn't any logical reason she should be calling to consult with me. I am not sure she realized how strange this whole conversation was. She talked to me as if I were her old friend and colleague. None of this made any sense unless you subscribe to the theory that there are never any accidents in life, and that everything has a meaning and a purpose. Since I believe that nothing does happen by accident, I listened to her concerns. She went on to tell me about a 17-year-old black girl in Sacramento. She happened to be a friend of one of the girls in their group home and was desperately in need of some help. She was in great physical danger from her stepfather, who had pulled a knife on her and threatened to harm her. The social worker went on about all the problems facing the girl; then, she asked me what I thought I could do to help her.

The question at first floored me, since she could have called any number of qualified sources. She had the phone numbers of many professionals who worked for the county and the agency that she was employed with. Yet, she was calling me, a total stranger, to ask for help and assistance with this child. This was not something that I could turn down. I felt there was a higher power at work in this phone call. The young girl needed help, and there was no way that I was not going to try. I told the woman not to worry about the situation, that I would take care of it. She gave me the address where the girl was hiding from her stepdad.

The address didn't seem right when I wrote it on a piece of paper. I looked at it, and I knew that I had written it down correctly, but I knew it was wrong. I set out driving to Sacramento on a cold, foggy December night a week before Christmas.

When I got to the street of the address I had, I saw two police cars pulled into a shopping center parking lot. The officers were talking to each other. I could barely make out their cars in the fog as I drove up beside them and asked for their assistance. I told them what I was trying to do and gave them the address. They punched the address into their computers and found that it was a wrong street number. They volunteered to help me find the girl by going door to door down the long street of apartment buildings.

They had knocked on about seven apartments, waking up people, when they found the girl and brought her to me. She was a large, athletic-looking young girl with an innocent child-like look about her. She trustingly got into my pickup truck, and we drove off into the fog together toward Elk Grove.

She introduced herself to me and sat there staring at me as I was driving. She told me that she had been dreaming about me ever since she was a small girl. She said she had seen my face many times in her dreams, and that she knew it would be okay to go with me. I was a little stunned. I was not sure if this was some kind of a foster-kid con job or if she was telling me the truth. From all of her body language, I thought that she was being very open and honest. I did not know what to say, so I remained quiet, eventually dismissing her words from my mind.

When we got to my house it was around midnight, but everyone was still up, waiting to see the girl I had brought home. My daughter welcomed her with a hug, and my wife gave her some hot chocolate and cookies. My daughter and wife needed to rise early for school and work, so we took only a few minutes to talk with her before they had to go to bed. We listened to her explain all the problems that were going on in her life. She told us it was just past her birthday, which she didn't get to celebrate with much joy.

I wondered about leaving her alone in our house while we were off at school and work the next day. I no sooner had that thought when she said, "I know what you are all thinking about me, taking your things if I am alone in your house; please trust me, I won't do you any harm."

I was impressed that she could pick up my thought since I hadn't given her any indications of my concern, but I thought maybe that was a logical guess.

After my daughter and wife had gone to bed, the young woman and I sat in the family room. She sat in a big, soft easy chair and I sat across from her on our long sofa. On the other end of it sat our fat, old family cat. All of a sudden, she stopped talking and looked directly at the cat whose hair was standing straight up in the air. The cat was focused on a spot between us on the sofa. The young girl pointed to the cushion, which was pressed down as if someone had just sat on it.

"There is someone sitting here on the couch with you. Can you see anyone?" the girl asked.

All I could see was the cushion pushed down and the cat totally freaking out with its eyes fixated on the spot. A slight breeze passed, sending chills up and down my spine. I didn't move as I tried to shift my attention back to this young woman sitting across from me. The conversation continued on, but every once in a while I glanced sideways to observe the slightly crushed sofa cushion and my cat still sitting there with her fur straight up in the air.

Her conversation style was very child-like and simplistic. It was like talking to a seven-year-old child instead of a 17-year-old! Yet, she and I discussed some very deep principles of Zen and yoga along with different spiritual theories and concepts, which even though she did not use any big words she seemed to have a deep intuitive understanding. She was able to sense and grasp what I was saying. It was as if she were a spiritual savant, and it left me wondering who she really was. I finally left her to go upstairs to sleep.

I had put her in my spare bedroom downstairs, which also had been my personal meditation room for 20 years. The room would be a quiet and peaceful place for her to sleep. The next day when we talked again, I found out that it also was a place for visions. She told me that when she had gotten into bed, my mother had come to her and tucked her in. She described how a dark-skinned, long-haired woman wearing an orange robe made her feel safe and at peace.

I stood there listening to her and wondering if she was talking about my guru, Paramahansa Yoganada. I grabbed a copy of his *Autobiography of a Yogi*, which has a color photo of him with long black hair and wearing an orange robe. I asked her, "Did she look like this?"

"Oh yes, that is her! She was there last night and helped me get to sleep. Was that your mother?" she blurted out.

I had to explain to her that "she" was actually a "he," and it was my guru and not my mother. He had passed away many years before.

We got into a long spiritual conversation about reincarnation, forgiveness, karma, and a host of other subjects. I was so surprised that this young girl had been gifted with a visit or a vision of my very own guru. She took it all in stride as if it weren't anything out of the ordinary.

She was only able to spend three days with us before I eventually got a phone call from the Sacramento County Child Protective Services wondering why I had this girl in my house and why the foster agency had called me instead of them. They told me that I had no legal right to keep this young girl at my home; they were sending a police car to pick her up later that day. I knew in my heart that she needed to go, but this was just a few days before Christmas. I hated to see her spend it at the children's shelter.

When I broke it to her that she couldn't stay with us any longer, she began to cry. She had really enjoyed her short stay with us, and it was killing her to have to leave. She told me a story of what had happened to her that morning when I was at work.

She said that she was sitting on the edge of the bed looking at an old photo I had of my mother. It was actually a black and white photo of my guru taken just minutes before he died. It shows a much-aged guru, and that is why she did not relate it to the photo of the young man in the orange robe that I had shown her the day before. While staring at the photo, she said she became relaxed and felt at peace. Then, she felt something pressing on her upper leg. When she pulled up her pants leg, she saw what looked like the impressions of a face of an owl (like the impressed lines one gets when sleeping on something and it leaves lines for a while on the skin where it touched). She said the owl's face made her feel loved.

I explained my lifelong history with owls and symbols representing owls. It seems that whenever something very special and spiritual is going to happen in my life, or when I need a sign to refresh my faith, an owl comes to me in some form. Sometimes it might be a real owl flying across my windshield or overhead as I drive down the road. It might be the hooting or screeching of an owl outside my window. It might be a photo of an owl that someone gives me, or any number of other ways, but always it is an owl. When I get this symbolic visitor in my life, I know things are okay, and that was what I told her.

She sat there crying, both for joy and for the sadness of having to leave me. Soon it was time to go. The police arrived and took her, making her sit in the back seat as if she were under arrest. It was so sad for me to see. She reached up and pressed the window with her hand. I touched it on the outside. I looked at her for that last time as the police pulled away; her face was all wet as tears flowed down her checks. I could hardly see her face through all my own tears. I watched her leave, feeling as if I had lost an old friend.

Who was this young "ebony angel" who spent a few days in my life and who has never left my mind since? Why did the group home call me out of the blue? Who was on the sofa with me and my cat? Why did she see my guru? What caused her to have an outline of an owl's face on her leg? Did she really dream about me for years as a child? I still do not know any of the answers. All I know is that there are no accidents in life, so for whatever purpose we each served each other, I am grateful and feel blessed to have had those few days with my ebony angel.

#

Author's note: This young man claimed he saw me in a "real-life dream" and it gave him hope when he had none. He was a stranger I will never forget. Perhaps he was much more than meets the eye?

The Hitchhiker

For several days I had a nagging feeling that I had someone special waiting for me. In fact, I couldn't get the thought out of my mind. Hebrews 13:2 kept coming to the forefront of my thoughts. It was a mantra playing in my mind, overshadowing all my other thoughts: "Be not forgetful to entertain strangers; for thereby some have entertained angels unawares."

When I went to the local bookstore, I picked up only one book. It was Linda Goodman's *Star Signs*. It was stacked on a lower shelf, and I had to actually stoop down to see it there. I reached down and pulled out this one particular hardback that was among dozens of other books. For whatever reason, this book acted like a magnet. I felt drawn to it. I quickly opened it at the beginning of the book, and jumping out at me was the Bible quote from Hebrews 13:2, which had been ever present in my thoughts all week long. I could not believe that the first book I picked up, on the first page I turned to, had this verse sitting right there in front of me to remind me of "my appointment."

I did not know what specifically I was to do or whom I was going to run into. I was trusting that my inner feelings would lead me to the right place and the right time to make "my appointment." I relaxed and let the thought go.

Later in the week, while at work in downtown Sacramento, I got an urge to leave work early to head home. The feelings were too strong to ignore. I left work, heading south down Highway 99. That Bible passage kept coming back to me as I drove. I knew something was about to happen, so I was on the lookout for what it might be even though I was not totally certain of what I was looking for. My feelings got stronger the farther I drove south. I felt I was about to make my appointment and very soon.

When I passed the South Sacramento Kaiser Hospital, which was only about five miles from my house, I saw a hitchhiker alongside the highway.

It was illegal to be hitchhiking on that stretch of the highway. He was not near an on-ramp, and he was standing along the highway where no one could safely pull over to give him a ride. It was obvious that this young man did not have a clue as to how to hitchhike.

I decided that I should pull over and give him a ride. It just did not feel like an optional thing to do. My feelings were very strong that this was something I needed to do. I pulled over as close to where he was as I possibly could. Even then, he had to run about 100 feet to get to my pickup truck. When he got up to my side window, I could see how young he was. I later found out he was 22 years old. He looked beat-up by the weather and life in general. He was soaked from sleeping in a field alongside the highway the night before. The rain had continued to dampen him and his spirits all day. He was wearing a short sleeve shirt, and he didn't even have a jacket. He had taken a pair of white socks and had fashioned gloves over both of his arms. It was apparent that he was trying to keep warm, but the socks were soaked, as was everything else he was wearing.

He looked in at me through my truck window, but then he pulled back with a strange look on his face when he got a good look at me. I asked him where he was heading. He replied that he was trying to get to Texas, to find his stepdad. I was only going a couple more exits down the highway, but I told him to hop in the truck and I would take him a short way.

He smelled like someone who had been living out on the streets for weeks without a shower. He had a rancid body order that emanated in all directions. It was a musky, foul smell like a pile of unwashed gym clothes stuffed in a locker for months. His clothing was drenched and more than just dirty; he was filthy from head to toe. He was so cold and chilled that he was actually shaking. He did not say too much as we made it to my exit ramp. When I took the turnoff, I impulsively asked him to stay in the truck. I took him to my home so he could warm up and eat.

When we got to my house and my daughter saw the young man coming in with me, she made an expression that I knew meant she wondered what in the heck I was doing. His odor permeated the house. I showed him the bathroom where he could take a hot shower. I gave him some of my clothing to change into, tossing his spent rags in my garbage can. When he was clean and freshly dressed, I took him to my garage and pulled out my camping equipment. My thoughts were that if this kid were going to survive out on his own, he needed some basic equipment.

I pulled out a backpack and filled it with camping gear, including a waterproof tarp that he could use to make a shelter. Back in the house, I packed a wool blanket and some other comfort items into the backpack. I went through my clothing and gave him some underwear, tee shirts, sweaters, socks, extra jeans, and most important, a jacket. I also gave him an old Oakland Raider's baseball cap and a bag to carry extra food and clothing. I made sure that he was fully equipped.

He was grateful and polite when I made him lunch. He looked at me in the same way he had when we first saw each other on the highway. I asked him what he was thinking.

He told me that he had left his grandmother's house up on the northern coast of California because she had died. He had no one to turn to and no place to call home. He told me about all his time spent in foster homes and about the lousy life he had been living. He was now trying to hitchhike to Texas to see if his stepdad would take him in.

He went on to tell me how he got to that place on the highway and what had happened to him the night before. He told me that the rainstorm had drenched him. He was unable to stay dry because he had no tent or rain gear. Everything he owned had been totally rain soaked. His sleeping bag was ruined, so he had thrown it away. He had no jacket or spare clothing. He went on talking, and it was easy for me to see that he was desperate and depressed. The night before, he had felt that he had absolutely nothing in his life for which to live. There was nobody in his life to help him or care about him. This caused him much inner pain. I could empathize since I'd felt this way many times during my younger years.

As he talked about his night of despair, I could tell how close this young man had come to thoughts of suicide. I thought on that night of his young life when all he wanted was to end all the suffering. He had felt so unloved and unwanted, even the weather was against him. At

241

this point in his conversation, his eyes got that fixed look on me again.

He told me that at his very lowest point of despair the night before, he had some kind of "real-life dream," as he called it, while he was totally awake. He saw a man who looked just like I did: same clothing, same beard, hair, eyes, and voice. He believed I was the one who had been in his real-life dream the previous night. He did not understand how or why. He went on to say that "this man" came to him with a smile on his face as he reached out and said something.

I stopped his story at this point. I opened a kitchen drawer, reached in and pulled out an opened pack of sugarless chewing gum. His eyes opened wide.

"Some people have said that I have a special psychic gift. When I hand you this, you will understand more fully what happened to you last night," I said.

I reached out and put the pack of gum into his hand, and his eyes began to tear up. Why I had said and done this, I was not even sure myself, but the words just came out.

He stated that in his real-life dream, the man who looked like I did, had put the package of chewing gum into his hands. Then, the man in the dream went on to say something to him.

"And the man said that everything would be all right. God loves you," I finished his sentence for him.

The young man let out a gasp. He said that was word for word what the man in his dream had said to him. Those were the exact words that the night before gave him enough hope to continue his journey to Texas. My daughter, who had been watching all this transpire, couldn't believe all that she heard. The kitchen was very quiet for a few moments as we tried to figure out what had taken place. We had just witnessed something incredibly special. We did not have a clue as to how or what had happened or even why.

I gave the young man a hug. We got back into my pickup truck, and I drove him to the best spot to catch a ride heading south on Highway 99. I put a few dollars in his pocket and handed him a raincoat so he would be comfortable. He got out of my truck, and I watched him walk away down the road. He turned one last time to look back at me, sitting there in my truck.

"Thanks," he called out.

"Thank God," I replied.

He walked over to the on-ramp for the highway to continue his journey. I started up my truck and turned around to head home. My eyes were beginning to get moisture in them. I figured it must have been all the rain, but I knew this was much deeper. I knew God had given me a special gift that day.

That happened back in 1991, and I have been sending out prayers for this young man ever since. I do not know his name or where he is, but I know that in some strange and wonderful way our paths had crossed. Our lives have been forever changed because I listened to that voice within me. How many more strangers are waiting out there for others to discover and help? How many are "angels unawares?"

#

Becky as a toddler with her brother, Billy.

Author's note: This was the hardest story to write and the last one I included in this book. I realized how terrible the disease of AIDS really is and how little compassion there is for people who have it. The death of my 30-year-old-niece, Becky, taught me some hard lessons about life and myself.

Goodbye, Becky

My sister's oldest daughter was a wild teenager to say the least. She was no virgin to the world of drugs and sex. She also was very angry at the world and could at times be mean and abusive. Now that Becky was lying before me, dying a slow and painful death, all of her transgressions meant so little to me anymore. I tried to remember that young, innocent girl that I once took to Marine World to ride an elephant. I tried to picture her as a little toddler with that huge smile and healthy laugh. I will always remember her as the little angel she once was.

She was only 30 years old and should have been just starting her life. She had already suffered through a decade of illness with HIV and now full-blown AIDS. I had watched her change over the years from an angry young person to an old and helpless skeleton. My heart was breaking for her. I wondered if someplace along the way I had missed a connection with her. Was there something more that I should have and could have done to help her as her uncle, as her friend, as another human being?

I was at my little sister Marsha's apartment spending time with Becky, as she was now down to her last three or four days of life. She was actually getting stiff, almost as if she were slowly dying from the feet up. I couldn't move her legs; they were locked stiff already. She could barely talk anymore; if she did, it was impossible for me to tell what she said. It all sounded like muffled cries to me. It was so painful to observe her in this sad condition. I was holding back my own emotions so as to not give her any fears, but inside I was repulsed and sickened by the vision of this dying soul in front of me. She looked terrible. Her eyes were sunken into her thin skull; she looked like a WWII photo of a Nazi extermination camp victim.

I held her cold hand, and I knew there was no more hope for her. I believed she was holding on for her little six-year-old daughter, Marcella. She was such a beautiful little girl. I was glad that Becky had been able to take one last trip to Hawaii with her daughter that fall, creating lasting memories for the whole family. That was where she wanted her ashes taken.

I talked to Becky, giving her permission to leave, to give up the body and go "home." She was suffering and in so much pain, I didn't want her to continue living in her present physical state.

I couldn't hold back my emotions any longer. When I left her apartment and got into my car after those last visits with her, tears rolled down my cheeks. I sobbed not only for Becky but for her daughter and for my sister. It was painful for me to continue seeing her in such physical and emotional agony, but I went back each day to offer whatever support I could. I felt so inadequate; I had never had any experience dealing with this kind of killer disease before.

It also hurt that others seemed to be afraid to see or visit her. And God help them if they had to touch her. There was and is a great deal of fear about AIDS and not much compassion for those who have it. I must have heard over and over from people who knew her and from relatives that she got AIDS because of her lifestyle, it was her choice.

That made my heart sick when anyone said that. Where was the compassion?

I was forced to examine my own thinking as well during this time. Had I also been a little less than sympathetic toward people with AIDS or even those with lung cancer who happened to have smoked? They all created their own health problems, but so do overweight people dying of heart attacks. Had I allowed myself to blame these people and thus reduce my compassion level needed for each of them? After all, they were responsible for their own situations, weren't they? Watching her dying taught me as much about my own self as it did about others.

When Becky finally died in the early morning hours just a little over a week before Christmas Day, I felt such relief for her. I knew that her suffering was over.

Now when I hear about someone with AIDS, I have a whole different attitude. And I will never tell a person with lung cancer that it was their own fault, that their smoking did it to them. Too bad it took the death of my niece Becky to educate me on the necessity for compassion for everyone.

Author's footnote: The following was from the memorial service I gave Becky at my house just days before Christmas.

Thoughts and Remembrances A Celebration of Becky

Becky would not want us to be saddened or spend our holidays weeping, not at this most holy and joyful time of the year. She did not want a funeral or people with black clothing and solemn faces and words mourning her. So, I am here to honor those wishes of Becky's to facilitate and participate in a celebration and remembrance of her life, not her death.

Becky left us to go home once again. I am sure that if she could be heard by all of us right now, she would tell us to get down and party. She believed in life being eternal. She believed in the power of God's love. I hope all of us here today share those same beliefs and can feel the peace that comes from knowing that life is never-ending, and that it does go on and on. And since we are made in the image of God, then we are forever; we are eternal. Life has no beginning nor will it have any ending.

Becky's family links go back to the islands of Hawaii. Her father's family had their roots on those sandy shores. She took pride in being a part of that Hawaiian heritage. Her last trip, just weeks ago, was to go back to Hawaii and to spend time there with her daughter and mother. They watched the most beautiful of sunsets and enjoyed the sounds of the surf washing up on the beaches. She wanted Marcella to share that experience with her. I am sure that is going to be a long and loving memory for Marcella to keep within.

The Hawaiian spirit of aloha fits very well with what we are doing here today. The word has so many meanings including goodbye and love. What better word could we use this day to say farewell, goodbye, and I love you than "Aloha!"

In the old days in Hawaii, death was considered just a journey from these earthly shores. They would think of their loved ones as rowing their outriggers out beyond the reefs and the horizon. They believed that even though they could no longer see that boat, it was still sailing onward in the company of God. So it is now with Becky, and it is we who are on these earthly shores. We must realize that

247

even though she has sailed out beyond our limited horizons, she is more alive than ever and now resides with angels and with her savior, Jesus Christ.

Becky wanted all of us to live our lives with joy and peace this holiday season. That is why this is a celebration and not a memorial service. She wanted all those who came here today to enjoy each other's company and to feel at peace. So with that in mind, she did not want her uncle to go on and on, so enjoy the fellowship of this gathering; eat and drink and be happy. If we party well, I am sure that this will honor her memory and please her.

To her mother, father, daughter, sister, brother, family, and friends, I offer this short prayer.

Heavenly Father,
Bless this family and their friends with peace,
Let them know joy this holiday
Let them feel your love surrounding them
Let them know that life is eternal and everlasting.

We ask you in the name of Jesus,
Amen and Aloha.

Author's note: My cat was more than just a pet; she was my divine friend!

Cat Angel

We once had a very fat and lovable tabby cat called "Critter." She belonged to my son before he left to go into the Army and eventually off to the Gulf War. That is how my wife and I became the caretakers of this furry feline.

Over a short period of time, Critter took over the house not by being bossy but by being so loving. She knew how to get anything she ever wanted just by turning on the old charm. This cat was not a fighter but definitely a lover. She got along with all of the neighborhood cats and dogs, allowing any of them into our yard.

When I went into the garden, she followed me all around, stopping where and when I did. She lay or sat at my feet as I worked in the garden, sometimes almost causing me to trip over her fat little body. She was a people cat and loved to be around us all the time.

I had a room built into the attic space above my garage ceiling. This little room was my sanctuary, a place where I could find quiet for prayer and meditation periods. I put a couple of chairs in there right under the skylight I had installed in the roof. I would sit in one chair and old Critter often wandered up the pull-down steps and climbed onto the other chair, which had a soft cushion on it.

She always lay there, silent and still, no matter how long I was meditating or praying. She really enjoyed being up there with me, as evidenced by her purring. She never left until I was finished, and we went into the house together. If I left the stairs down when I went to work, she often wandered back up there and sat in "her" chair.

I enjoyed her company at night the most. Her nightly routine began when she jumped up on our mattress and pounced along from the foot of the bed to our pillows. She circled around a few times, rubbing her furry body into our faces before she settled down between our heads. I loved to pet her soft body, which started her purring like a small motor. But in order to get any sleep, I had to nudge her toward our feet, where she eventually curled up into a small ball of fur and slept. Around four every morning, she wanted to be let outside for her morning social time.

One day while I was away on a business trip, my wife called me with bad news. Some stray dogs had been running loose and got into our yard. They had attacked and killed our friendly, little tabby cat. My wife said that she was not home when it happened. It was our neighbor who stopped the attack and took the cat to the vet's office where she died. At least we were spared from having to see her bloody body or hearing her cries for help. I felt an emptiness inside because I never got to say goodbye to her. There was no closure for me.

Not long after Critter's death, something happened to help me with my closure. I had been sleeping in late on a cold Sunday morning when I felt a familiar bounce at the end of the mattress. It was followed by the pouncing of little cat-like feet walking up the bed toward my head. I felt the touch of fur on my neck and the back of my head. I could hear the loud purring and feel the warm breathing in my ear of a cat. I reached behind my head expecting to stroke my cat, but when I did, there was nothing there. No cat. No nothing at all.

A gentle current of energy flowed up my spine as I realized what had happened. I knew my cat was no longer alive. Yet, I knew that what I had felt were very real sensations. I knew then that my cat had come back just to say goodbye in the only way a cat angel could. I felt at peace once again. I had my closure.

#

Author's note: There is no way to classify this whole experience; but once again my daughter played a significant role in my life.

Voices, Thunder, Light, Death, and Healing!

It was one of the strangest and most difficult of times for my relatives and family. Our son was in Saudi Arabia with the Army as part of Desert Storm. My wife and I were concerned for his safety. My brother-in-law was on his last leg in his long fight against cancer; and there I was, 3,000 miles away in Washington, D.C.

My family really needed my presence at this time, but my job demanded that I be gone for three weeks that January. I had left knowing that many things could happen while I was gone. The first day away, I got a phone call informing me that my daughter got a speeding ticket. The next day, I got a phone call telling me that she had a skiing accident and hurt her knee so badly that she would need an operation. Later that first week, my wife called again to tell me that she had given permission to allow a young boy, whom I was mentoring, to move into our house. He had been kicked out of his group home and was now 18 years old. A few days after that, I received a phone call informing me that my brother-in-law had died.

That was the background for my first couple of weeks away from home. But the real story is what happened to me during this time. My small hotel room had a desk with an overhead lamp. I put a photo of my guru on the desk so that the light could shine on it when I was meditating in my room. The problem was that the light did not work, no matter how many times I fiddled with it. So, I left the photo there without the light.

Around four in the morning, on the day I later learned that my brother-in-law had passed away, a thunderous sound shook me wide-awake.

"It is only a dream!" thundered words that filled the room.

Then, the light fixture came on by itself, lighting up the photo of my guru. I knew that things would turn out all right, after all, life is only a dream.

When I finally got home, I saw my daughter on crutches and with a temporary cast on her leg. She told me that she needed an operation

251

on her damaged, painful knee, but I informed her that there was nothing wrong with her knee. She gave me a look that asked, "What are you talking about, Dad, are you blind?" I had her go to my old meditation room on the first floor of my house and lie down on the rug. I held her knee with both hands and began to concentrate on pushing energy into her injured knee. I tensed up and my whole body trembled as I visualized energy and light moving into her knee for about three minutes. Then, I rested and told her to stand up and walk. She did just that, leaving the crutches and temporary cast on the carpet.

Later in the week, I took her back to Kaiser Hospital to see a knee specialist. He examined her and stated that there must have been a mistake in the first medical review of her condition. She had nothing wrong with her knee at all. She did not need an operation.

A footnote to this healing took place about a month later at my house. My daughter had fallen down a full flight of stairs. She ended up at the bottom, screaming and crying in great pain. The foster kid we had taken in saw it happen and ran to get me.

When I found her, she was in terrible pain. I could move her whole knee back and forth. I could feel small pieces of cartilage or bones moving around inside her kneecap. Her whole knee seemed to have exploded and was now much worse than the first time she had injured it. However, I told her nothing was wrong with it.

I again began the whole process of taking her into my meditation room and putting my hands on her knee. The pain stopped and she was once again able to get up and walk. She told me she was only about 90 percent better, just a slight stiffness and soreness remained, but nothing that would prevent her from doing normal physical activities. The knee was on its way back to normal health. For whatever the reason, she had to go through the injury and healing process twice. Maybe that is what she needed to really believe that the first time was not a wrong diagnosis by the doctor, but that it had indeed been a real healing.

#

Author's note: I loved this story that my son was able to share with me as my real Christmas gift.

The Prodigal Son (A Christmas Story)

Several years ago my son, Josh, who is a police officer, gave me a most wonderful gift. I had asked him to do a kind deed for the Christmas holidays; then, tell me about it, if he could, and that would be his gift to me. I really did not want anything that he could buy me. I wanted him to experience the gift that comes from giving of one's self. Let me tell you what happened one cold, wet December 25th.

My son had been patrolling in his squad car along U.S. Highway 101, just up from the Golden Gate Bridge. It was raining and fairly cold outside as he cruised along looking for any signs of trouble on this Christmas morning. He was not really that happy about working the holidays, but it went with the territory. He noticed a young man walking along the side of the freeway. Not only was it dangerous but also illegal.

He pulled over, put on his lights, and called the young man over to the car. When the man stood close to him, he could see they were about the same age. When he checked his identification and had the dispatcher run a check on him, he found out he was only 22 years old and was on parole. The report said that he had been out of prison for a couple of months.

Upon questioning, the young man stated that he had no place to go. He had been living along the freeway, sleeping under overpasses. He was all wet and very dirty. My son did not want to cite him or gave him a bad time, especially since it was Christmas morning. He took the guy a short distance off the freeway so that he might not be in as much danger of getting hit by passing cars.

He again looked at the report and noticed that the address listed was no more than two or three miles from where he had been sleeping on the freeway. The young man told him that it was his parent's house, but they had no idea where he was or what had happened to him for the last four years. He said he was afraid to go home and see them since he had been in so much trouble and had been in prison. He felt much shame and guilt about it. He would rather live on the streets alone than be rejected by his parents.

My son was not going to let the possibility of a reunion on Christmas Day slip away. So, he had the man sit in the back of the squad car, and off they drove. The address was in an upscale Mill Valley neighborhood where million-dollar homes were the norm. My son located the address of record and stopped in front of an expensive home. The nervous young man wanted to leave. My son left him in the back seat and went to knock on the door.

He was not sure what type of reception he might receive. He had dealt with cases where the parents had thrown out their son and did not want anything to do with him ever again. He also thought about the possibility that these people could get upset with him for attempting the reunion. If they called his sergeant, he could be written up for not following policy and procedures. He kept telling himself that it was, after all, Christmas Day. He had to at least attempt to drop off this young man here. He could not bear thinking that this guy who was about his own age would be sleeping out in the rain on the most holy of holidays. He knocked on the front door and put his faith and the outcome in the hands of God.

It was about 7 a.m., and lights came on inside the house a few seconds after he knocked. The door latches clicked, and an older man stood there looking at my son in his police uniform. My son quickly got to the point of the visit. He told the man that he had found his son wandering along the highway and asked him if it was all right to leave him there.

The man's eyes grew wet as he yelled for his wife to come to the door. The man shook his head to affirm that it was okay to leave his son. The parents stood in the doorway, looking at the young man who was looking out from the back seat of the police car. Everyone was visibly shaken by the turn of events. They had been sad on this Christmas morning, as they had been for the past four years, not knowing if their son were alive or dead. They did not care about gifts or money; they missed their son. Now their prayer for the holidays was actually coming true.

My son walked back and opened the door to let out the young man. He walked slowly toward the house. My son watched from the curb as they joined together in a hug. He could see the love and joy as the three of them cried, then disappeared inside. He stood there wondering at how it had all turned out. He got back in his patrol car and sat there for a few minutes. He drove off knowing that he was going to have that gift of a good deed to tell his dad.

#

Josh, Syd, and Spencer McDonald, 2001.

W.H. McDonald Jr.

Author's note: I had never felt so much love in all my life as I did when my church friends had a special prayer and meditation night for me. There is so much power in prayers but also so much LOVE!

Surrounded by Love

On the morning of August 15, 1998, I had reached what I thought was the end of my ropes. I could no longer endure the pain and suffering alone. In the early morning hours, I sat at my computer and sent out a message that was a cry for help to my closest church friends. These people were going to see a much different side of me than they ever had before.

I have always been a strong pillar in times of crises or emergencies. I was raised to suffer quietly alone, never asking anyone for help. I was always the giver. I was the one who was there for the other guy, the one who visited and prayed for the sick, the one who gave or did whatever it took to lend assistance to those in need.

In Vietnam, during the war, I was the one who stayed calm under fire. I was the one who took the risks to give aid to the wounded. I was the one who never showed any soft emotions—men do not cry and men do not need hugs! On this hot summer morning as I sat there in great pain, I opened up a part of myself that I had never explored. I was going to tell my closest friends that I was weak and in need of their love. I was concerned that my tough-guy image would be ruined forever. The following is some of the edited e-mail message I sent out that morning:

Friends,
My skin cancer treatments have become very aggressive and painful. I just wanted to ask you guys for your supporting prayers. My face is very raw and painful this morning. I am feeling like I need a group hug to keep going on. So, when you are doing your meditations, take a few minutes and send me some of your loving energy. I must admit that my inner child wants to cry this morning, but that macho guy on the outside will not allow him to do that.

256

I got up after not sleeping very well and showered. It was all I could do to stand the pain as the water hit my face. I let the water run over it for over an hour to get off all the old scabs and skin. My face bled and really hurt. It is still bleeding now.

I cannot breathe without it causing me pain. My face feels like it is in a frying pan. It is so sore and raw from the treatments I have been taking for the last five weeks. The face no longer seems to have any surface skin on it—it looks like raw meat that is all bloody. I am unable to continue this treatment because it is just too painful to do so. I must see my doctor as soon as possible.

I feel like such a wimp this morning. Me, the guy who faced 500 North Vietnamese with just an M-60 machine gun on my hip and a few thousand rounds of ammo; me, who is not afraid to jump out of an airplane or face troubles head-on. Now, I am admitting that I am in so much pain and discomfort that I no longer care about curing this cancer. I just want the pain to stop! I sure hope that this does not destroy my image, but this morning I just feel like rolling over and saying enough is enough!

Okay, I know it is the lack of sleep and all the pain that is talking here, but this tough guy is listening to his inner child this morning, and that child wants to sit down and cry his little old heart out!

Anyway, I am just feeling sorry for myself this morning and am reaching out for some hugs. Even tough guys want to be hugged once in a while. I just needed to share with you this morning; hope none of you minded being a part of my coping process. I just wanted someone to listen to me. I guess I am still a little boy on the inside. It just seems to be easier to handle this pain if others care about you. Thanks for listening to me this morning.

Your friend, Billy

I had been battling this skin cancer problem since 1980, but it was only getting worse. When I went to my dermatologist that July, she told me that unless we took some very aggressive treatments immediately, I might lose my nose to the cancer. This meant having to surgically remove all or a large part of my nose. The thought of dying never bothered me, but having my nose cut off and disfiguring my face made me depressed. Call it vanity or ego, but I kind of liked my nose just the way it was, right in the middle of my face.

I began the treatment during the hot summer of 1998. As the Sacramento Valley was having record hot temperatures, the chemicals were slowly burning my face. I was willing to endure whatever I had to do to save my face. By the third week of the treatment, my face was beginning to bleed and was all blistered. When I showered, pieces of my flesh fell from my face and nose. It was very raw and hurt so badly, but I continued doing what the doctor told me to do.

What the doctor did not know was that by week three, my face was totally infected with two different infections: one was a bacterial infection and the other was a herpes virus that covered my entire face and nose. Around my eyes it was so crusted from the infection that it hurt to open and close my eyes. This treatment was to continue for three months, and I was only in week three and already in trouble.

I kept calling my HMO to see my doctor, but I kept getting the advice nurse. She told me that I was okay and to continue the treatments. I kept calling back trying to talk to the doctor. The nurse told me that the doctor was very comfortable with my treatment, and I was to continue.

My face looked so bad by week five that I looked as if I were wearing a Halloween mask. I kept going to work but was having a difficult time concentrating on my job. Finally, I reached that weekend when I lost control of my tough-guy image and sent out that e-mail message. After that, all kinds of things began to happen. When I went to church service the following Sunday, I was amazed at the reception I got from close friends as well as from others I really did not know. My friends had shared my message with other concerned and caring people. What I was beginning to feel that day continued to grow into the most precious moments I had ever had in all of my then 52 years of life.

When the word got around that I was asking for prayers, people began to send phone calls, letters and cards, e-mail, and prays my way. I was still in great pain, but within me there were great things taking place. The healing processes were going to start with my emotional and spiritual illnesses first, a healing from the inside before the outside.

The day after the services, I went to my HMO and demanded to be seen by a new doctor. I made an early morning appointment, and when I saw the new doctor, I felt my guru was working behind the scenes on this. In walked a young, beautiful Indian doctor. She took just one look at my face and knew what the problem was. She cut off some of the flesh to run tests on it, but she was sure it was both a viral and a bacterial infection. I felt confident that my situation was going to change for the better. She stopped my previous treatment altogether and put me on medication for the infection. She also told me not to go back to work. Had I waited much longer to get this treated, I could have been disfigured. I went home to rest and recover. My body was completely exhausted, and I had no energy to do anything. I was still having a great deal of pain, and I was unable to sleep for several days. Nevertheless, I felt that I was on the road to recovery even if it was a slow cure.

The following Tuesday, I got some messages about a special healing prayer service at the chapel that night. Two dozen members of the Sacramento Meditation Center got together for the purpose of praying for me and sending me healing energy and love.

I was deeply touched by the actions of these people. I had never had other human beings do anything like that for me. I reached out to them that night as I sat in my own home, allowing their love to flow my way. I felt surrounded by so much love coming at me at once. I felt loved and as if the universe were giving me a hug. The energies they were sending me from the chapel hit me with full force some 25 miles away. I even forgot about my pain. I thought about it the next day while looking into the mirror; then, I remembered the pain, and it came back. So, I decided not to spend much time looking in the mirror, and not to think about the pain.

During the next few days, I felt like a child wrapped in the arms of a loving mother. I wanted to let the others know what I was feeling, so I wrote a poem and sent it out to them. This is the first verse:

Enclosed in the Hands of God

Stepping out from my long sleep,
I finally opened my eyes
And found myself enclosed
And wrapped in the loving hands of God.
Oh, how long was I asleep?
How deep was my darkness?
Love completely surrounds me
Now that I know ALL
Is but a part of you, Lord.

I had never felt so loved by so many people in my whole life. I felt much peace and joy within. I began to see things about myself and the illness that helped me come to a realization. Before the cancer treatment, I was only a giver and never a receiver. It was as if I had been unworthy of such a gift. The love I was feeling and that was being expressed from others showed me that love is really a cycle. In order to complete this spiritual cycle, you cannot just have people willing to give, but you need someone to be open and receptive to receive all that love and healing energy. If you are not willing to receive, you are not completing the cycle, and you stop the flow of love and energy. I found this thought most interesting, and it brought me much peace.

During this time, I was able to open up some old childhood wounds and explore my past while being held in this envelope of peace and love that I was experiencing. While in this process, I discovered that my healing was not for me alone. From the e-mail and other communications I received, it was obvious that others were being touched in their own ways. People began to open up and share parts of themselves that had remained hidden from me. The door was open for healing to come to many of the group. Many who had sent me so much love and healing energy were now engulfed in a healing process themselves.

Each day during my convalescence, I heard stories about how my illness and healing had affected others in some positive way. It was really very amazing how all this was unfolding. I also was getting better each day. The pain went away, and in just a matter of days my face began to really heal. I continued to feel so much peace and love. Let me share some excerpts from the following e-mail message I sent out to those praying for me during this period:

> Prayer Circle,
> Last night I felt so loved and full of peace. Those of you who have been praying and sending me energy have succeeded far beyond your realization. I felt as if I was in a cocoon of love all night long. I had a great sleep and awoke this morning with my face looking even better than yesterday. It is okay to look in the mirror now. The infections are losing their battle to all your energy and the power of your love.
> You guys are better than family; no, you guys are family in the real sense. I feel so much closer to all of you.
> I am filled with awe and joy this morning. I wanted to share this with all of you, so you can realize how powerful your prayers have been. We are not talking just on the physical level but deeper within me there has been great healing. You are all a part of this drama and all a part of my "good karma."
> Billy.

I have learned so much from this experience. Yes, there was pain, but in the end I found that all that pain was nothing more than "spiritual growing pains" as I continued to grow. I can honestly say that I would not have changed anything that happened to me. I would not give up a minute of the pain if it meant giving back all that I had learned and experienced. Being loved by others is truly the greatest healing gift God can give us. The love that surrounded me during my illness made me feel that God's own loving hands had caressed me.

#

Author's note: This is a follow up to my five-month battle with skin cancer and my recovery, although it may not sound like it.

The End of the Rainbow

We had been married almost 30 years when my wife and I decided to take a trip to Washington and Oregon in the early autumn. We packed my pickup truck with clothing and items for the trip; of course, my wife always ensures that we have plenty of snacks and drinks along the way. We took in some wonderfully beautiful sights on this trip along the Columbia River Gorge. We spent a couple of days exploring waterfalls and hiking in the rain forests. I believe that there are few places on earth that can surpass this area for its pure breathtaking beauty.

We headed north, driving along a road that took us toward Mount St. Helens National Volcanic Monument. It was rainy outside as we wound through a landscape of both destruction and regeneration. It reminded me of nature's own life and death mosaic, representing the struggle for all life. It was all so symbolic, as I had just spent five months off work fighting to recover and heal from my skin cancer. I was taking this trip partly to help regenerate the inner joy I have always felt for life.

As we were driving up one hill, we looked out our car window and saw a bright, deeply-hued rainbow that stretched across the entire horizon as far as we could dream. I thought that this was a very special mystical vision of color and hope. I felt differently about this rainbow than any I had ever seen.

I thought about how destructive the skin cancer had been to my face and how I must have looked to others. I could hardly bear to look in the mirror because my face had become so disfigured by my battles with this disease. My face was much like Mount St. Helens, having been almost destroyed, but now it was in that regenerative state where I was getting new skin and overall renewed health.

I was looking at the rainbow, the promise of hope and second chances, when the strangest thing happened. As my wife and I were watching the rainbow, we reached the peak of the hill and saw the actual end of the rainbow hitting the road just ahead of the truck. Of course, that was not possible, so I expected to see the rainbow image keep moving out in front of our view. Now, here is where it got strange; we actually drove right past and under the rainbow. It was suddenly directly behind us. We had actually seen what we knew to be the very beginning of the rainbow hitting the ground; then, somehow we had magically driven directly under it.

I have never known anyone who has found the actual end of any rainbow. In fact, I always thought it was impossible to find let alone go under, but on this rainy day on the road to Mount St. Helens Volcano, we both experienced a very special moment. It was then that I knew real healing was taking place within me. I felt renewed with joy and peace about my own life once again. I knew that rainbow was both a sign and a gift to my very own spirit.

#

Author's note: This happened at work when I was with the type of guy who doesn't believe in these kinds of things at all. That is what made it even more special for me.

The Car Crash That Never Happened

I remember the moment as if it were yesterday, but I still do not understand what happened or why. If there had been no other witnesses to what happened that day, I would be questioning myself about what I thought I saw.

Let me start at the beginning of this story. My work as a senior safety specialist with the USPS (United States Postal Service) took me to the little valley town of Modesto, California. I went there with Sam, a fellow safety specialist and good friend. Sam was driving about 45 miles per hour in our government staff car as we headed down a busy street on our way to one of the post offices across town. Everything seemed normal and ordinary that morning.

When we entered the middle of an intersection, a large 24-foot recreational vehicle turned directly across our path. It must have happened very fast, but at the time, it all seemed to be in slow motion. It felt like several minutes for us to move forward just a few feet.

I remember looking directly into the eyes of the RV driver as we were just a few feet from impacting the front section of his traveling home. I could see there was no way to avoid a major collision. At our speed, we were certain to be seriously injured or worse. I was an' expert on safety and knew from my years of accident investigations that this was going to be a bad crash. There was no time for Sam to brake or slow down.

I was frozen with anticipation of what was supposed to happen next. What is odd is that everything should have been happening in mere hundredths of a second. But, I seemed to have had plenty of time to think, and all I could think of was God's love. As we reached the point where the two vehicles should have impacted, the RV disappeared from our view. We passed directly through where it should have been on the road, and we were instantly past the point of collision. We looked back to see that the RV was now on the other side of the road.

Sam made a quick U-turn and headed back to where the RV driver was pulling into a parking lot to get his breath back. We pulled up next to him and sat there for a few moments looking at each other before we got out of the car. We asked the RV driver if he had seen what we thought we had witnessed. We all agreed that we should have hit in that intersection. We all should have been either killed or injured, not standing in the parking lot safe and unscratched.

The driver of the RV confirmed that he thought it was impossible for us to have not hit the side of his RV. We all agreed there was no way it could have been avoided—but it didn't happen! The driver said he saw us; in fact, he had been looking directly into my eyes. The next thing he knew was that his RV was out of the way. It was as if we had passed directly through where he was, he said.

Sam and I sat in the car for a few minutes gathering our thoughts. We both knew from all of our training and experience that what had happened was not explainable, nor were there any logical reasons for it. It was a moment in our lives that defied time and space. It was as if we had gone through the RV or it had jumped out of our way. In either case, we felt that there were powers at work in the universe that had saved us from a terrible fate. I felt that God was once again protecting me, and I felt blessed to have experienced this moment. It truly was a gift.

#

Author's note: I feel that I have had a special bond with my first grandson, Spencer, even before he was born. I seemed to have been picking up energy from him even prior to his birth. I was able to go into the delivery room just several minutes after my daughter-in-law gave birth. They were still cleaning him up and had just put him down in a bassinet. I was close by looking at him when he turned his face toward me. We made eye contact and held it for the longest time. It was like acknowledging an old friend back to the family. It just had that kind of feeling. The two instances in the following story may at first seem totally unrelated to what I have just said, but my feeling is that they are connected somehow.

Two Encounters with Tibetan Monks

I went to an art show in San Francisco to view paintings by a famous European artist. I really wanted to see the show, and my sister-in-law invited me to come along with her.

At the end of the row of art exhibits there were several Tibetan monks working on a sand painting of a holy symbol. They had already spent a couple of weeks on the design and were going to keep working on it until it was finished in another two weeks. When I saw the scene, I immediately flashed to a dream that I'd had that week. In this dream there was a wild, crazy woman who jumped up on the monks' platform and messed up their art. I saw it as clear as day in my mind as I thought of my dream.

We left the museum while they were still adding more grains of sand to their sacred artwork. That would have been the end of it, but the next day I read in the newspaper that some angry woman, acting in an insane fit of rage, had jumped onto the platform and destroyed all of the religious sand art. She had to be pulled off the platform and restrained. The story went on to say how the monks just quietly swept away the old sand and began to create a new holy symbol made of sand. Her protest didn't seem to upset them at all.

Several years later, my wife and I were driving back up to Truckee to take our 10-month-old grandson home after we'd had him for a couple of days at our house. We stopped at a rest area so we could change a dirty diaper on a picnic table. We chose to stay a little

266

farther away from the crowd, so we went to the end of the rest area with our diapers and grandson in tow. Carol had him lying down and in the process of getting changed when I felt someone looking at us. I looked around and then down the hill at a group of four Tibetan monks all wrapped in their orange robes. One of them was standing, facing my direction, but he was focused on my grandson, Spencer. He saw me looking, and he smiled while he bowed slightly with his hands together as if he were in prayer. He had old wooden prayer beads hanging from his neck (these beads are used by the monks to count their repetitions of prayers or their mantra that is chanted silently or out loud). His head was clean-shaven and smooth, but it was his eyes that caught my attention; they radiated a smile. We both stood looking at each other for several comfortable moments; then, I returned the same folded-hands greeting gesture that he had given to me.

He put one hand up as if to bless us and say goodbye. I looked at my grandson who was now standing up on the tabletop and holding onto my wife's hand. Spencer was focused on the monks down the hill as he returned their smiles. We got back in the car and drove off, but I could not shake the good feeling that something special might have just happened. It was all very gentle and causal, as if it were normal. But how often do you meet four traveling Tibetan monks at a roadside rest area on your way to Truckee; I know it was only once in a lifetime for us.

#

Spencer surrounded and protected by his parents.

Author's note: My best friend from childhood was Bob Brooks. Our association goes way back to third grade in Sunnyvale, California. We went through all of school together as friends and then went our separate paths for a while; he went on to college and I went to Vietnam. However, we were always friends even when we did not see or hear from each other for years at a time. I also knew his sister, Sharon, and had actually become great friends with her in the last decade of her life. No recalling of my life journey would be complete if I did not relate some of the experiences that I shared with this family.

Sharon and the Butterflies

All of us were at the Carter Center in Atlanta, Georgia, to listen to President Jimmy Carter talk about our dear friend Sharon Brooks. President Carter was naming and dedicating to her the only lake at the Carter Center. This was really a great honor, and Karen Wilson and I were there to support our old friend and Sharon's brother, Bob. He was there with his wife and about 25 others in a private ceremony. What also made this an interesting moment was that I had brought a guest with me, Robert Reese, with whom I had traveled back to Vietnam a couple of months before.

I was sitting next to Karen, remembering when I had first met Sharon and her family back in the 1950s. They had moved next door to my mother's old high school friends, and so there was a connection between all of us even back then. I became good friends with Bob, and it wasn't until my last year in high school that I paid attention to his little sister (she was just one year younger).

The first summer out of high school I had moved to Hawaii. It was there one week that Bob, his sister, and parents got together with me to tour the island of Oahu. I was working my butt off at minimum wage jobs to live there, much in contrast to their flying over on free airline tickets (Mr. Brooks worked for United Airlines as a pilot) and staying at a ritzy hotel. We went around the island, and I couldn't believe how bored Sharon was acting. That was my last impression of her until a family crisis brought us all together again many years later.

269

Sharon was working for President Jimmy Carter in the White House when her mother took an overdose of several poisons in order to kill herself. She didn't die right away, but was comatose. Her death was a slow process for everyone involved. I was at the hospital every day or night and spent time with Sharon's father. Mr. Brooks and I became much closer during this week than I ever expected. He confided things to me that he was uncomfortable talking about with his children. He knew that his shared information was safe with me, and I continue to honor his wishes.

Sharon's mother had taken her life, and it changed the chemistry of the whole family in ways that would only come out later. Sharon and I talked during this time, and she often invited me to have a lunch or dinner in the White House, but I couldn't afford to fly back there with my family. Soon our correspondence ended, and she and I went back to our separate lives once again.

The next time I saw Sharon was a few years later at her father's funeral in San Jose. Something very special happened that day that I will never forget.

When Mr. Brooks' casket was in the church, and the pastor was giving his talk about him, a large Monarch butterfly floated high up by the stained glass windows and the ceiling. The early morning sunlight filtering through the windows cast spotlights on the dancing butterfly.

The minister paused from his prepared speech and pointed out the butterfly to those who had not already become aware of it flying so angelically and free above everyone in the church.

At the gravesite, we noticed another large Monarch butterfly patrolling the skies around us. I tapped Bob on the shoulder and pointed it out to him and Sharon. Soon everyone was smiling and feeling good about the funeral as they watched the butterfly.

After the funeral, we went to Mr. Brooks' house for refreshments and to talk. My wife and I and a small gathering of close friends from high school were there with Bob and Sharon and their families. Then, it happened again. To my great amazement and delight, another butterfly was inside the house and flying around the room. It came and sat on my shoulder. I got chills up and down my spine. I put it on my finger and sent it off to fly around the room. Eventually, we decided to let it go free and soar to the heavens. It seemed like the right thing to do.

Now, I was sitting there listening to President Jimmy Carter talk about my old friend and how valuable she was to his administration. I kept thinking back to how she had ended her own life almost 20 years after her mother's suicide.

I felt bad because during the last few months of her life, I felt that this was what she had intended to do; even my friend Karen knew it. I had flown all the way back to Washington, D.C. right after she quit working for President Bill Clinton and talked to her. I spent a week trying my best to change her fate. I told her I thought she was going to do this, but she protested and said, no, she wasn't. I knew that she was depressed. I could feel the end coming. I knew it was going to happen, and yet I was helpless to stop it!

So there I sat, thinking about Sharon and the fact that I could not stop her suicide. I felt a great sadness. I looked up and her brother, Bob, was speaking to the group and to President Carter who was now sitting down with his wife just in front of me. Behind Bob and out of his sight was a large Monarch butterfly flying gracefully over the lake and around the back of his head. I smiled and poked Karen who was sitting next to me, but she was already smiling. I knew then that everything was as it should be at that moment. I sat back and sent Sharon my prayers.

Author's footnote: At the memorial service in California that Bob had given for his sister Sharon, there was a comforting event that took place. We had pulled into the parking lot where the memorial service was to be held. I was with my old high school friends Karen and Mahaila. I had just been explaining to them about the importance of owls and their symbolism in my spiritual life. I had given them a few examples of how they have appeared to me at various times to give me comfort, a message, or reassurance that what was happening would be all right.

We were standing next to the car in the parking lot when I noticed the tall chapel bell tower. There, up high on the ledge was a huge owl, hooting for her mate. A second owl, apparently her mate, appeared. They began to mate right there in the broad daylight on the ledge.

We were all fascinated by the possible spiritual connections with Sharon. We wondered why owls would be out in the daytime having sex. It was not something that most people have seen.

It occurred to me that sex represented the creation of life and this was perhaps Sharon's way of letting her best friends know that she was still eternally alive. I shared this thought with both of them. Mahaila fully agreed. We intently watched the owls, which everyone else seemed to totally miss or ignore, for several minutes until they both disappeared inside the bell tower. I felt at peace and knew intuitively that Sharon was okay.

#

Sharon's Suicide

I stare at my monitor screen
Still expecting you to answer
My last e-mails.

I am hesitant to delete
Your e-mail address,
It would leave me without
A gravesite or place of entombment
To kneel at and whisper
To you my words
Of poetry and love.

You never answered
My last e-mail.
Were you already fading beyond
Into that darkness?

I wish I could have held you
Just once more,
To tell you
How much we all loved you.

But you had already
Bought a ticket out,
And you did not want to wait,
So you left us all a note
And so many wonderful memories.

But I would
Rather have you here tonight.

Notes are such a lousy way
To say goodbye
Forever!

#
For Sharon Brooks
273

W.H. McDonald Jr.

Part 4

Return to Vietnam, 2002

The Peace Patrol with an NVA Veteran.
Bill McDonald, NVA veteran, Robert Reese,
Richard Webster, and Dave Gallo.

"Sometimes you need to go back to the old battlefields to embrace your enemies, so you can move forward with the rest of your life."
Bill McDonald—Memorial Day Speech, 2002

Vietnam during the war years.

The Peace Patrol
Dave Gallo, Bill McDonald, Robert Reese, and Richard Webster with
Vietnamese greeters.

Author's note: I finally went back to Vietnam in April and May of 2002 with three other veterans. We called ourselves "The Peace Patrol." The local NBC TV station interviewed me before I left and when I returned. It was a trip of a lifetime, and no one was shooting at us!

The Flight Back to Nam—The Flight from Hell, Part II

I was planning on going to India that year for a couple of months, but the events of 9-1-1 changed that when my tour company cancelled the trip. I now had the time and the money and no scheduled place to go. So, it was fortunate that I happened upon a website of a small group of veterans who were planning on returning to Nam in the spring of 2002.

A veteran named Dave Gallo of San Francisco had put together a nice tour package for interested veterans. The final group consisted of him, me, and two other veterans, Richard Webster from Illinois, and Robert Reese from Georgia. We had all served in the same basic area of operation in Vietnam during the war. They were all former members of the 1st Infantry Division. Each of our reasons for going back were individual, but all of us wanted to see what had happened to the old base camps, the battlefields, and most important, the people. We also wanted to go to make peace with ourselves and to see what had happened there since the end of the war.

The beginning of our trip felt as if I were reliving my first Pacific crossing to Nam back in 1966. This flight was going to make me wonder about my sanity for going on this journey.

The plan was for me to meet everyone at the airport for our flight, which left about 30 minutes after midnight. I got there way too early, thinking that I could check in at the airline ticket counter to get rid of my bags and go relax. I found out that they didn't even open until a couple of hours prior to the flight. I had nothing to do all afternoon but sit around with my baggage. My old classmate and friend Karen, who sent me off the first time I went to Nam, wanted to carry on the tradition, so she came to the airport and had dinner with me.

Eventually, I was able to check in. I said goodbye to Karen and went to the boarding area where I met my fellow travelers for the first time. I was instantly impressed with the guys I would be spending the next three weeks with. I felt good, but I had a nagging feeling about getting on this airplane. I chalked it all up to a case of emotions since I was going back to a place and time in my life that might open some emotional and spiritual wounds once again.

As I waited to board, the nagging got even worse. Something was wrong with this flight, I knew it. Once I was on the plane and it lifted off the runway, there was nothing I was going to be able to do about it.

The plane was full and I was uncomfortable already, and we had only begun. There was not that much space for my legs or my butt, and I am a little guy. I tried to take my mind off of it and thought back to my original flight back in 1966. That was a big mistake because that "flight from hell" was plagued with nothing but troubles.

I tried to sleep and forget about it, but it kept coming back to me that something was wrong with the flight. I looked out of the window and saw jet fuel freely flowing from the wing tanks. It looked as if someone were pumping the fuel out of the tanks to lighten the load for a landing or to crash. We were over the Pacific Ocean, two and a half hours from the coast of California, so landing did not sound like a great option. My mind was really going to town with this. I poked my travel mate Robert and told him what I saw. He looked out and confirmed what I was worried about as the aircraft was making a slow180 degree turn. The captain spoke over the intercom, telling everyone that they were experiencing "some minor technical difficulties," and we were returning to the San Francisco Airport.

I was wondering why we had flown so far out over the Pacific Ocean before turning around to return to where we had begun. That was five hours going nowhere! It had to be more than a "technical problem." I wondered what might happen next.

We finally arrived off the coast of California and circled around the Bay Area sky several times. I looked down at the airport and saw the red flashing lights of emergency vehicles sitting at the edge of the runway. I assumed it was for our landing. That didn't make me feel good about the "minor technical difficulties."

We finally made our approach and touched down. I was relieved to be on the ground, even if it was where we had started. I went forward to ask what had happened. The door to the flight cabin was open, so we could hear some of the conversation about a broken windshield. The "minor technical difficulties" were their concerns about having the windshield blown out and sucking all of them out of the cockpit. I am glad that I didn't know all of this while we were still in the air.

We had to find a place to sleep for half a day before catching a late afternoon flight to Hong Kong. We missed all our connections and had to spend a night there as well. By the time we got to Vietnam, it was already a two-day adventure. I was tired and was still wearing the same clothing since all of my bags were on the original airplane. I wondered what great adventures awaited us. I was ready for anything.

Welcome back to Nam!

#

Bill with former VC double agent and his family.
Tano, the guide, on far right.

Author's note: Meeting old enemy veterans whom we had fought against was like meeting old friends. There is a unique bond of fellowship and brotherhood between old warriors.

A Dream Reunion in the Iron Triangle

We found the weather just as we remembered it, hot and humid. The humidity was the biggest factor, as my shirt seemed to be glued to my skin. However, in this modern, present-day Vietnam, there was air conditioning in our rooms and even in the van that we were taking around the countryside. Thank God for the blessings of civilization!

We stayed a short while in Saigon before heading out to see the country that we all thought we knew. Each of us wanted to see where we had been stationed, so each day we went to see our old base camps, airfields, and battlegrounds. It was amazing how much everything had changed, and for the better. Old airfields were now reclaimed fields of natural grasses and trees. Base camps were either completely gone or now occupied by the new People's Army, which was the case for Phu Loi, my old base camp.

On one of our trips through our old area of operation, we were heading back to Saigon down old Highway 13, Thunder Road as we called it back then. This road travels right through the heart of the old "Iron Triangle," where I was shot down on April 16, 1967. It was now April 18, 2002, and it seemed like a strange anniversary. As we drove down the road, I had a flashback of a dream I'd had 10 years before. I had dreamed about this trip down this road and a house that was on it. In my dream we had stopped to chat with an old VC veteran and his family who invited us inside his house. I could still see the images from the long ago dream. I was getting that feeling that I had been here before in the dream experience.

I told Dave, who was leading the tour, that I wanted to stop up ahead at one of those houses along the road to talk to the people and possibly to go inside. He looked at me with an odd half smile and said something about that being strange because he was about to have the driver stop so we could do exactly that. Dave had planned on stopping at this veteran's house, which was across the road from a destroyed ARVN tank that had been left as a monument of the war.

Dave told me that he always stopped at this vet's home for the tours he gave to American veterans. The man was a former VC officer and a double agent. During the daytime he had been an ARVN (South Vietnamese Army) veterinarian doctor who took care of the guard dogs and other animals. At night, he rendered first aid and medical care to the VC in the tunnels.

Dave was a little shocked by the timing of my request to stop, as we were only a short distance from the house. He had never informed us about this extra stop on our journey. He wanted to surprise us with this visit when we got there. I told Dave that I had already seen this in a dream. I am not sure what he thought about that statement at the time.

We stopped, and the three of us played around on the old tank and took photos. Dave went across the street to see the Vietnamese veteran and get us an invitation to come over. He cordially invited all of us into his home. There was an outside courtyard in front of his home that led to his front door. Decorated with fresh flowers, a small personal shrine to Buddha sat near his doorstep.

When we walked inside, we faced another altar with religious pictures and statues. There was a table next to it where we sat down. His lovely wife, who stood less than five feet tall and was about 70 years old, brought us each a glass with ice cubes. She also gave us each a bottle of American cola. I would normally avoid drinking anything with ice in a third world country, but this was given with so much loving care that I was not about to insult them by refusing it.

We went on to have a wonderful conversation about what he did during the war years and how that affected his family. He asked us about America, where we lived, and what we did. His daughter and a grandchild also came in to see us. Spending that afternoon with him and his family was a pleasant experience, and I was happy to have had such a unique opportunity.

It was hard to believe that 35 years before I had crashed no more than a few hundred yards from his home, and he had been my enemy. Now we were sharing a soda with ice in what used to be the least secure place in all of Vietnam. This was where the Japanese and then the French had lost hundreds of men well before the Americans set foot there and lost lives as well. It had been a stronghold for the VC, as they had always owned this territory. The irony of it amused me, but also made me feel good that real recovery from any war is possible. Here were all of us old warriors sitting around a former VC's dinner table talking about our grandchildren. What a difference 35 years made!

We got up to leave and went out to his courtyard for photos. He wanted to have us in his photos with his family. I told him that I had dreamed about his house and his family and this day's events some 10 years before. He and his wife lovingly looked at me, and he replied, "Yes, I believe that is true." Neither one of them doubted nor even thought it was strange that I had made that statement. It was as if I had said the sky is blue. They fully understood what I had told them, and both of them gave me long hug.

I left there feeling much better about life, the aftermath of wars, and the hope that people could learn to live together in peace. This showed me that forgiveness and understanding were as much a part of nature as were the devastated forests and jungles of Vietnam that are growing back. I still can see that old man's face with his smiling wife at his side. They have lived through a history of violent times and events and seemed none the worse for it. In fact, they seemed to enjoy life. There was no bitterness about the many years he had spent fighting the Japanese, the French, the Americans, his own countrymen, and the Cambodians. To him and his family, those wars were long over. He now lived in the present moment, and that has been his secret to finding peace within.

#

The famous Peace Patrol

Author's note: This was such a simple act, but it seemed to have a much bigger meaning and impact on our communist escorts than anything else we could have said or done to impress them.

A Sacred Ceremony in an Old Graveyard

Our group had just come back from spending an afternoon along the Cambodian border area looking at the old Viet Cong headquarters. These were the same headquarters that were hidden from us during the long years of the war. Now it is a national historic site.

We had to have special permission to see this historic site; and as it turned out, we were the only tourists there that day. Part of the required procedure for visiting that area was we had to pay two young communist "expert tour guides." It was more about them watching us than guiding us around. We already had a tour guide and a driver, now there was one Vietnamese guide for each of the four of us. One of the young communists had a camera to take our photos for a local publication, he told us.

We did not let any of the red tape or bureaucratic crap get to us; we played the games and enjoyed ourselves. After all, we were not spies or the enemy. We established a good and warm relationship with these three men and one woman.

On the way back to our hotel, after spending a long and exhausting day in the jungle, it was beginning to get dark. I wanted to visit one of the war graveyards that was off the highway we were on. The one we stopped at had huge Soviet-made statues that looked very impressive as they cast long shadows over the graves at sunset.

We convinced the group to get out so we could walk around and visit the graves. This particular cemetery was filled with soldiers from both VC and NVA units. The dates on the gravestones indicated that our own wartime units had possibly killed these men and women. It seemed that each of us had some direct or indirect responsibility for those buried there. It was rather emotionally moving to think about it in that way. We decided that we could not ignore what had happened to their warriors as well as ours. We decided to perform a simple ceremony to honor all of those killed from both sides.

Darkness had fallen on the cemetery by the time we got a large handful of incense together. Our guide, Tano, lit the bundle on fire. A blazing bright light of fire and smoke billowed up from the incense in his hands. He waved the sticks around until the ends were no longer flaming but were red smoking embers. He handed each of us several dozen of the smoking incense sticks to carry inside the little temple. Situated on a small rise of ground above the graves, the temple had open spaces instead of doors or windows. It was covered with a tile roof and had clean, shiny marble floors. Inside was big enough for only a dozen people. The Buddha sat at the front of the temple, facing directly toward us as we walked in.

We added to the sacred and holy ambiance of the temple with our smoking incense sticks. The temple became cloudy and surreal as it filled with the mysterious mist of our fragrant incense. We stood in front of the Buddha statue, and each of us said a few words. We spoke with the greatest devotion and respect to all the fallen warriors, soldiers from our units as well as their old comrades who had lost their lives in battles long forgotten.

We each placed some of our smoking incense in the sand-filled bowl in front of the large Buddha statue. We bowed and silently said our prayers. We walked down to the gravesites and placed the remaining sticks of incense at several hundred grave markers. The red glowing sticks sent the mystical smoke wafting slowly skyward into total darkness.

We stood quietly, each in his own thoughts. I noticed that our guides were reverently observing us. I do not believe that they had ever seen anything like this done before by Americans. I know that they were moved by this small gesture; I just hope that perhaps they came away with a newly-found respect for American veterans.

We got back in the van. No one said a word. It was a quiet and peaceful ride back to the hotel as we felt the spiritual connection with this place and with each other.

#

Peace Patrol in Phu Cong, along the Saigon River:
Bill McDonald, Robert Reese, and Richard Webster.

Old warriors meeting on Black Virgin Mountain. Bill with NVA veteran from Haiphong. who showed his wounds from a B-52 attack during the war.

Author's note: Meeting this woman warrior was a real surprise and a true honor. Our timing was perfect so that we were at the right place and at the right time, but of course there are no accidents in this world!

A Chance Meeting at Black Virgin Mountain

The mountain was officially known as Nui Ba Den, but it was known locally as "Black Virgin Mountain" because of an old legend about a woman who jumped off the mountain to avoid marrying someone she did not love. The mountain itself is said to still contain her feminine energy. It was the location of many fierce battles during my Vietnam tour of duty. In fact, we had lost a Huey and its entire crew on this mountain. They were shot down and crashed into the side of that great mound of earth and rock. We may have been on the top of it in 1967, but Charlie and his friends owned all the real estate from the bottom of that hill right up to the edges of our barbed wire fence at the top.

The mountain was honeycombed with natural caverns where the VC could safely hide during the war. We learned from a metal plaque on one of the caverns that there was even once a hospital there. We could still see bullet pockmarks on the rocks.

This mountain landmark is visible from anywhere in the south area outside of Saigon. It stands out like a large sentinel watching over all the flatland around it. Yes, it was a very special and sacred place, and we wanted to go back to visit. We were warned that it was not like we remembered it. When we saw it, I couldn't have been any more surprised; you could have knocked me over with a feather.

We pulled into a parking lot at the bottom of the mountain and saw all the signs; it had been turned into an amusement park! I couldn't believe my eyes. Never in my wildest imagination could I have envisioned this transformation from wartime to peace.

We got onto, of all things, a children's train for a ride to the cable car, like the ones at Disneyland or a ski resort. The cable car took us up a long elevated ride over the tops of trees and rocks on a steady climb to the summit area. The cars hang by a thin cable high up in the air. My buddy Robert wasn't too happy about going up on it. I

291

watched his cable car in front of me rock and roll from side to side as it slowly lurched forward on the cable.

I could see for miles around as we got higher up the side of the mountain. It looked like it did when I was flying over it in a Huey during the war, but no one was shooting at us now. I looked below me and saw people walking up thousands of stone steps hidden under the canopy of trees. I could barely see them because of the dense cover even though we were only a few feet above the treetops and going very slowly. It was no wonder that I could never see anyone down there when we flew over at much higher altitudes and faster speeds during the war.

Next to the cable lift was their newest attraction, a slide that tourists rode down in a little car-like vehicle on small wheels. They were testing it the morning we were there. We watched as these "cars" whizzed by right under us on their way down the mountain. It was opening that afternoon, and there would be a ceremony and some local celebrities. That was one sight I never thought I would live to see at this mountain.

We got off of the cable cars near the top and had to hike up many more flights of rock stairs to reach the mountainside temples. The eastern grandeur and elegance as well as the spectacular works of art and devotion were awe inspiring. The pilgrims that we saw making their annual trek obviously thought so, too.

There was a building next to the temple for the weary to rest, but we took off our shoes on the outside steps and went right into the temple. We walked softly, trying not to disrupt the tranquility and peace that we felt inside. There was a little bald headed monk standing by a large gong that was hanging from a wooden frame at the back of the sanctuary. When we bowed to the large golden Buddha, the monk rang the gong. It sent chills up my spine when it happened so unexpectedly. I offered my incense, and another monk gave me fruit to put on the altar. He also gave me a folded, old paper currency note and a small amount of rice to keep.

The monk seemed to be intrigued by all of us, me in particular. He kept his gaze focused on me while I sat on the floor and said a short prayer and meditated. When I had finished and bowed to the altar, I could see and even feel that he was still watching me. I exchanged direct glances with him. He smiled back at me and put both his hands together as if praying and slightly bowed to me. I returned the same gesture and slowly backed out. I sat down on the step outside and put on my shoes. I was emotionally moved by the whole place. It felt peaceful, satisfying and welcoming.

We went to a couple more temples that were located higher up the mountain. We had to negotiate a steep climb up more rock stairsteps to get there. On the way to the last temple, a young man selling birds approached us. Actually, he was asking for us to pay for their release back into the wild. These birds had been captured, or bred and raised, and it was good luck and a spiritual gesture to pay for their release. We were to say a prayer for someone we loved, and then let the bird go.

I decided to release two birds, one for each of my children. I offered a prayer for each one as I released the little birds from my opened hands. They both quickly soared skyward, racing with my prayer, no doubt, to heaven. I watched the birds flying away with my prayers across the same skies from which only 35 years before I had fired machine gun bullets onto this mountain. I was hit with the symbolism of it all. I stood there absorbed in the moment.

We met several old NVA veterans who were on tour from Hanoi and the northern area. They were on a holiday, enjoying the peace and serenity of this sacred mountain, just as the four of us American veterans were doing. Each of us was having our own experience and handling it a little differently. We approached one of the veterans who had on his old medal-decorated uniform. We all hugged and talked and took photos together. He pulled up his shirt to show us where he had been wounded by a B-52 bombing raid on the Ho Chi Minh Trail when he was coming down from the north. There was no anger from him at all. That amazed me.

We eventually came down off the mountain. As we were walking around the concession area by the cable car entrance, our old NVA friend found us. He now wanted some of his buddies to meet us and get their photos taken with us. We were all in the moment and enjoying each other when a guy in a military uniform approached me. He invited me to please come and meet a famous woman veteran who was in the back of a small limo. The car had blacked out windows, so I could not see inside. I walked over to the car and the door swung open. Inside was an elderly, heavyset woman with rows of medals draped on her jacket. She had a walking cane next to her, so I assumed she had a physical problem. Her hair was white and her teeth slightly stained, but her smile was truly genuine and warm. She extended forth her hand to shake mine. I shook her hand and stood at attention. I gave her a crisp military salute. She cupped her hands together over her mouth as an indication of her surprise and the joy she was feeling. Her tear-glistened eyes said it all and she returned my salute. It was just a gesture of friendship and respect between old warriors, but it meant so much more to both of us at that moment.

I stepped back and happened to look at the bus that was parked alongside her car. There were several dozen veterans in their old uniforms standing near the windows saluting me. I whipped my hand to the brim of my hat and returned the gesture. Everyone smiled; we had all bonded. We looked at each other for several more seconds until I slowly turned to rejoin my friends. I heard loud cheering coming from the bus. I turned around to see that all of them were waving goodbye to me. I waved back at my newfound friends.

There was a feeling of love in the air. I do not know any other words to explain it. All my feelings about my former enemy and the war melted into an understanding that we are all just brothers and sisters on this small planet of ours. I loved these people, and it seemed they loved us too. Perhaps it was respect born out of battle, but whatever it was, I was happy to have shared that moment in time with them.

#

In the Delta drinking tea.

W.H. McDonald Jr.

Part 5

In the Shadow of the Blade

A Documentary Film and Journey

Our Veteran Crew
Mike Venable, Bill McDonald, and Bob Baird;
the missing veteran is Gary Roush, who was taking this photo.

"Healing—that is what this mission was all about;
I saw it every day on this journey,
and it still continues like ripples on a pond."
Bill McDonald

The Shadow 091 passing over the LZ at Demorest, Georgia.

W.H. McDonald Jr.

Author's note: I had the good karma of getting involved with a documentary project called "In the Shadow of the Blade." It was a film that recorded the experiences of people who were affected by the Vietnam War, either as veterans or noncombatants such as family members. This film took all of us who were on the crew over 10,000 miles across America in an old restored Huey helicopter that had actually been used in combat. In fact, it was from my old sister company, The 173rd Assault Helicopter Company (The Robin Hoods) out of Lai Khe, Vietnam. I had seen this aircraft after it had been shot down and sling loaded back to our airfield. We had a "bone yard" made up of destroyed and damaged helicopters that were all piled up together. It looked very much like a car wrecking yard. We used some of those old birds for spare parts, and we shipped the salvageable ones back to the states. Our old aircraft was one of those that survived the "bone yard" and was shipped back to the states to be rebuilt. Now, it was once again back to its old glory as the centerpiece in our movie. This was truly a journey of a lifetime.

The Concept is Born

It took Patrick Fries and his wife, Cheryl, several years of soul-wrenching work to finally make their dream come to life. They had a concept for a documentary film they believed in so strongly that they did not give up on the idea, even after one roadblock led to another. They wanted to fly a Huey helicopter around America, bringing it to veterans and others affected by the Vietnam War. They thought that once these people heard the familiar "whop-whop-whop," ran their hands along the OD (olive-drab) green fuselage, and strapped in to relive the rush of warm air at takeoff from a hover, their stories would fly as well. They were right, we found thousands of stories out there in America's heartland just waiting to take off and soar.

I got involved at the earliest stages of this dream when they contacted me to give them names of veterans who might be interested in being interviewed. They became interested in my poetry and stories, and one thing led to the next; I was to be one of the people interviewed for the movie. The original plan was for the Huey to fly from Texas to California, up to Washington, and across the northern states before dropping down the East Coast to Florida. That plan fell through because of the tremendous costs involved.

At one point in the summer of 2002, Pat and Cheryl's project was "grounded" for lack of funding. I kept e-mailing them that it was going to happen. In fact, it had already happened in the future, and they just had to continue working to make it materialize. I had been acting as their spiritual and emotional cheerleader for the past two years, and I wasn't giving up on them or the project.

Finally, the project plans went from idle to full RPM as funding became available and the right people added their talents and other pieces of the puzzle. Soon it began to look as if they could launch the Huey, but they still did not have enough money to complete the cross-country trip. There also were a lot of risks and unknowns involved.

"Take a leap of faith, and go for it!" I told Pat and Cheryl by phone. "Let the universe find the missing parts of the puzzle."

One Sunday night in August 2002, Pat called me, asking for two minutes of my time. He asked if I were willing to fly to Fort Rucker, Alabama, to offer a prayer for the mission's takeoff. It was fitting that the mission should begin at Fort Rucker, the Home of Army Aviation. I told him yes, I was willing to give him anything he needed, even after he told me I would have to pay my own expenses. I, too, really believed in their dream.

Then, we talked about Pat's personal life, and two minutes turned into two hours as he opened up. Toward the end of the conversation, I explained the meaning of the recurring dreams about flying he had been having over the years. He was experiencing these nighttime adventures in his sleep and wondered what they all might mean. I told him it wasn't about flying but about his spirit. I went into detail about what I sensed as the meaning of these dreams and mentioned some other aspects about his life.

He mentioned that he was upset about his young daughter, and he had left his house without resolving a conflict. He was at his office in downtown Austin. I told him to go home, hug his daughter, kiss her right between the eyes on the forehead, and tell her, "I love you." I also told him the importance of the dreaming experience itself and in particular, his dream of flying. I told him to expect something to happen soon dealing with dreams about flying. I felt that something would transpire that night that would relate back to this dream of flying.

The next day he called to tell me that his daughter had crawled in bed with him and his wife early that morning. She was excited and wanted to tell them about her dream of flying. She had never talked about her dreams before, and for her to wake him up to share it was very special to him. He now understood what my words meant.

He also asked me to come along on the crew. Arrowhead Film Company took an entirely different route with this movie than most other documentary filmmakers. They added a compassionate touch to the interviewing process by appointing me as their flight/mission chaplain. My job was to render emotional support as needed by those interviewed. Pat and Cheryl didn't want the people who had vented their souls to be left emotionally abandoned after all the cameras and lights went off. They really wanted this whole documentary process to be a part of a true healing mission for everyone involved.

#

Film Director Patrick Fries and his daughter, Claire.

Author's footnote: Several weeks after we began, I had a dream in which I saw Pat's black SUV get into a minor car crash. I sent an e-mail warning him to stay alert and be careful. He never had any accidents, so I wondered how I could be so wrong about my dream. When I talked to Cheryl, she mentioned she had been in a car accident while driving Pat's black SUV. Right car, but I had warned the wrong person. I felt really bad about it, but nobody is right 100 percent of the time. I had assumed that because it was his car that he was the one having the accident.

Bill McDonald and Cheryl Fries in Austin, Texas.

"I am centered in my belief that God called us to make a film because that film has a mission of its own. Beyond the film...the mission is not ours; it belongs to the veterans. If we can help—and it is God's intention that we do so—we will."
Cheryl Fries

Author's note: This documentary was a pure labor of love for all of us. But it did zap our emotional and spiritual energy. We met thousands of veterans and their families and supporters of all kinds in every LZ. Everyone had a story. Some could not talk in front of the camera, but they did unleash their emotions and tell their stories to me. Some days, I felt as if the weight of the world were on my shoulders; I always felt that I could have done more or said something more to some of these people. We also experienced so much love from everyone that it helped us to continue each day.

We had two helicopters on our journey, our Huey and a Bell JetRanger that we used as a camera ship for aerial photos and movies. We also had three to five vehicles following us on the ground with all of our equipment and personal items. We picked up other fixed-wing aircraft and helicopters along the way. We had National Guard helicopters, sheriff department helos, and all kinds of other TV media and government aircraft tagging along on various legs of the flight.

We Begin the Journey

Our Huey took off October 2, 2002, from Fort Rucker, Alabama, the Home of Army Aviation. It was a most fitting place to begin our journey. The Army had given us a huge party with several hundred invited guests the night before at the Aviation Museum. It was fully catered and was all first class.

I finally got to meet Eric, the son of one of my unit's pilots who was killed in Vietnam in 1967. Now an Army career man, Eric had never gotten to know his father. We had met on the Internet several years before and had become good friends. I was able to get him interviewed for the film. We both hugged, and I got to meet his beautiful wife. I felt bad because I couldn't talk much with him as I had many people to visit, but it felt good to finally connect with him.

The next day the Army had a band and color guard unit to send us off. There were speeches and a half dozen modern Army helicopters to escort us on the beginning leg of our journey. Mike Novosel, a Medal of Honor recipient and dust off pilot, was flying in the left pilot's seat. (Novosel Street at Fort Rucker is named after him.) In our chopper, we also had an honorary crew of Vietnam veterans representing each branch of the military service. I was pleased that the film company had chosen my old buddy Private Doug Ward from the Robin Hoods (173rd Assault Helicopter Company) to do the honors of representing the U.S. Army. It was the greatest of honors to sit in this aircraft with such a fine group of soldiers. Before taking off, our crew and passengers were introduced to a gathering of several hundred people. I gave a blessing for the mission, and then we marched out to the aircraft while the Army band played. Film crews from CNN and four other networks shot footage of the event. It was a moving moment for me that morning. After all the years of no recognition for my war experiences, I was now being honored as a Vietnam veteran and a hero. The band was finally playing for me! When we lifted our skids from the ground, it finally hit home that we were actually beginning the journey.

Our first official LZ was at the South Wall in Florida. It has a scaled down replica of "The Wall" in Washington, D.C.; however, it is no less emotionally powerful. When we made a low pass over it, our blades made the popping sound that is so familiar to any GI who ever served in Nam. It is a distinct "whop-whop" sound that one can never forget. All eyes were on our Huey as we made another low-level run over the group standing around the LZ, which was right next to "The Wall." We gently landed in the middle of a grassy knoll, and the men and their families slowly approached the helicopter as the blades came to a stop. Our honorary crew members got off the aircraft, and our film crew interviewed them. (We repeated this process at each LZ, picking up passengers and taking them to the next LZ. Riding in our Huey was part of the healing experience that we wished to capture on film. We had two cameras mounted on the inside of the Huey to record their various emotional reactions. For some of these men, it was their first ride in a helicopter since leaving Vietnam 30 to 35 years before.)

One man told me he did not know we were coming. He had come down to "The Wall" as a way to better understand his father who was dying in the hospital. He came to find some quiet time at "The Wall" and certainly hadn't expected to find a Vietnam War helicopter landing right next to him. He was emotionally overwhelmed by the coincidence of our landing there at this exact moment. He had been depressed and was looking for some support and perhaps some answers. I put my arm around his shoulders, and we walked away from the crowd of people gathered around the Huey. I asked him to tell me about his dad, which he did.

I asked him if he would like me to pray for him and his father. He softly replied that he would really appreciate that, so we prayed together out of sight of the cameras and the media. He immediately broke down sobbing and I held him. I gave him some words of comfort, then I had to leave him because I could see a line of others waiting to talk to me.

Next, the wife of a Vietnam veteran approached me. She was unsure what was wrong with her husband. She told me that he had not cried or spoken about Nam in 35 years. Now, she was watching him crying just a short distance away from the helicopter. She asked me to talk to him.

When I put my arms around her tear-choked husband and told him, "Welcome home, brother," he really broke down.

"Bill, don't worry about me. These aren't sad tears, but tears of joy for bringing the Huey here and for coming to honor us veterans," he said.

We had a long conversation, but there were so many others, several in wheelchairs. We had less than an hour to spend there before we had to make it to our next LZ, so I tried to comfort all I could in that short period of time. The blades began to rotate, and we were jumping in for another LZ. There would be other groups of men and women waiting for us there and at every LZ we landed in the entire journey.

As I looked out from my seat in the helicopter, I saw the young man who talked to me about his dad. He saluted me as I did to him. I wish I'd had more time there; too many broken hearts for such a short stop. I knew that the next 10,000 miles we were going to see many more people in need of spiritual and emotional healing. I prayed I would be up for the job.

#

The Robin Hoods at Fort Rucker, October 1, 2002.

Author's note: I had some old images of the South that had formed and embedded in my memory from the 1960s when I was there in the Army. I remembered the police calling me "boy" and places I could not bring my black friends to. I also remember seeing four restrooms at gas stations in Florida and couldn't figure out why. The old South was not a safe place for young California liberals back then, so my whole image of the South was biased when I began this trip. This LZ in Georgia changed my thinking radically. There really was a new South with a whole new attitude. If I hadn't seen it myself, I would never have believed it.

Southern Hospitality

We flew up the East Coast of Florida along the long, beautiful, white beaches where the gentle, blue waves licked the shoreline. It was one of several inspirationally scenic parts of our journey. We had made many stops at various LZs, including an aviation school for new commercial airline pilots. After almost four nonstop days of activity, we were going to land and spend the night in a rural area outside of Savannah, Georgia. The place wasn't even a town; it was in Liberty County.

We had a last-minute invitation from a couple of veterans to land at a farm out in the middle of nowhere and join the locals in a big "Low Country" community feast. We had no idea what was waiting for us there, but what we found was much better than we imagined.

It looked as if everyone who lived in Liberty County was at the farm. They had set up several picnic tables under the huge trees. There were large cooking pots with shrimp, potatoes, and corn boiling away. They also had food of all kinds everywhere. I especially liked the sheet cakes with images of our Huey in different colored icing. The number of people there was difficult to estimate because everyone was all over and moving around talking to their friends. I guess there were several hundred people of all shapes, sizes, races, religions, and political persuasions. There were black families sitting and talking to white families; there were Asian and Hispanic families, too. There was even one Hawaiian veteran who came to see his friend and join the welcoming party. There were poor farmers and rich people too, but it was hard to tell one from the other. Everyone was mixing together and enjoying each other's stories and company.

The local fire department had parked their truck with the ladder fully extended into the sky with an American flag hoisted on the top rung. This made finding the LZ a little easier for our Huey crew. They also popped colored smoke when the Huey got close.

Everyone was waiting for the arrival of the helicopter, and all eyes searched the skyline as our blades began "popping." As the ship came over the treetops at over 100 knots, it buzzed the farm and all the people cheered. On this particular day, I was with the advance party who had come to make sure the LZ was set up and safe to land in. I was on the ground watching as our Huey took another lap around the sky, giving everyone another rendition of the "whop-whop."

I saw our host, Bruce, the veteran who had invited us there and set up everything, walking away from the crowd and the LZ. He was totally overcome by his emotions. I walked with him to the back of the crowd and spent some time soothing his nerves as the Huey landed on the ground. By then he was composed enough to walk to the helicopter.

The crowd gave the Huey a big touchdown, team-winning cheer as it landed. Everyone wanted to meet the crew and touch the aircraft. Our cameras were rolling, recording all the action and friendly people around us. It was a big party, and we were the guests of honor. We ended up spending the night in a Southern mansion on the bay. What impressed me the most about this whole event was how totally real the people were to each other. There wasn't a lot of pretentiousness that I normally see and feel at gatherings.

One of the veterans that greeted us, Rodney Riley, was so moved by our mission that he wrote and recorded a CD of original music for the film. He neither wanted nor asked for anything in return; it was a pure gift from his creative and grateful heart.

That was the kind of excitement that this whole trip produced. When we flew into airports to get jet fuel for our helicopter, we always got it at a discount, at cost, or on more than one occasion paid in full by someone. The Huey holds 220 gallons of jet fuel, and it burns about 200 of that in two hours, so this was a considerable kindness. Almost all of our hotel rooms and meals also were discounted or paid for by strangers who asked for nothing in return.

We gave them a flight crew member patch or two as thanks. The South proved truly to be "the queen of hospitality." There is no place better in the world!

#

Bill McDonald and Johnny Hobbs.

Bill at Fort Worth, Texas, in front of old 091.

Johnny Hobbs, Bill McDonald, and Keith "Hacksaw" Bodine in
Texas during the filming.

One of the many different helicopters and aircraft that
accompanied us along our cross country journey.

Author's note: We heard a story on our journey about a rescued baby girl from Nam in 1969. This led to an even bigger story and eventually became a national story on the CBS Early Show. I gave a speech at the California State Vietnam Veterans' Memorial on Memorial Day in 2003 about this story. I also had the privilege and the honor of introducing the father who adopted the baby girl and also the young woman herself.

Baby Kathleen

We began that day very early in the morning. The crew was at the aircraft as the sun was rising in the sky. It was hot and humid, and we knew it was going to rain sometime during the day. We loaded both of the helicopters with camera equipment and people, and fired up the engines. Then it happened; a red indicator light began flashing on the helicopter's cockpit dash. The tail rotor chip detector was indicating trouble. We shut it down and waited while Bruce, our aircraft commander and a certified aviation mechanic, climbed up to examine the magnetic plug in the gearbox. He cut the safety wires and pulled out the magnetic plug to examine it for any metal shavings or chips of metal.

The visual examination yielded nothing; it was all clean oil. We had to make a choice; did we believe the warning light or did we put our trust in what appeared to be a clean plug? If there were metal chips in the gearbox, that would have indicated that the gears were failing and could freeze up in flight. That would cause a tail rotor failure, and we would be in serious trouble.

We gathered around Bruce, our leader and the man to make the final decision whether we went forward with or canceled our flight plans. There was much more involved than just being late or a no-show at the next LZ if we had to cancel the flight. A large part of Kennesaw State University's student body along with an ROTC color guard and a band; many veterans, some waiting to tell their stories; and camera and sound crews, a director, and other media were all sitting outside in the rain waiting to see our Huey. This was no small decision, but as Bruce reminded us, safety had to be the number one priority. It didn't matter what or who was waiting for us, he would cancel the flight if he felt it was unsafe to fly the aircraft.

Bruce told us that any one of us could veto his decision. He didn't want to make us go on the aircraft if anyone was uncomfortable about the warning light. One veto and we would all stay on the ground. We each gave our opinions. As a former crew chief, I told him I felt perfectly safe after looking at the plug. There was no doubt in my mind that it was a defective warning light and not the gearbox. Everyone else felt the same way and stated that we should go. We all boarded and took off with the red light still flashing on the dash.

When we got to the university, it was pouring rain and we were late, but there was still a crowd waiting for us. We had a nice ceremony followed by a free lunch in the cafeteria.

Afterward at the helicopter, a woman approached us with a photo album tucked under her arm. Donna Rowe asked if she could share her story with us. We got the camera rolling as she began her spellbinding story about a 1969 rescue of a three-week-old baby in a village in Vietnam.

Donna was a nurse with the 3rd Field Hospital in Saigon in 1969. She opened her photo album and turned to a page with a picture of an infant. She said that she was tired of hearing stories about American "baby killers." She had a story that proved the opposite.

When she began the story, the crowd around the Huey grew quiet. She told us how a group of infantry soldiers from the Big Red One (1st Infantry Division) came across a small hamlet that had been attacked by the VC about three days before. There were dead people and animals scattered everywhere on the ground. The huts were burned and the livestock was slaughtered. Everyone and everything was dead—men, women, children, and animals. The soldiers had been saddened by what they saw as they walked among the dead corpses of what was once a happy and peaceful hamlet in the mountains of Vietnam.

Then, the soldiers heard a muffled sound of a baby crying. They rushed to a body of a young woman grasping something in her arms. She was lying face down, so one of the soldiers turned her over. That violated one of the golden rules of combat because the VC sometimes attached explosive devices to dead bodies. If a soldier moved the body, he could be killed or maimed. This mattered not to the young

313

soldier because he was reacting to the sound of a helpless infant, and he and the other soldiers wanted nothing more than to help this child.

The three-week-old baby was tightly wrapped in the arms of her mother who was now a three-day-old corpse. The baby had several wounds and was bleeding; however, the pressure being applied by the mother's grip was holding the baby's blood pressure and had actually helped to keep her alive for almost three days.

The soldiers immediately called the 3rd Field Hospital and asked them what to do. Donna, the triage nurse, broke the rules by telling them to transport the child with the mother's body to the hospital. American medical facilities were only for American GI casualties. Normal procedure would have been to transport this child to a Vietnamese hospital for treatment, which Donna knew meant certain death for the baby.

The soldiers brought the child and mother to the hospital, and the medical personnel went to work trying to save the baby. They knew that they had to act fast once they broke the mother's arms to remove the baby, because the child's blood pressure would begin falling rapidly. Nurse Rowe also decided that it wasn't good enough to just save the baby's life, she also wanted to ensure this little girl had a chance at a decent life. She knew that if she could get her baptized as a Catholic, she could negotiate with the local Catholic orphanage to take the baby once she was well. She had hoped that someone might adopt her and give her that better life.

She sent for the Catholic chaplain and gathered some of the staff. While they were moving the baby to the operating room, the chaplain baptized her. Everyone became a godparent to the child, and Nurse Rowe named her Kathleen Fields: Kathleen, from the old Irish ballad "Take me home again Kathleen," and Fields because she was at the 3rd Field Hospital.

As Donna was telling us the story, there were many wet eyes among the group around the Huey. She went on to tell us how they made diapers for her out of women's personal hygiene products and medical rags. Several days later there were three young, muddy and dirty soldiers asking to see their baby. They were the ones who had found little Kathleen in her mother's arms. Some of the staff took them to the baby's room with her makeshift crib so they could see their baby. The nurses left the soldiers alone with the baby, so Donna did not know what happened. But when they walked out of the room, the soldiers all had big smiles as well as moist eyes.

I listened to her story and couldn't help thinking of the three wise men who came to visit baby Jesus. I was moved by this powerful story, and as I looked around I saw that so was everyone else.

Donna said she wasn't sure what had happened to the baby after she left the hospital, but she heard rumors that a Navy officer had adopted her and taken her to the United States. She finished telling her story, and I was left still wondering about baby Kathleen. Did she really get adopted and come to the states?

We shut down the filming and Nurse Donna Rowe left, but her story stayed with us for the next five months. Then, something wonderful happened.

The *Atlanta Journal-Constitutional* ran a story about "Baby Kathleen" as told by Donna Rowe. The story appeared a day or two after we had left town and were headed to another LZ. It also was posted on the newspaper's website where someone discovered it and notified our crew five months later.

"I am that baby Kathleen," was the message posted on our movie website. She was now a young woman, living in California with a family of her own. She stated that she wanted to make contact with Donna and the others who had saved her life. We were all happily surprised by the good fortune of it all. The director of the film immediately contacted Kathleen, as I did. We talked to her and found out that she was now living in my part of the world, a short drive from my house in northern California. Her dad, the Naval officer who had adopted her in 1969, was living on the edge of my town in the Elk Grove area. We lived no more than three or four miles from each other.

Arrowhead Film Company quickly began to put together a plan for a reunion in San Antonio, Texas, of those involved in the rescue. Although the documentary filming was completed, they reassembled the entire crew for the reunion.

This was going to cost well over $35,000 to get everyone there, including the helicopter. The film company didn't have that kind of funding left, so they asked for help. Several people stepped forward to assist in the reunion plans. Southwest Airlines donated 17 roundtrip airline tickets and even some cash for hotel and food for Kathleen and her family. The spirit of giving and helping was wonderfully abundant. What amazed me was that none of these angels who helped us with the reunion asked for a single thing from anyone, not even a mention in the media that they were paying for it.

We had been able to get in touch with almost all the parties we could identify who aided in some way with the rescue effort. We even found the actual helicopter pilot who had transported baby Kathleen to the hospital. When we contacted him, he was elated to find out that something he had done in the war had a positive impact on someone's life. He had been suffering from depression for many years and drank very heavily, according to his friends. He had never really gotten over the effects of the war, and he had become an unhappy soul since his homecoming. This news was a gift of sunshine for him. He was excited about coming out to meet everyone at the reunion. We arranged for an airline ticket for him, but a few days before he was to fly to Texas, he caught pneumonia and died a day or so later. He never made it to the reunion, but his friends said that he died a much happier man for having heard about baby Kathleen and the reunion.

The reunion took place April 14, 2003, at Fort Sam Houston, Texas. It was an event that took over 34 years to happen. All of the media including CNN were there to cover it. The timing, however, was such that all the news' focus that week was on the ongoing war in Iraq and the release of our POWs (prisoners of war). In spite of that, CBS arranged for Kathleen, Donna, and one of the medics to go to New York City to do a 15-minute segment on the CBS *Early Show*.

Kathleen and I talked on the phone several times about how she had spent years trying to find out something about her life. She wondered who the people were who had helped her when she was an infant. Now, she finally had some sense of fulfillment. She said she has often expressed her concern about why this happened to her and what it meant. I do not have all the answers, but I do know that her story has brought much inspiration to many veterans who now feel that they did something of real value during their tour of duty in Vietnam.

Author's footnote: During all the rush for the reunion with Kathleen and her rescuers, no one thought to include her dad, Marvin Cords. The dashing and loving Naval officer had to fight through almost a year of paperwork, which included getting the president of South Vietnam to sign off on the adoption. The birth certificate also was a problem, but the medical staff put pressure on the orphanage by letting them know that if they did not provide Kathleen Fields with a birth certificate, they would no longer receive free medical care and supplies from the 3rd Field Hospital.

Marvin Cords already had adopted three children (he eventually had six adopted children) when he happened to hear baby Kathleen's story from the chaplain during a church service in Saigon. It was then that he began his long quest to bring Kathleen home.

In one of my phone conversations with Kathleen, she mentioned that her father was feeling rather rejected and left out of the whole reunion process. No one had even called him or interviewed him. He wasn't even offered a ticket to fly to Texas.

I decided that Marvin deserved his day in the sunshine. When I gave my Memorial Day speech in Sacramento's State Capitol Park, I told Kathleen's story. At the end of speech, I told the audience and the media that I had a very special treat for them, and I introduced Marvin. The crowd of mostly wet-eyed veterans gave him a three-minute standing ovation. Marvin was a humbled man. Afterward, many in the crowd came up to give him a handshake or a hug.

Finally, I introduced "baby Kathleen," a 33-year-old mother of three daughters. She walked up to the microphone and offered the healing words below to an attentive and respectful audience of veterans. When she finished, not even I was dry-eyed. There was so much joy, love, and healing taking place. There wasn't a person who was not emotionally affected. Even the MC for the event, local CBS TV newscaster Dave Bender, was moved.

Kathleen's speech:

"Hello, my name is Kathleen Cords-Epps, and when I was just three weeks old, my tiny life was saved by American GIs, nurses, and doctors who took great risks to save me.

I am tired of hearing in the media about American "baby killers!" I was an orphaned baby in Vietnam. My mother and the entire village were killed by the VC, and I am alive and healthy today because of veterans like you.

When you came back you were never welcomed home as the heroes that you were, and I have never had the opportunity to say what I have wanted to say for so many years.

Welcome home and thank you very much! God bless you and your families."

Photo Credit – Johnny Hobbs
Baby Kathleen getting hugs from the crew.

Photo Credit – Sarah Beal
Reunion at Fort Sam Houston, Texas, for baby Kathleen (center) with former Army medic Richard Hock and Army nurse Donna Rowe.

318

Photo Credit - Johnny Hobbs
Kathleen with her youngest daughter.

Wedding Ceremony

Author's note: We meet people as we travel along our journey in life, and sometimes we instantly bond as if we had been friends for years. This was the case with several people on my trip across America in the Huey. In Demorest, Georgia, I found a pair of new "old" friends waiting for me, a couple of artists known professionally as Aurence and Biegun. They asked me to consecrate their marriage by giving them a formal wedding ceremony and reaffirming their vows—not in a church but in the presence of our old Huey helicopter. It turned out to be a joyous celebration for everyone. Our friendship continues today, even though we are a couple thousand miles apart.

A Wedding in the Huey

This was the most physically demanding LZ that we attempted to land our Huey in during our entire 10,000-mile odyssey. For a while, it was questionable if we could actually drop into this tight opening in the forest.

Waiting for us there was a group of veterans who had gathered to honor our coming and to attend a wedding celebration. The LZ setting was on a small, forested parcel of land along the banks of the Chattahoochee River, up in the wooded mountains of northeast Georgia. It belonged to two extraordinarily gifted folk artists, Larry and Patty Hancock, better known professionally as Aurence and Biegun. Larry, a Marine veteran, told us that our coming to his home was very special for him. He had invited all of his veteran friends and family to witness our arrival and to celebrate the occasion. We had been invited to drop in and party with them, and that was what we were going to do. Our very capable aircraft commander, Bruce Lemonie, made sure that we had successfully landed, to everyone's great amazement and entertainment.

One of the men there, Ben Purcell, was a former POW. He was the oldest POW held during the Vietnam War and one of the prisoners held the longest. I had talked to him on the phone several times and had exchanged some e-mails with him. I was looking forward to meeting him and his wife, Anne, in person. This was a man I admired not only because he survived captivity, but also because he didn't let it dampen his love of life or of his country.

We all gathered around the Huey late that afternoon to witness the blessing of Larry and Patty's marriage vows. They had decorated the inside of our helicopter with candles, incense, and flowers. They had a young girl playing the flute, and the bride wore a traditional Vietnamese wedding dress of bright orange and other vibrant colors. The groom wore his old USMC fatigues with his Purple Heart pinned to his chest. The crew joined the invited guests in a large semicircle around the side of the helicopter. I was standing there with my black clergy shirt and white-tabbed collar showing from underneath my flight suit.

The ceremony encompassed their values of love, friendship, and spirituality. I administered the vows to reaffirm their marriage, and they recited personal vows, which they had written for each other. Instead of rings, they exchanged white roses in honor of their long, successful marriage. The wedding was covered by the local TV station's news show, and the *Atlanta Journal-Constitutional* had a nice story about it with a photo in that Sunday's edition.

The bride and groom embraced and kissed like newlyweds as their guests celebrated their happiness. It was a highlight of the trip for me. I was honored to have given them the gift of the service.

That night we had the cameras rolling as Ben Purcell and his wife, Anne, told us their spiritually moving story of how they both handled his captivity for over five and half years in a North Vietnamese POW camp. Most of his time was spent in solitarily confinement without any access to other human beings except for his interrogator and guards. Anne never knew his status, since the North Vietnamese never listed him as a POW.

For almost his entire time in captivity he was listed officially as an MIA (Missing in Action). That meant that neither of them was able to exchange mail or information with the other. Anne had to keep her faith alive that Ben was coming home.

Ben told us that his last helicopter ride was the one he was shot down in and captured. We wondered how he would feel the next day when we took him up for a flight to Augusta, Georgia. But this night belonged to Ben and Anne. They held everyone's attention captive as we listened to their tale of courage and love. What struck me the most was his compassion and lack of hatred or even anger about what had happened to him. He is truly a man of great faith and forgiveness.

As a great example of not only courage but of love, he inspired us all. He demonstrated with his own life that it is not what happens to us, but it is our attitude about it that makes all the difference in the world. He loved God and prayed each and every day he was imprisoned. He never lost his faith, and now he is out spreading it to many others through his book and his public talks at churches and other gatherings. I am honored to have met such a man!

#

Photo Credit – Patty Hancock
The Shadow 091 at the LZ at Demorest, Georgia.

The bride and groom being filmed for the movie.

Old 091 sitting in the sunrise at Angel Fire, New Mexico.
Ernest Dogwolf Lovato and Fidel Gonzalez.

Author's note: I felt the greatest spiritual energy at this most sacred place—a place that gave birth to the first Vietnam Veterans' Memorial of any kind in the world. It was a place made sacred by ancient Native Americans many centuries before, and now it was a place that would capture the emotional heart and soul of our documentary film, "In the Shadow of the Blade." It was up over 9,000 feet in the mountains of New Mexico, and it was covered in powdered snow when we landed there. Our parked helicopter was a sparkling jewel on the hillside as ice and snow crystals caught the early morning sunlight and reflected it like diamonds. It was here that I met an Apache Indian Vietnam veteran who made a lasting impression on me.

Angel Fire, New Mexico

I had been looking forward to one of our last LZs because of what it promised to be. This LZ was filled with much love and spiritual energy. We had people working for us in New Mexico who had put their full heart and soul into making everything right for us when we got there. One veteran in particular, Earl Waters, unselfishly devoted time, effort, and money into making our stay there the most memorable possible. I knew when I met him that he was a good man.

I first saw Earl with a group of veterans waiting for us at the Tucamcari Airport above Albuquerque, New Mexico. We landed our Huey, refueled it, and loaded him and his buddies onboard for the ride of their lives. We rolled over the mountains and swooped down toward our next LZ where well over 1,000 people were waiting to greet us, including a bagpipe player. He played "Amazing Grace" while standing in the shadow of our Huey to a tear-filled group of veterans and their families.

The next morning, the Huey lifted off and headed to Angel Fire, the site of the world's first Vietnam Veterans' Memorial. The helicopter climbed up and over the snow covered Sangre de Cristo Mountains before landing at close to the 9,000-foot level in the snow. It was an inspiring sight with a Veterans' Day crowd of around 800 people all huddled on that cold, snowy little hilltop next to the Memorial Chapel that was built as part of the monument.

The helicopter made several passes playing that "sound of freedom" as the blades popped and the engines roared. Our aircraft was escorted to the LZ by a formation of New Mexico National Guard UH-60 Black Hawk helicopters. It was a beautiful sight, flying over the white-covered hill. The other helicopters broke away and our Huey came in for a landing. The snow flurry from the rotor wash created a spectacular entrance in our own personal snowstorm.

There was a ceremony and many speeches, including one from me. The thrill of the morning for me, however, was seeing in the front row a dozen of the last living code talkers from WWII and Korea. These old Native American heroes sat there wrapped in their colorful native blankets in the cold to honor our crew. We were the ones, however, truly honored by their presence.

After the ceremonies were finished and everyone had left the hillside, our parked Huey sat alone in the snow for the night. The next morning the director of the documentary, Pat Fries, took a couple of cameramen and a soundman to the top of the hill to film the sunrise. I went along to be a part of that golden (literal and metaphorical) moment.

On the hilltop, two Native America musicians greeted us. One of them was my new friend, Vietnam veteran Ernie Dogwolf. We had instantly bonded the day before when I had met him and his wife. Meeting him was so natural and familiar, like old friends or kindred spirits seeing each other again. I sensed he was spiritually sensitive to life and the world around him. I found him to be someone who commanded others' attention and respect. He did this not by being aggressive or bold but by being tranquil and by projecting an aura of being in tune with his surroundings. He had the look of being a courageous warrior, yet at the same time there was a soft gentleness about him, a rare combination. We quickly became good friends as we spoke the same spiritual language from our hearts.

The director asked the two men to play their musical instruments and to do and say anything they wished. Pat wanted to capture the early morning moments as the sun peeked over the mountain, making the snow and ice on the helicopter shine like priceless gems. Ernie blew steam with each breath in the cold one-degree temperature as the sunrise brought the promise of the new day. He raised his arms skyward and held his Native American flute in one hand as he offered some thoughts about life and God. Out of the sky flew a large black raven that circled behind him. He addressed a message to the bird who slowly descended to a perch on the chapel steeple. The bird sat and watched like a sentinel as Ernie turned his attention and focus to his music. The film captured these magic morning moments along with the sounds of drums and flutes and the image of the Huey parked in the background covered with ice and snow.

Ernie and his friend walked slowly down to the aircraft. He took out from his leather bag, a large bundle of sage that was tied together. He set it on fire and shook it until it was smoking. As the drums were beating, the two men chanted and offered prayers for our Huey and for all the men who had ever flown in it. Ernie walked along the body of the aircraft, blessing it with the smoke from the burning sage bush and continuing his prayers and chanting.

When he reached the front of the Huey and put his hands on the pilots' windshield, his head dropped and he began to weep. The music and the chanting had stopped, and the cameras had finished rolling. I walked down the hillside to where he was now walking back up. His eyes were wet with emotions. He and I embraced as he very softly wept. He told me what had happened and why he was emotional.

He stated that when he had touched the Huey, he saw the spirits of the many men who had flown in this helicopter, and they were pleased with the blessing ceremony. He saw their eyes and felt their presence. He was visibly shaken but not saddened, more spiritually awakened might be a better way to describe his feeling. We stood there looking into each other's eyes. He and I both knew what he was talking about and feeling. He didn't have to explain it to me, we both understood.

#

Bill in Angel Fire, New Mexico.

Our Huey sitting in the early morning sunrise at Angel Fire, New Mexico. We had just finished filming the blessing of the helicopter.

Bill with a couple of the last surviving code talkers

Filming morning sunrise in Angel Fire, New Mexico.

Ernie Dogwolf playing his flute for Dr. Victor Westphall,
the founder of the Angel Fire Vietnam Memorial.

Bill with Dr. Westphall who died before the film was released.

Bill with Earl Waters and his friends.

Pat Fries with soundman Mack Melson

Helicopter landing in the snow at Angel Fire, New Mexico.

Bill with friend Lynn Raymond, at Machu Picchu, Peru.

Author's note: After all the months involved with the making of the documentary "In the Shadow of the Blade," I was emotionally exhausted and in need of a spiritual rest. My friend Lynn Raymond and I flew down to South America to spend most of the month of December 2002 exploring the Andes Mountains and Inca ruins in Peru and Bolivia. We thought of ourselves as the spiritual version of Butch Cassidy and the Sundance Kid.

I needed a rest away from people, and this afforded me a great opportunity to reflect on the past year: my trip back to Vietnam, meeting former President Jimmy Carter, my daughter's wedding, and working on the documentary while flying around the country in a Huey helicopter. It was a year in which I was interviewed by 35–40 newspapers, 75 or more TV stations including a couple of times for CNN news, and I gave at least a dozen public speeches.

I had listened to the thousands of stories from countless veterans, families of veterans, widows, and orphaned sons and daughters of veterans. I had shared their tears and their pain. I had embraced their suffering and had given all of myself in an effort to help them move past their pain. I was not always successful, but for many, our journey across the nation meant that spiritual and emotional healing could begin for them. We witnessed many miracles of the heart and soul, but it took its toll on me. By the end of the year, I needed to get away and recharge to get back my energy. That last year I allowed myself to become a spiritual and emotional sponge, but I had no regrets. I had a year like no other Vietnam veteran could have ever dreamed. Come to think of it, I did dream it.

Reflections from the Andes—An Epilogue

I had to get away. I was pleased that I was able to find a traveling companion as easy-going and tolerant as Lynn. He was a retired schoolteacher whom I had enjoyed serving with on church committees.

He and I took the trip of a lifetime to a place of the soul that I had only dreamed about as a child. The trip was more than about seeing places; it also was about reflection and introspection for me. This was the perfect way to end the year and perhaps a good place to take a look back on my whole life's journey.

We flew down to Lima, Peru, at the beginning of December 2002 and found there were few other Americans traveling at that time of year. I discovered that the entire country had a friendly feel to it, at least for the two of us. Moreover, the higher we traveled up into the Andes Mountains, the friendlier the people were to us. It also became much harder for us to breathe when we were hiking at the 13,000-foot level. We were both well past what we considered our best youthful days, and the high altitude mixed with being out of shape made for some slow yet scenic walking.

To me, this was an accumulation of my whole life. I had just finished one of my busiest and most interesting years, and now I was heading to see "the Lost City of the Incas." It seemed totally surreal.

We eventually found our way to the Sacred Valley and saw what we thought were impressive and massive Inca ruins everywhere. We were about to be even more impressed. We took the train ride to Machu Picchu, which takes tourists within a short hike, or in our case, a bus ride from the mountainside ruins.

We spent the night in the village at a cheap hotel next to the railroad tracks. The next morning we got up early and were greeted with a heavy rainstorm. The rain was pouring buckets, so most of the tourists stayed in their rooms. We walked in the rain to the bus that went up the mountainside to the ruins. We boarded the 40-passenger bus, which only carried us and four other people. The bus snaked along a narrow jungle road next to the Urubamaba River, which is in a deep gorge at the base of the mountain that we were climbing in our bus.

When we arrived, we eagerly began our hike up a trail that led us though a shroud of fog and rain. As we ascended, the dense fog clung tightly to the mountainside. We had no idea where we were or what the scenery around us looked like. We reached a restored hut with a thatched roof on it, so we climbed inside to get out of the rain and fog. Lynn and I found a dry spot and meditated while we waited out the weather.

It felt sacred and special to be there meditating with my friend in a hut that was hundreds of years old. When the rain eased up, we ventured back out on the trail and met some incoming hikers who had arrived via the old Inca Trail. We walked along an ancient rock wall, and we wondered where the main view was that we had seen flashed across hundreds of travel brochures and travel books.

We had taken a rock-paved trail along a hillside when we came upon a pack of llamas. Lynn began taking photos as they jumped down from the ledge almost into my front pocket. Their sudden movements startled me, but I thought it was a most exciting encounter on that old foggy trail.

We finally made it to a peak that overlooked the major part of the main ruins. There was an old hut called the "Caretaker's House" from which many famous photos have been shot. For us, however, there was no view thanks to the cloud-covered mountaintop that we were now slightly above. The main ruins were actually much lower than we were and hidden in the fog. Our patience paid off as the wind tossed the clouds apart below us and we could glimpse the ruins. It was a wonderfully enjoyable show when we found the "Lost City" as it became slowly visible to us in all its glory.

It stood out like a mysterious citadel below us. I was at a loss for words, which Lynn may have noticed. While he shot photos and tried to capture the right lighting and shadows, I immersed myself in thinking of the past year and my whole life in general. I found that this was a crossroads on my journey—no longer was I a young man and no longer would I see the world as I once had. I had changed and so had my world. I was very much like that "lost city," shrouded in my own fog. Now, from the vantage point that comes with age and experience, I was able to see the view much better and the purpose of my life much more clearly.

I realized that my childhood, even though it had a certain amount of sadness and pain, had helped to educate and shape the person I was who had gone to Vietnam. My experiences in Nam taught me valuable lessons of life and death and sharpened my faith. Those experiences created who I was when I got married and became a father. All those years and experiences as a young man and a parent molded me and gave me insights that I did not have when I was younger. This past year with the movie making and all the flying around the country meeting people, taught me that wounds do heal and that people can overcome anything once they make up their minds to do so.

I realized that I am the luckiest man alive. I would not trade any one experience or event in my life because all of them created the very me that sat on this mountaintop. I liked this person I was now and enjoyed my own company. I realized that I was still in love with life and that I still had things I wanted to do, one of which was to record for my family and friends these stories of my journey. I wanted to share what I had learned and what I had seen along the way. I think everyone has a song in them that needs to be sung. I hope you enjoyed mine.

So ends what I hope was just the first half of my life. What wonders still wait for me to discover in the second half? More important, what wonders and glorious things still wait for you to discover? Will you learn to sing your own song? Do not wait too long; we do not know how many of these wondrous days we are given. If my time is over tomorrow, I will be fulfilled and satisfied. Please let my epitaph read:

> He was a spiritual warrior who sang his own song.
> He loved his children and grandchildren without measure.
> He was a faithful and loyal husband, citizen, soldier, and devotee.
> He came. He saw. He helped. He believed!
> Honor, courage and faith were his creed.
> But love motivated everything he did!
> And by the "amazing grace" of God, he lived his life.

Bill McDonald with former President Jimmy Carter, July 2002.

W.H. McDonald Jr.

About the Author

William H. McDonald Jr., better know to his friends and those who seek his advice as Bill McDonald, is a published poet and author. He was part of the flight crew for the Vietnam War documentary *In the Shadow of the Blade*, released for theaters in the fall of 2003 by Arrowhead Films. He also does public speaking for veterans' causes and events.

Bill is a Vietnam veteran who did his tour of duty with the 128th Assault Helicopter Company in Phu Loi, South Vietnam, from October 1966 through October 1967. He has counseled several thousand veterans over the past three decades and offers his own support group on his website. He is no stranger to combat and was shot down several times while flying as a crew chief/door-gunner on a UH-1D Huey helicopter. He was awarded many medals including the Distinguished Flying Cross, the Bronze Star, the Purple Heart, and 14 Air Medals.

He earned his B.A. degree at the University of San Francisco and his A.A. degree at San Jose City College.

His website, the Vietnam Experience www.vietnamexp.com, has received well over 3,000,000 visitors as of October 2003.

He is still married to his high school sweetheart, Carol, since 1970. He has two grown children and two grandchildren. He lives in the Sacramento area of northern California in Elk Grove. He also is retired from a 30-plus year career in postal management with the United States Postal Service.

In his quest for peace and understanding for all veterans, he is active with the International World Rose Peace Gardens. The organization plans to build a new Peace Garden in Vietnam in 2004–2005. If you wish to contribute any time, effort, or money to the organization for this or any other future projects, you can contact Bill McDonald for details.

If you wish to send comments or ask questions of the author
His current e-mail address is on his website.
www.vietnamexp.com

<u>Mailing Address:</u>
Bill McDonald
P. O. Box 2441, Elk Grove, CA 95759-2441

Author's note: Don't follow me; I am still on my own journey looking for truth and enlightenment. Seek your own path and be true to yourself. Believe and have faith that everything happens for a purpose and a reason. We are all ONE, connected by God's love.

I Am but a Poet

I am but a poet,
Not an angel,
Or prophet.

I am just a pilgrim
On a journey of words,
Not an enlightened guru
Able to give you
Dream-maps of heaven.

I am only a fugitive
From future funeral fires.
An ornament of faith, illusion
Skin and bones.
Just a house
To shelter my soul.

I am but a poet.
I create humble mindscapes
Out of ordinary words,
To show you that there is a path
Through our emotions
And dreams.
It is called love.

#

Printed in the United States
18699LVS00004B/28-39